CLASSICS & FEMINISM

Gendering the Classics

The Impact of Feminism on the Arts & Sciences

Claire Sprague, General Editor
New York University

History & Feminism
Judith P. Zinsser

Biology & Feminism
Sue V. Rosser

Philosophy & Feminism
Andrea Nye

Political Science & Feminisms
Kathleen A. Staudt and William G. Weaver

Classics & Feminism
Barbara F. McManus

CLASSICS & FEMINISM

Gendering the Classics

Barbara F. McManus

Twayne Publishers • New York
An Imprint of Simon & Schuster Macmillan

Prentice Hall International
London • Mexico City • New Delhi • Singapore • Sydney • Toronto

Twayne Publishers
An Imprint of Simon & Schuster Macmillan
1633 Broadway
New York, New York 10019

Library of Congress Cataloging-in-Publication Data

McManus, Barbara F., 1942–
    Classics and feminism : gendering the classics / Barbara F.
McManus.
        p.   cm. — (The impact of feminism on the arts & sciences)
    Includes bibliographical references and index.
    ISBN 0-8057-9757-2 (alk. paper)
    1. Classical philology—Study and teaching—Social aspects—United
States.   2. Classical philology—Study and teaching—United States—
Sex differences.   3. Civilization, Classical—Study and teaching—
Sex differences.   4. Women—Greece—History—To 500—
Historiography.   5. Women—Rome—History—To 500—Historiography.
6. Feminism and education—United States.   7. Women classicists—
United States.   8. Women—Education—United States.   9. Women and
literature—Greece.   10. Women and literature—Rome.   I. Title.
II. Series.
    PA78.U6M38   1997
    480'.07'073—dc20   96-36021
                                                                                    CIP

The paper used in this publication meets the minimum requirements of American National Standard for Information Sciences—Permanence of Paper for Printed Library Materials. ANSI Z39.48–1984. ∞ ™

10 9 8 7 6 5 4 3 2 1

Printed in the United States of America

To the memory of
Patricia L. Wismer
1949–1993
beloved sister,
feminist, teacher, scholar

*Accipe germanae multum manantia fletu
atque in perpetuum, soror, ave atque vale.*

CONTENTS

FOREWORD

The contemporary women's movement has entered its third decade. We can now take a longer and larger look at what has been happening to traditional modes of research and evaluation in the universities. The Twayne series on The Impact of Feminism on the Arts and Sciences represents a unique contribution toward an assessment of more than 25 years of feminist activity. It addresses the complex questions as well as the uncertainties and possibilities that are raised by the meaning of feminist impact. Which disciplines can claim to have been altered as a result of feminism and which cannot? How can we measure feminist impact? What biases or gaps in scholarly thought are still there? Are we creating new ones? Has a gendered approach developed in the field? What are the major areas of resistance to change?

The scope of the series is ambitious. Over the next several years, we envision the publication of individual volumes on anthropology, art history, bioethics, biology, classics, drama, education, economics, film, history, law, literature, music, philosophy, political science, psychology, and sociology. The decision to have one volume for each field rather than an anthology or anthologies means that each author will have the opportunity to develop a position in some detail. The series will not follow a uniform format or approach. The belief behind this approach is that feminism is a plural adventure. There are feminisms; there is no single feminism. We anticipate that each volume will combine the virtues of accessibility with original interpretations of central issues of gender, genre, methodology, and historical perspective. These are the areas that feminism has explicit and implicitly unsettled in every field of knowledge, forcing us all to reconsider how we learn, how we choose what we learn, and how we change what and how we learn. We hope that the series will be both charting change and making it happen.

The fifth volume in the series, *Classics and Feminism,* takes on the field that American higher education still considers the centerpiece of a liberal education. The very word *classics* is charged with a point of view; it is not neutral. No other academic field is called by so biased a name, one that represents, as Barbara McManus puts it so well, "both chronological priority and normativeness." The paradox of a disciplinary label that makes no pretense to objectivity is compounded when we consider that the study of classics, meant to be "useless," was required of men in power. Women did not share in its power and prestige. Perhaps only in the sciences have women had so thoroughly to become "disembodied scholars" or "honorary men" in order to succeed.

As Barbara McManus knows and shows, classics is intimately tied into our conceptions of what education is all about. Its study has a complex social and political role. The tables and graphs assembled in *Classics and Feminism* are thorough and original; they give us crucial information about faculty, students, scholarly publications, curricula, dissertations, and professional associations. McManus's interpretive skills show to perfection in her analytical overview of the state of classical scholarship since the 1970s and in her discussion of transgendered moments in Vergil's *Aeneid.*

Her Vergil chapter is the high point of the book. In an epic considered so masculine, so focused on the construction of Rome's claim to surpass the Greek achievement, Vergil gives to his hero distinctly unmasculine moments. Such moments effectively redefine our conceptions of heroism. Aeneas has "feminine" traits that do not feminize him, while Dido and Camilla have "male" traits that do not masculinize them. Achieving what McManus calls transgendered moments, these characters earn the homage that sex-role crossovers do not.

Classics has changed significantly since the 1970s. While it is not a field in which new texts are likely to be uncovered, how we see old texts, what we bring to them from our knowledge of noncanonical texts, nonliterary texts (inscriptions, papyri, medical and legal texts, magical spells) and material evidence (vases, paintings, sculpture, coins, the remains of private homes) continues to enlarge our knowledge of gendered issues in antiquity. In that larger undertaking, Barbara McManus has made an exceptional contribution. No one can read her book without an awareness that "gender is a crucial category of analysis and that modes of knowledge that do not take gender into account are partial and incomplete."

Claire Sprague
Series Editor

PREFACE

Seeking to measure and evaluate the impact of feminism on the discipline and profession of classics in the United States is a formidable task, requiring a knowledge of classics, the historiography of women and gender, and feminist theory and methodology. As I undertake this task, I think it is appropriate to explain a little about my own experience in these areas as well as the standpoint from which I approach this study.

Although initially trained as a classical philologist and literary comparatist, I have been extensively reading, writing, and teaching about ancient women since 1983, when I participated in the National Endowment for the Humanities Summer Institute on Women in Classical Antiquity at Hunter College, directed by Sarah B. Pomeroy. I was also one of the founding members of the women's studies program at the College of New Rochelle, the liberal arts college for women where I have taught since 1967. Both of these interests provided the impetus for acquiring an intensive familiarity with current scholarship on feminist theory, academic feminism, and disciplinary transformation, which in turn led to this volume in the series The Impact of Feminism on the Arts and Sciences. I have also been very active in the national professional organization for classicists, the American Philological Association (APA), first as a representative of smaller classics departments, later as a member of the Committee on the Status of Women and Minority Groups, and currently as a member of the board of directors. My active involvement in the Women's Classical Caucus began in the early 1980s, and I have since served as secretary-treasurer and cochair of that organization.

I present this information in order to clarify my standpoint: I make no pretense of approaching this task as a disinterested, "objective" observer. I am deeply committed to the goals of modern feminism, as I am deeply committed to the discipline of classics and to the teaching profession. These three loves have shaped my life and my outlook and thus all of my judgments. My position in this study is that each of these areas needs the others, and so inevitably this book will present the story of how well they have been integrated. I do not, however, rely solely on my own experience and judgment to tell this story; not only is this the first book-length study of classics and feminism, but also it is the first to attempt to document its assertions. To this end I have conducted many statistical studies of various aspects of the profession and of patterns of scholarly publication. These may make for some heavy reading, but I believe that they provide a necessary foundation for my conclusions, and I have included many tables and charts to aid in understanding them. I have also conducted a nonscientific survey of individual classicists; a substantial part of chapter 5 is devoted to their voices. In the several years I have worked on this study, I have come to conceive of the relationship of feminism and classics as a complex chorus of many voices singing in counterpoint, and I have relied on the words of the many respondents to my survey to ensure that this book is not a solo performance.

The book is organized thematically rather than chronologically. Chapters 1 and 2 are built upon the distinction between discipline and profession. In chapter 1, I provide background on the nature of classics' disciplinary self-definition. After analyzing the characteristics of prefeminist treatment of women and gender in classical scholarship, I explain the dramatically new features of the feminist scholarship on women in classical antiquity that began to emerge in the United States during the early 1970s. Chapter 2 considers the profession of classics in the United States, proposing that the unusual educational opportunities open to women in nineteenth-century America created a unique double legacy for female classicists in the United States. After discussing the role of women in the American Philological Association, focusing particularly on two feminist organizations (the Women's Classical Caucus and the Committee on the Status of Women and Minority Groups), I present a statistical profile of women's current situation in the classics profession in the United States.

Chapter 3 focuses on contemporary classical scholarship, presenting the results of several studies I conducted of gender-related publications (including books, journals, and dissertations) and then analyzing in some detail the nature of feminist classical scholarship, particularly with regard to the study of ancient Greek and Roman women and sex/gender systems. Chapter 4 abandons the wide-angle lens for a telephoto focus on a single, canonical literary work, as I demonstrate how feminist theory has changed the way I read Vergil's *Aeneid*. Finally, in chapter 5, I present the voices of many individual classicists, respondents to my survey, describing in their own words how they have been influenced by feminism. The chapter ends with a look at resistance to feminism in classics graduate programs and thoughts about the need for feminist classicists to communicate more broadly outside the discipline.

When I refer to *feminism,* I am not envisioning a monolithic, well-defined entity or theoretical position. I use this term in its broadest meaning, as a movement to create equal opportunity for women as well as men in all areas of life and as an intellectual commitment to transforming androcentric structures of knowledge, both of which began to take shape in the United States in the late 1960s and early 1970s. In chapter 3, I describe in more detail what I believe to be the defining characteristics of feminist scholarship. I am deeply indebted to various feminist theorists, but my sense of what makes an approach "feminist" has been particularly influenced by three disparate works: Joan Wallach Scott's *Gender and the Politics of History* (Scott 1988), Evelyn Fox Keller's "Gender and Science: An Update" (Keller 1992), and Sandra Bem's *The Lenses of Gender* (Bem 1993).

In a book such as this, many important considerations are inevitably left out, and feminist theory has taught us to pay attention to what *is not* as well as what *is* said. This study focuses on the discipline and profession of classics in the United States, not only because that is what I know best, but also because there is a distinctive story to tell. Women entered the classics profession earlier and in greater numbers in the United States than elsewhere; more importantly, modern feminist scholarship on women in classical antiquity began in the United States. The nature of this story also requires a concentration on the philological and historical branches of classical scholarship instead of the archaeological and art historical branches, although I have included information about these areas as they bear upon the story I have to tell (see Brown 1993 for an introduction to the troubled relationship of feminism and classical archaeology). Furthermore, I have chosen to exemplify the characteristics of feminist scholarship by focusing on current social/historical work on women in classical antiquity rather than on literary studies, although these characteristics are of course present in all types of feminist classical scholarship. There are a number of reasons[1] for this choice: (1) studying ancient Greek and Roman women provided the initial impetus for feminist scholarship in classics and is still the dominant strain of feminist work; (2) a social/historical approach enables a more gynocentric perspective, since the vast majority of classical literary texts are male authored and distinctly androcentric; (3) modern literary theory has been relatively hospitable to feminist approaches, and literary scholars from a number of disciplines have developed feminist rereadings of canonical texts from all periods of history. But feminist classicists have learned to read ancient literature as well as ancient lives against the background of a vast cognitive grid of Greek and Roman conceptualizations of sex and gender. I believe that classicists have made their most distinctive contributions to the general feminist enterprise through piecing together tiny bits of evidence from many diverse sources in order to illuminate the structure of this grid, and it is this process that I have highlighted in chapter 3. I have included an example of a feminist rereading of a canonical literary text, Vergil's *Aeneid*, in chapter 4, and the interested reader can find many other examples in the bibliographies provided on the web site *Diotima: Materials for the Study of Women and Gender in the Ancient World*.[2]

Furthermore, I have chosen to emphasize the characteristics that feminist scholars in classics share rather than their inevitable theoretical and methodological differences, because without these commonalities (and the ability to recognize them as unifying factors), there would have been no story to tell. Since one of my purposes in writing this book is to make feminist scholarship by classicists more visible both within and outside our discipline, I have featured writing by classical scholars rather than the better-known studies by feminist theorists from other disciplines. Finally, I have concentrated on questions of gender rather than related constructions of race and ethnicity, class, and sexual orientation. This is not because I fail to recognize the importance of these other constructions or their interconnection with gender; however, race, ethnicity, and class have been significant in the history of classics because of the *homogeneity* of the profession, which has been overwhelmingly white, upper and middle class, and Euro-American. The story of race and ethnicity, class, and sexual orientation is just beginning to emerge, and feminists in classics recognize the importance of these other constructions for their own future. But that story awaits its own chronicler.

The research for this book would not have been possible without New York University's Faculty Resource Network: by offering faculty from smaller colleges access to the NYU research libraries and opportunities to participate in collaborative projects, the Faculty Resource Network has made a major contribution to the academic community, providing a model of responsible citizenship for research universities. I am deeply appreciative of the support I have received from the network, including a scholar-in-residence grant in the summer of 1992 and participation as a University Associate since 1989.

I am grateful for the advice of Sarah Pomeroy, Judith Hallett, Marilyn Skinner, and Amy Richlin, who read drafts of this manuscript; any flaws that remain are due to my own stubbornness. Their friendship and encouragement, and that of the whole community of scholars in the Women's Classical Caucus, have meant a great deal to me—considerably more than any formal acknowledgment can convey. I thank also my dear friend and colleague Ann Raia for her unfailing support, and Sandra Schnaithman for serving as an able research assistant. Claire Sprague, our series editor, has believed in this project from the beginning, and for that I am grateful. My family deserves a medal for putting up with my enslavement to the library and computer, especially my husband Jack, my sine qua non.

Finally, I thank all the classicists who took the time to respond to my survey with such thoughtfulness and openness. Statistics and scholarly studies can document the influence of feminism, but voices like these give it life:

I wanted to find out more about Second Wave Feminism, so I accepted last year an offer to deliver a paper at a Women in Archaeology conference, where I was one of five men at a conference with 250 women—boy! did I learn a lot, and it completely turned me around. [male professor]

Thanks to the rise of feminism, I see almost everything I do and experience differently than I did thirty years ago. I try to get my students to see that in everything they read, there are points of view that are not expressed, and that thinking about what these might be can shed a new light on just about everything. I am much more interested in the role, the lives, the experience of women in ancient societies, and I try to give that a place in all of my teaching to the extent that it is relevant. I work hard at making my classroom a good place for girls and boys to learn, . . . and I have become much more aware of sexism throughout the educational process, in all areas of school life. I really did not think much about these kinds of things when I was in college, or just beginning as a teacher. I am immensely grateful to the women's movement for all that I have learned and am learning from it. [female high school teacher]

My scholarship is probably the arena in which feminism has most profoundly impacted on my "classics" life. I attended the Cincinnati "Feminism and Classics" conference as an undergraduate and was impacted beyond measure by the kind of work that I saw being presented there. I have been working on sex and gender issues ever since. [female graduate student]

I was introduced to feminist study in classics only recently. I was ignorant of any of the modern approaches to classical studies until my professor turned me on to them, the feminist approach being the first. A whole new world has been opened up for me thanks to the work of people like the feminist classicists. [male undergraduate student]

1

THE GENDERING OF
"THE CLASSICS"

The discipline of classics presents a particularly challenging field for feminists. Its very name[1] suggests both chronological priority and normativeness; what is classic not only "has stood the test of time" but also "sets the standard" of quality and rank. Hence, the discipline has always asserted a claim to privileged status as the most broadly humanistic of all academic studies.[2] In 1909, Mitchell Carroll, a professor of classics at George Washington University, stated this claim unequivocally: "It becomes us as classical teachers to recognize that our strongest weapon in this material age is the fact that we stand for humanism and all that the term implies far more than does any other branch of knowledge. We must respond to the call for the discipline of cultured manhood" (Carroll 1909, 156). Though Carroll's title was "The New Classical Philology," his underlying assumptions were as old as the discipline itself. Writing in the same journal 62 years later, Charles Segal, then a professor of classics at Brown University, revealed the same assumptions despite his avowed emphasis on

1

"modern problems and perspectives": "The Classics, then, will have ever changing meanings for the changing needs of our society. One perennial need in any society is an image of man, and here our humanistic legacy from the ancient world is particularly precious. Despite their notorious cultural bias, the Greeks developed an idea of the unity of mankind based upon man's common participation in suffering and mortality" (Segal 1971, 31–32).

More insidiously, both quotations virtually equate classics with humanism; although historically appropriate when speaking of Renaissance humanism, which was a direct outgrowth of the renewed focus on Greek and Roman culture at that time, such an equation in the twentieth century is inaccurate as well as elitist. Furthermore, although the term *classics* reveals its own bias to the discriminating observer, the word *humanism* does not, suggesting rather a universal, inclusive focus on all things human. The identification of classics with humanism actually promotes a kind of blindness, since it renders invisible all who do not fit within the concept of "cultured manhood" fostered by the discipline of classics and strengthens modern biases by fusing them with ancient Greek and Roman ones.

The gendered nature of this blindness is particularly apparent in the article by Charles Segal because he acknowledges one form of exclusion practiced by the Greeks, their "notorious cultural bias" against non-Greeks, but appears totally oblivious of the complete exclusion of women both from the ancient "image of man" and from his own language and concepts.[3] Although the words *men, man,* and *modern man* are ubiquitous, the word *women* appears only in a reference to a play *(The Trojan Women).* The word *woman* is never used, and the only references to females anywhere in the article occur in the mention of the British scholar Jane Harrison and of a few literary characters whose gender is never noted as significant.

Only seven years after writing this article, Segal began another article, which was published in a special journal collection dedicated to the study of women in antiquity, with the following statement: "Greek tragedy, like Greek myth and literature generally, presents a complex and ambivalent image of woman" (Segal 1978, 185). The distance between these two articles, in which gender has moved from complete invisibility to focal point, testifies to the changes that were occurring in the American classics community during the 1970s. But before we can examine this process in detail, it is necessary to sketch in the background against which these changes took place.

THE DISCIPLINARY CULTURE OF CLASSICS

When we consider the history of a field of study, distinguishing between the concepts of *discipline* and *profession* provides a useful analytic tool. A discipline involves a shared tradition of methodological and theoretical procedures for resolving problems or answering questions; a profession involves the people who carry out these procedures and the organizations in which they do it (Toulmin 1972, 142).[4] In other words, an academic discipline includes a common field of study, the accepted methods and theories employed to analyze that field, and the body of scholarship already produced in that field. An academic profession includes the practitioners who study that field, the institutionalized roles through which they study it, the groups into which they are organized, and the accepted channels through which they communicate their views. The first is intellectual; the second, institutional. Although they can be separated for the purposes of analysis, they are highly interdependent. Any disciplinary history that focuses on one to the exclusion of the other will be incomplete and inaccurate. Therefore, although this chapter concentrates upon the gendering of classics as a discipline, the developments described here are part of the same process as the changes in the classical profession detailed in the next chapter and cannot be fully understood in isolation from them.

The history of classics reveals a "diffuse" discipline that thinks of itself as "compact" (for the distinction, see Toulmin 1972, 378–95). In a compact discipline, practitioners employ an authoritative paradigm and share generally accepted goals, ideals, and standards; because of this theoretical agreement, their debates usually focus on specific empirical findings and how they are to be interpreted. Diffuse disciplines, lacking such agreement, tend to be held together by a common field of study or subject matter; thus, disciplinary controversies often involve rival assumptions, approaches, and perspectives. Modern languages are admittedly diffuse disciplines, but classics stubbornly promotes an image of itself as the most objective and scientific of the humanities despite its lack of an authoritative paradigm.[5]

The only thing that all classicists share is a common subject matter—a focus upon some aspect of the civilizations of ancient Greece and Rome, using the Greek and Latin languages as a primary means of access. The breadth of this object of study has led to numerous subdivisions and subspecialties within classics, which can be roughly grouped under the headings of *philology* (linguistic, textual, and literary studies), *ancient history* (including history, law, philosophy, medicine, religion, etc.), and *classical archaeology* (including archaeology, art history, numismatics, epigraphy, etc.). Since mastery of ancient Greek and/or Latin, languages existing only in written form, is a prerequisite for entrance into any branch of the field, much of classical training and research has centered upon written texts. Moreover, many academic institutions group all these specialities in a single department; even when this is not the case, practitioners' primary disciplinary identification is frequently with classics because of the bond provided by the ancient languages.[6]

One strong feature of the disciplinary self-image of classics is provided by positivism. Many classicists see themselves as participating in an empirical, unmediated encounter with the textual and material remains of ancient Greece and Rome. Using precise intellectual tools to evaluate and assess this evidence, philologists attempt to establish definitive texts; historians, to establish the "facts" of the past as it actually was; archaeologists, to establish definitive catalogues and analyses of the material record as it exists today (see Blok 1987 for a discussion of the role of positivism in classical philology and historiography and Morris 1994 for its influence on classical archaeology).[7] Yet these positivist principles do not constitute an explicit and generally accepted theoretical paradigm in classics because they conflict with another, equally strong strain in the discipline, its claims to present the highest literary and humanistic values (see, e.g., the quotations that begin this chapter).[8] A recent article comparing classics and anthropology (Redfield 1991) reveals the way these two strains can coexist with no apparent recognition of their inherent opposition. On the one hand, the article claims that classical study, which is "constantly engaged in a struggle with hard, recalcitrant facts," is more of a science than anthropology (14). On the other hand, classical criticism is characterized as "holistic, meditative, and humane," and philology is said to "define civilization in terms of a privileged ancestor culture which is before us not as a problem to be understood but as a model to be emulated" (12, 18). The discipline can suppress the contradictory nature of these two tendencies only by failing to examine their underlying assumptions. To preserve its "scientific" self-image as well as its humanistic claims, classics has consistently refused to theorize its own practice and has characteristically resisted all explicit forms of theory; even today, a large number of classicists would probably agree with the following statement by William M. Calder III: "I am an historian and philologist and therefore by nature skeptical of theory" (quoted in Richlin 1988, 21).

EARLY STUDIES OF ANCIENT GREEK AND ROMAN WOMEN

It is essential to understand the disciplinary culture of classics before one can appreciate the complexity of "gendering the classics," for specific resistance to feminist theory has been interwoven with and complicated by the discipline's paradoxical self-concept and hostility to theoretical discourse in general. In fact, these disciplinary characteristics greatly influenced early writing about women in classical antiquity. For classicists did not totally ignore ancient women.[9] It is the nature, rather than simply the presence, of scholarship on women that manifests the impact of modern feminism on classics. Much of the major early work on this subject consisted of debates about the "position" or "status" of women, especially in Athens. Since the significance of these debates has been analyzed in detail elsewhere (most notably Katz 1992 and Blok 1987; see also Versnel 1987, Gould 1980, Arthur 1976, Just 1975, Pomeroy 1973), the following discussion will sketch the major characteristics of this early scholarship on women and then consider some publications by American scholars that have not received much critical attention but that help to show the influence of the debate on scholarship in the United States.

Ancient Greek and Roman Women in Mainstream Classical Scholarship

A major characteristic of early work on women in classical antiquity is its isolation from work on every other aspect of the ancient world. Mainstream classical scholarship paid little attention to women. Traditional historical studies simply ignored women unless they had played a major role in political events (as, e.g., Cleopatra VII did); traditional literary studies presented the masculine perspective as the only (read "universal") perspective. The revered nineteenth-century German classicist Ulrich von Wilamowitz-Moellendorff even pointed to the absence of women as one of the main attractions of Athenian history. After denigrating both the character and influence of Pericles' mistress Aspasia in a footnote, Wilamowitz concluded,

> I am not so foolish as to bear ill-will to a dead female, but one should leave her as she is—dead and a female. People who don't want to sniff out any history without women's perfume and don't consider their heroes to be human unless they coo and bleat from time to time may read Hamerling instead of Thucydides. But it is no small sign of the dignity of Attic history that only one woman is found in it, although she commands it all—the maiden of the Acropolis [the goddess Athena]. (Wilamowitz-Moellendorff 1893, 2:100 n. 35)[10]

The scorn in this passage may be extreme, but not the attitude toward women's role in history. A good example is provided by the first edition of *The Cambridge Ancient History,* published in the 1920s and 1930s. In volume 5, dealing with fifth-century Athens, the general index contains no entry for *women,* and the detailed, 11-page table of contents does not refer to a single historical woman by name or implication, although Aspasia is briefly and dismissively mentioned in the text: "there is no reason to suppose that her attractions deflected the compass by which [Pericles] steered the ship of state" (Adcock 1927, 175). The word *women* does appear once in the table of contents, in a chapter comparing the historians Herodotus and Thucydides: "Gods and women excluded from the world of Thucydides." The author of this chapter, R. W. Macan, maintains that the exclusion of deities and women marks Thucydides' "silent protest against the pietistic and the feminist motives, as historical mechanisms." In contrast, he states that Herodotus always produces "a woman to account for the trouble" in his "racy" early sections and relies on divine influence to shape his accounts of more recent history (Macan 1927, 405–7). Macan's coupling of women and gods as similar categories, equally undifferentiated and existing somehow outside normal historical processes (emphasized by his use of the phrases "Das Ewig-weibliche" and "cherchez la femme"), reveals a pattern frequently found in these early studies. This pattern may be seen as stemming from the ancient Greeks themselves, who conceived of women as a thing apart, as essentially outside the boundaries of civilization and thus the processes of history (Arthur 1973; 1987).

In volume 11 of *The Cambridge Ancient History*, published in 1936 and dealing with the Roman Empire from 70–192 C.E., the table of contents does contain the heading "Women," placed between a section on "The Social Grades" and one on "Slaves and Freedmen" in the chapter entitled "Social Life in Rome and Italy." This method of organization doubly isolates women; not only are they omitted from the chapters discussing the progression of historical events, but they are even considered apart from the structures and divisions of Roman society, as though women were not found throughout the ranks of Roman society. In the four pages that the author, J. Wight Duff, allots to women, his real interest lies in evaluating their morality or immorality, so their treatment is dramatically different from that accorded to historical men in the rest of the volume (Duff 1936, 752–55).

Writings Devoted Specifically to Ancient Greek and Roman Women

In view of the idea that woman is a category that can be understood best in isolation from history, it is not surprising that most studies of ancient women were presented outside the mainstream of classical scholarship—in lectures, articles, and monographs that treat women as a special problem. Many of these studies were intended for nonspecialist audiences and employ a light, popularizing tone quite foreign to professional classical scholarship (Blok 1987).

Ancient women as a vehicle for ideological debate. The most striking characteristic of classical studies of women prior to the 1970s is the fact that they are not really about the historical recovery of ancient women, though that is their ostensible subject. Instead, in much the same way that Greek and Roman writers did, the modern classical scholars were using ancient women as a category to think with, to consider and debate issues of modern ideology. The research questions that came to dominate this literature—what was the status of women in Athens and how should we evaluate it—were determined by these underlying ideological issues.[11] Put very briefly, a good deal of what classicists wrote about ancient women from the late eighteenth century until the early 1970s either defended or attacked the view that Athenian women of the citizen class in the fifth and fourth centuries B.C.E. were uneducated, kept in "almost oriental seclusion," and generally regarded with contempt by the dominant Athenian males.

Marilyn Katz (1992) argues that this "status debate" began in mid-eighteenth-century Europe as part of the Enlightenment discourse about freedom, equality, government, and civil society. Because of the normative value of the classics, ancient Athens played a significant part in this discourse, and writers like Rousseau began to refer to concepts about Athenian women to justify their own views about women's nature and proper role in society. As these concepts became part of the general intellectual discourse of the time, a few nineteenth-century German classicists began to investigate the "position of women" in Athens using the premises of this discourse in a basically circular fashion: they invoked the example of women in classical Athens to justify the exclusion of women from their own civil society, but the vision of women in ancient Greece that they used as justification was itself filtered through contemporary assumptions and rhetoric about their own practice (Katz 1992, 70). One significant strain of this discourse sought to explain the origin of civil society by positing a dialectical historical development from matriarchal societies to patriarchal ones. The chief exponent of this theory was the classicist and jurist J. J. Bachofen, whose work *Das Mutterrecht* (1861) was highly influential, though more so outside the discipline of classics than within it. Aspects of Bachofen's theory entered Marxist historiography through Friedrich Engels's work on the origins of the family (1884), and one can still find traces of Bachofen in contemporary (nonclassicist) writing on mythology and on matriarchy.

Judith Zinsser's description of the invisibility and/or dismissive treatment of women in traditional historical studies of later periods (Zinsser
1993, 5–15) is generally applicable to work on classical antiquity, particularly her observation that these histories often identify women with "latent,
potent sexuality" (9). There is, however, a very significant difference, for
publications about women of later periods do not typically manifest the ideological compulsion and emotional investment found in work on ancient
women, stemming from the way Greek and Roman women served as coded
signifiers for modern concerns about civil society in relation to gender, race,
and sexuality. Hence, although nineteenth- and early twentieth-century writings on ancient Greek and Roman women are not reliable sources for a study
of women's history, they do provide valuable clues about the tangled roots of
modern ideological constructs. The emphasis on Athens instead of Rome is
tied not only to Enlightenment discourse about democracy and civil society
but also to pervasive European (especially German) concepts about linguistic and racial origins and purity that developed during this period.[12] This
implication with modern ideological constructs is an important reason why
we need to understand the historiography of ancient Greek and Roman
women. As Christiane Sourvinou-Inwood notes, "There are many reasons
why the study of the Classical world is a privileged locus for thinking about
thinking; not least among them are its many histories, constructed over many
centuries in different cultural milieus, each refracting ideological constructions of its present and shaping the constructions of the ancient past by subsequent generations" (Sourvinou-Inwood 1995, 111).

Ancient women as justification for modern gender practices. In addition to these ideological implications, there was another subtext in this early
work on women. One of the driving impulses behind early classical writings
about ancient women was the need to vindicate male cultural practices, both
those of the ancient Athenian men and those of the modern men who ideal-
ized and identified with them. The topic of women necessarily involved
assessing social practices and relationships between the sexes, the very areas
of modern life that were increasingly under scrutiny as the nineteenth century progressed, particularly in Britain and the United States. Hence these
studies of Greek and Roman women continually refer to "normal" practice
and compare ancient and modern situations as though the terms were identical. The influence of early feminist agitation for women's suffrage, increased
economic rights, and access to education are especially obvious when modern phrases and words such as "the emancipation of women," "women's
movement," and "feminist" keep cropping up in this literature as if they

applied equally well to the Athenian situation. The topic of ancient women also seemed to evoke a judgmental and moralistic tone not usually employed in classical scholarship.

United States Publications on Ancient Greek and Roman Women

The earliest study of ancient Greek and Roman women I have found that was published in the United States consists of the first two volumes in a multivolume series entitled *Woman: In All Ages and in All Countries,* privately printed "for subscribers only" in Philadelphia in 1907. The beautifully printed, leather-bound volumes both have as frontispieces reproductions of nineteenth-century paintings featuring bare-breasted women who are represented as Greek or Roman prostitutes, and this moralizing and universalizing tendency is continued in the "General Introduction" to the series (written by a man identified only as G. C. L. of Johns Hopkins University). The following sentences are characteristic of this introduction: "The typical woman, as she is seen in the pages of history, is either very good or very bad," and, "The passion of man for woman has been the underlying cause of all history in its phenomenal aspects" (Carroll 1907, vii, xi).

Greek Women, the first volume of the series, was written by Mitchell Carroll, a professor of classical philology at George Washington University and frequent contributor to the journal the *Classical Weekly* (see the quotation that opens this chapter). Although Carroll does treat "woman" as a universal category ("The Spartan Woman" and "The Athenian Woman" are chapter headings) and uses literature uncritically as direct evidence for life, his work has a number of surprising features. In contrast to typical writing on this subject, which is preoccupied with "woman's position" and "the attitude of Greeks toward their womenfolk," Carroll sets a broader goal, emphasizing "the subjective side" of women's lives:

> . . . how they regarded themselves, and were regarded by men; how they reasoned, and felt, and loved; how they experienced the joys and sorrows of life; what part they took in the social life of the times; how their conduct influenced the actions of men and determined the course of history; what were their moral and spiritual endowments;—in short, we should like to know the Greek woman in all those phases of life which make the modern woman interesting and influential and the conserving force in human society. (Carroll 1907, 3–4)

Except for the last part of this quotation, Carroll's aim is not so very different from that of modern feminist historians; for example, Sarah Pomeroy's groundbreaking study begins with the words, "This book was conceived when I asked myself what women were doing while men were active in all the areas traditionally emphasized by classical scholars" (Pomeroy 1975, ix). Unfortunately, Carroll is not able to fulfill his goal, but the very fact that he has expressed it in more woman-centered terms is significant.

Carroll is also less moralistic than most other writers on this subject. For example, he justifies his long chapter on hetaerae ("companions," upper-class prostitutes) by stating that they "constituted a most interesting phenomenon in the social life of Greece, and played an important role in Greek culture" (14). His treatment of the subject is sober and serious (not at all like the titillating frontispiece), and although he includes obligatory condemnations of "the gross immorality of the sexes," he concludes the chapter with an aesthetic argument, stating that Greek hetaerism was "most advantageous for the arts of sculpture and painting" (235).[13]

Carroll is well aware of the debate about the status of Athenian women and opens his chapter on Athens with a summary of the contrasting positions:

> Many scholars have asserted that women were held in a durance not unlike that of the Oriental harem, that their life was a species of vassalage, and that they were treated with contempt by the other sex; while the few have contended that there existed a degree of emancipation differing but slightly from that of the female sex in modern times. (Carroll 1907, 159)

He argues for a middle ground between the two sides, rejecting the concepts of contempt and vassalage (and greatly downplaying the racial assumptions in the "Oriental" comparison) but arguing that Athenian citizen-women were "carefully secluded and restricted, under the rigid surveillance of law and custom" (161). Unlike most other authors on this subject, he attempts to analyze the restriction of women according to specific historical and cultural factors, attributing it especially to the nature of the Athenian city-state, which he calls "the feature of internal polity which had most to do with the seclusion of women" (8). While his analysis is neither detailed nor profound, it does anticipate directions that have proven fruitful in contemporary scholarship (see, e.g., Arthur 1973).

Carroll was clearly influenced by the suffrage movement and by the contention of the German Ivo Bruns (1900) that a women's movement similar to the modern one arose in classical Athens; he cites Bruns in his preface and entitles one chapter "The Woman Question in Ancient Athens." He maintains that dramatic and philosophical writings of the fifth and fourth centuries

B.C.E. were merely giving literary form to "a sociological movement of great import" (239), and that the comedies *Lysistrata* and *Ecclesiazusae* portrayed actual leaders of this movement (255). In contrast to other writers of the times, Carroll is at least conscious that he is applying modern terms to an ancient situation, for he ultimately concludes that, unlike the modern movement, in Athens "the agitation for the emancipation of woman seems not to have accomplished any demonstrable change in her social life. . . . Perhaps it was impossible for women to be accorded greater liberty of action while the ancient conception of the city-state obtained" (265–66). The influence of conditions in the United States at the turn of the century can also be discerned when Carroll imagines Sappho as leader of a "literary club" he conceives along the lines of the numerous American women's clubs dedicated to various cultural subjects (127).

Although Carroll was a recognized scholar, I have been able to find only two reviews of his book, both in relatively new journals representing regional classical associations. Both reviews are favorable, but their treatment clearly reveals the "beside-the-mainstream" status of the work. H. R. Fairclough writes of the book as if it were a woman, calling it "beautiful" and "charming." He says that Carroll "handles his subject *con amore*, treating it with uniform dignity and never allowing himself to sink into mere flippancy" (Fairclough 1908, 22). George Horton praises Carroll's "skill in attaining an interesting and entertaining style, commonly known as 'popular,' without sacrificing the demands of good scholarship," but allows himself a good measure of flippancy; for example, he disagrees with Carroll's characterization of Andromache as the "most lovable" of Homeric women with the dictum "in fiction as well as in real life, women are subjects of personal taste" (Horton 1909, 284). After these reviews, Carroll's book vanished from the scholarly literature. Though later classicists often cited another, more conventional study published in 1907 by the Englishman James Donaldson, I have never seen a single scholarly citation of Carroll's work, and I wonder whether this might be attributed to the book's more progressive features.

I have found no reviews in classical journals of the second volume in the series *(Roman Women)*, perhaps because its author, the Reverend Alfred Brittain, was not a professor, or perhaps because there was simply less interest in this topic. Unlike Carroll's study, Brittain's work does display most of the characteristic features of early classical writings on ancient women. His overall approach is highly moralistic (especially typical of writing on Roman women; cf. Duff 1936); one of his chapters is entitled "Woman at Her

Worst," and another "Good Women of Nero's Reign." He couples this moralizing with a treatment of women as a universal category isolated from historical specifics; for example, he claims that "a certain skill peculiar to their sex" (180) makes women especially adept at behind-the-scenes political management: "the rule was, and has been in all history, that the activity of women in State affairs was accompanied by an abundance of meretricious amatory intrigues" (198). He also assumes straightforward analogies between antiquity and the present ("the main features of a Roman matron's life were not essentially dissimilar from those which characterize polite feminine society in our own time," 55), including analogies with the feminism of his time: "The new woman had begun to make her appearance in Rome. This proverbial phenomenon, so greatly talked of in our own time, is by no means a modern discovery" (112). Finally, unlike Carroll, he explicitly invokes the racial theories so often coupled with early twentieth-century writing about Athenian women:

> Somewhere between the civilizations of Greece and Rome was the boundary line, starting from which the status of woman degraded to the Oriental or developed into the Occidental type. . . . While Greece looked to the East, and subjected her women to some of those customs which characterized the harems of Babylon, Rome was essentially Western, and its women enjoyed a goodly portion of dignity and honor. Both Greeks and Romans were of the same branch of the great Aryan race, and the indications are that in the earliest times their women enjoyed equal freedom; but Greece, to a certain extent, fell under the influence of Semitic ideas, which saw in the wife a voluptuous possession to be jealously guarded. (Brittain 1907, 127–28)

In 1925, an American journal, *Classical Philology*, published an article by a British classicist, A. W. Gomme, which became the rallying point for scholars who claimed a "high status" for Athenian women. This article is remarkable for the extent to which it makes a presumed affinity between "the Greeks and us" the cornerstone of its arguments, revealing an underlying need to justify modern social practices and attitudes by vindicating supposedly similar Greek ones. Many of Gomme's arguments draw on modern analogies, from the "'Ladies' Enclosure' at Lord's" to Oxford and Cambridge before the advent of the women's colleges (Gomme 1925, 11, 15). The article is full of comments such as the following: "not a sentiment, by the way, very foreign to our own or any other time" (8). Gomme's conclusion set the tone for subsequent Anglophone writing on the status of Athenian women: "I consider it very doubtful if Greek theory and practice differed fundamentally from the average, say, prevailing in mediaeval and modern Europe" (25).

Gomme's article was cited with approval by Kitto (1951) and Seltman (1955; 1956) among British classicists and by Post (1926; 1940), Shero (1932), Hadas (1936), and Richter (1971) among American scholars. Paradoxically, although these writers all claim that Gomme demolished the "low-status" view, they still feel the need to refute it again. With the exception of Richter, the American articles seem less passionate and doctrinaire than the British pieces. Hadas is closest to Gomme in his reliance upon analogies with the modern situation, though his comparisons are peculiarly American. For example, he sees a parallel between Greek social arrangements and the rural American division of the sexes between the "absolute sway" of the women in their kitchens or parlors and the "stag" gatherings of the men around the stove in the general store (Hadas 1936, 99). Hadas also implies that the American women's movement was responsible for current interest in the position of ancient women: "Accuracy in such matters is perhaps more important now than it was in earlier generations. Literate people are still anxious to get what lessons ancient Greece has to offer" (98). L. A. Post also reflects the influence of American suffragists, for he feels that modern China provides a better analogy with ancient Athens than the United States of his time because "the enlargement of woman's sphere within the memory of living men in our own land is probably greater than the difference between ancient Athens and Europe of two hundred years ago" (Post 1940, 422).

During the same period that American male classicists were writing about ancient women as a kind of sideline to their serious scholarly interests, a Vassar professor of classics, Grace Harriet Macurdy, was placing women at the center of her scholarship. Macurdy refused to treat women as a separate category, isolated from historical processes, so she focused her work on ancient monarchies, an area of traditional history in which a few women did play significant roles; she published studies of *Hellenistic Queens* (1932) and *Vassal Queens* (1937). She repeatedly emphasized the similarity of these women to the men of their rank and argued that they should be treated by the historian in exactly the same manner as other monarchs: "Of these few it may be said that if they were in nature and character the counterparts of the men, they should be judged by the same standard" (Macurdy 1932, x). Although she never challenged the methods or standards of traditional history, her work is remarkably free of the characteristics (discussed above) that marred other early studies of ancient women. Her books received favorable but brief reviews in a number of scholarly journals but did not alter the prevalent method of writing about ancient Greek and Roman women.

This method resurfaced with a vengeance as late as 1971, when Donald Richter attempted to revive the "status debate" about Athenian women. One wonders whether Richter's rather passionate insistence on the need to reopen this topic might stem from the resurgence of feminism in the United States during the late 1960s. Although Richter notes that "it is quite possible that the preconceptions of the late nineteenth- and early twentieth-century scholars regarding the proper place of women in their own society deeply influenced their reading of the Greek evidence," he does not conceive of any such motivation for his own "more objective inspection" (Richter 1971, 1, 3). Nonetheless, his reading of the evidence is largely based on an unexamined and unsupported premise about "the sexual laxity of Athenian women" (3):

> The protective solicitude that did obtain was not extraordinary. It was occasioned by a quite normal measure of husbandly jealousy. In view of the licentiousness for which Athenian women were notorious, the perennial suspicions of the husband were probably fully justified. . . . The young wives were as undisciplined a bevy of nymphs as Hellas ever reared. (7)

Although Richter warns against "accepting remarks in the area of female behavior at face value" from overwhelmingly male sources, he himself takes literally all the Athenian writers' negative characterizations of citizen-women, and he attributes "the healthy strain of misogyny and misogamy running through Greek literature" to the "impudence" of Greek women: "The targets of these diatribes are not quiet, tractable, cloistered" (5).

A NEW SCHOLARLY APPROACH TO THE STUDY OF GREEK AND ROMAN WOMEN

Using the method of reasoning that Richter himself employs, one might conclude that his own diatribe was occasioned by the increasing presence and activity of women in his professional community, for female classicists in America were no longer quiet, tractable, or cloistered. Besides the professional agitation detailed in the next chapter, there were many changes occurring on the disciplinary front, particularly the genesis of a new approach to the study of women in classical antiquity. New courses were springing up in colleges and universities: for example, Sarah Pomeroy, "Women and Slaves in Classical Antiquity," Hunter College, 1971–72; Meyer Reinhold, honors colloquium on "Women in Antiquity," University of Missouri, 1972 (Pomeroy

1973, 152); and Kathleen Berman, "Women in Antiquity," Lehman College, 1973 (Berman 1974). The newly established Women's Classical Caucus (WCC) began collecting and circulating syllabi for these courses, and an informal study group on women in antiquity was established in New York City. The first American Philological Association panel on the subject ("Ancient Greek Women and Modern Criticism," with papers by three women and one man) was presented in 1972, with annual WCC-sponsored panels appearing subsequently. The first conference on women in antiquity was held at the State University of New York at Buffalo in April 1973.

"Women in Antiquity" Issue of *Arethusa*

The Buffalo conference led to the publication of the first issue of a classical journal devoted entirely to the subject of ancient women, *Arethusa* 6.1 (1973), edited by John Patrick Sullivan, whose editorial statement began, "Like most things involving the liberation of women this issue of *Arethusa* comes late" (Sullivan 1973, 5). In addition to the novelty of its subject matter, this journal issue was unusual in the sex ratio of its authors—six women and one man (two spill-over articles on the topic were published in the fall issue of *Arethusa*, one by a woman and one by a man). The nine articles included five on Greek subjects, one on a Roman subject, one on an Etruscan subject, one including Greece and Rome, and an annotated bibliography covering the whole range of classical antiquity.

Although two of the articles focused primarily on imaginative literature and one on philosophic texts, all were directed toward the recovery of aspects of ancient life and *mentalité* relating to women and sexuality (one dealt with attitudes toward heterosexual and homosexual behavior and another with abortion). In contrast to earlier work on such subjects, these authors tended to be more sophisticated in their recognition of ambiguity and paradox in the sources and more cautious about correlating the ancient and the modern. The first article poses a question that clearly underlies all of the pieces: "can we seek to discover in classical antiquity an understanding of our present historical moment and a perspective on our own values, and yet remain both free from ideological compulsion and unburdened by the tyranny of raw data?" (Arthur 1973, 7).

In the subsequent issue of *Arethusa*, the editor comments with some surprise upon the popularity of the issue devoted to ancient women, noting that 399 copies of the 450 printed were sold, as compared with 286 of the previous issue. In fact, interest in the thematic issue ultimately prompted three reprints with total sales of approximately 2,000 (Skinner 1987b, 70), a double issue of *Arethusa* devoted to the same topic in 1978, and a book culled from both issues (Peradotto and Sullivan 1984).

Goddesses, Whores, Wives, and Slaves

Although the strength of the response to *Arethusa* testifies to the growing interest in women in antiquity, by itself this issue of a little-known classical journal did not have the clout or scope to constitute a disciplinary turning point. The book that did reach large numbers of readers both within and outside of the discipline was Sarah B. Pomeroy's *Goddesses, Whores, Wives, and Slaves: Women in Classical Antiquity*, published in the United States in 1975.[14] Unlike the separate and individual studies in *Arethusa*, Pomeroy's aim was comprehensive and synthetic—"to write a social history of women through the centuries in the Greek and Roman worlds"—although she recognized that it would be "impossible in a single book to fill all the gaps in the history of ancient women. Indeed it would be demeaning of the subject to attempt to do so" (Pomeroy 1975, x, xii). Fear that the book would not sell prompted the publisher to add the initial phrase to Pomeroy's original title, but that fear quickly proved unjustified, for this book has enjoyed a popularity unprecedented for a scholarly classical text. The book has been in print since 1975, with continuously high sales, and was reissued in 1995 with a new preface by the author. Two separate British editions have been published, as well as translations in Italian, German, and Spanish. It was widely and favorably reviewed in national and international journals from a number of scholarly disciplines, as well as more popular publications such as the *New York Times,* the *New York Review of Books*, and the *Times Literary Supplement*. Still serving as the standard textbook for courses on women in classical antiquity, the book has also influenced curricula of a broader scope, with excerpts reprinted in five general humanities texts. Its pivotal status in the discipline was implicitly recognized by Phyllis Culham in 1986 when she felt no need to explain the title of her article "Ten Years after Pomeroy: Studies of the Image and Reality of Women in Antiquity."

Examination of contemporaneous reviews of *Goddesses* provides illuminating glimpses of the disciplinary response both to this book and to the new currents of feminism in classics. As noted above, the book was favorably reviewed by classicists from many countries, including male and female scholars representing various disciplinary specialities and political inclinations. Indeed, two of the most lengthy and positive reviews were written by male classicists widely known for their exacting standards and conservative stance, the British philologist Hugh Lloyd-Jones (1975) and the American ancient historian Ernst Badian (1975). Although reviewers typically disagreed with individual points, they almost uniformly praised "the thoroughness of the author's research and the high quality of her own classical scholarship" (Balsdon 1977, 207), the "impressive array of information" (Dickison 1976, 62), and "the clear presentation of the extant data and the Socratic avowal of areas of collective historical ignorance" (Horowitz 1976, 825). Significantly, many reviewers predicted that the book would inaugurate a new era in research, most explicitly Ernst Badian:

> Like all important works, Pomeroy's is a beginning and not an end. . . . This modest and balanced summary of an immense and hitherto rather neglected area of the human past has both firmly established the history of ancient women as a legitimate field for future academic research (indeed, as one in which much further research is needed) and helped to remind us of the interest of the study of the past—even the remote past—in the present-day world. (Badian 1975, 31)

However, it was precisely this interest of the present-day world, "when the position of women is as much a burning topic as it has ever been" (Lloyd-Jones 1975, 1074), that made some reviewers nervous. Noting the wariness created by the rush "to fill the vast void in scholarship in the field of women's studies," Carole Trachy states that Pomeroy "manages to quell the uneasiness as well as to make a substantial contribution not only to women's studies but to classical scholarship. Professor Pomeroy makes her point without resorting to feminist rhetoric" (Trachy 1976, 87). Ernst Badian makes a similar observation: "The field was wide open for the romantic, the propagandist, and the fraud. It is a relief to see the fears dispelled by Pomeroy" (Badian 1975, 28).[15] The adverbs that keep cropping up in these reviews are also enlightening; the most common are *properly, rightly, cautiously,* and *prudently.*[16]

The frequency of such comments in the reviews provides one indication of why Pomeroy's book was so successful at starting a revolution—she presented her unconventional subject matter and conclusions within the rubric of scholarly conventions long accepted in the discipline. Since it did not explicitly emphasize the rhetoric of contemporary theory or feminism, her book was able to present an essentially feminist approach in a manner that ensured it would be neither ignored nor summarily rejected by the mainstream. These reviews confirm the efficacy of this approach; an overt and dramatic challenge to the disciplinary culture would have been premature and self-defeating.[17]

New Methodological Principles

Taken together, *Goddesses* and the 1973 issue of *Arethusa* were actually
establishing new methodological principles for the study of women in classical antiquity. These principles can be conveniently summarized under six
headings (cf. Skinner 1987b; Versnel 1987).

1. Women should not be treated "as an undifferentiated mass"
   (Pomeroy 1975, 60); groups of women (not "Woman") must be
   studied in the specific context of socioeconomic class, culture, and
   time period. Many reviewers of Pomeroy singled this out as one of
   the chief contributions of her book.

2. Sources must also be differentiated and interpreted with due respect
   for their individual codes, conventions, and biases, recognizing also
   the pervasively male origin of both the ancient sources and their
   later interpreters.

3. Because of the complexity suggested by the first two points, the
   most fruitful approach to studying ancient women will employ multiple viewpoints. Thus, a significantly novel feature of classical
   scholarship on ancient women is its *collaborative* nature. Sullivan's
   editorial introduction to the *Arethusa* issue speaks of a "venture into
   democratic editorship," with all contributors reading and comment-
   ing upon all articles in the collection (Sullivan 1973, 5).[18]

4. Unlike earlier studies, feminist scholarship will be interested in
   women *qua* women, not as a vehicle for the exploration of masculine ideology, whether ancient or modern, nor as a category to think
   with. Feminist theory and methodology will be essential to compensate for the biased and fragmentary nature of the evidence (as
   demonstrated, e.g., by the fact that Mitchell Carroll was unable to
   fulfill his professed goal of recovering "the subjective side" of
   women's lives because he did not have access to the modern conceptual tools provided by feminism). As Sullivan put it, "One deter-
   minant of our editorial choice was . . . the greater or less, deliberate
   or accidental, embodiment of a feminist perspective" (Sullivan
   1973, 5).

5. Such a feminist perspective is not monolithic but can encompass
   considerable diversity; in fact, respectful dialogue and debate open
   the most productive path to knowledge. Thus, Sullivan noted that
   "conflicting views . . . were deliberately left unreconciled" (Sullivan 1973, 5), and Pomeroy stated, "on issues where the evidence
   seemed to me to be insufficient to justify choosing one viewpoint
   and rejecting another, I have generally refrained from indicating a
   preference and arguing for it" (Pomeroy 1975, xii). Phyllis Culham
   admirably characterized such an approach as the ability "not only to

tolerate dissent on some fundamental issues but to foster debate on those matters in a public forum" (Culham 1986, 24 n. 1).

6. Work on women in antiquity must not be conceived solely in positivistic terms (whose hallmarks are conveyed by the adjectives *neutral* and *objective*); it requires an interest in theory, in conjecture, in "the discernment of patterns, inter-relationships, and chains of causality" rather than the mere accumulation of "facts" (Sullivan 1973, 5).

These new methodological principles were appearing in work on a number of different fronts (panels, conferences, articles) in the early 1970s; the immediate popularity of the *Arethusa* issue and Pomeroy's book indicate that they filled a need that had been building for some time. Marilyn Skinner feels that this period fostered "a spontaneous and widespread modification in disciplinary thinking" (Skinner 1987b, 71). Although she characterizes this as "a Kuhnian 'paradigm shift' in operation," I prefer Stephen Toulmin's concept of a "rational frontier." Such a frontier is reached in the development of a discipline when new and unforeseen problems or questions force a reappraisal of its methods, procedures, or criteria, leading to a potential redirection of the discipline or redrawing of its boundaries (Toulmin 1972, 241). When such a frontier is reached, professional developments in a field become crucial determinants of its future direction; the situation cannot be understood in isolation from the cultural, social, and institutional contexts of the disciplinary practitioners. In the 1970s, classics was poised at just such a rational frontier, and we must now backtrack to analyze the professional developments in the U.S. classics community before we can assess whether crossing this frontier has indeed led to a significant redirection of the discipline.

2

THE GENDERING
OF THE CLASSICIST

At its 1971 annual meeting, the professional organization of classicists, the American Philological Association (APA), sponsored a panel devoted to doctoral programs in classics, subsequently published in the *Classical World*. The four papers (all presented by males) expressed substantial criticism of graduate education in the field, pointing particularly to the lack of attention to the problems of teaching the classics. The panel's respondent, George Goold (then professor of classics at Harvard, later at Yale), reacted very strongly to this aspect of the papers, claiming "we did not take up classics in order to teach it" (Panel Discussion of Doctoral Programs in the Classics 1972, 258). In fact, Goold deplored the very existence of the panel as attesting that "professionalism is corrupting the American Philological Association," an association whose program in uncorrupted days had "consisted exclusively of papers submitted by scholars with something to say. The meeting revolved about disinterested scholarship" (258). At the climax of his polemic, Goold stated,

I deny that a doctorate in classics should include any teacher-training at all: I hold that the degree is and should remain a certification of academic excellence, open to any, not only blacks and women, but deaf-mutes as well, who provide evidence of the ability to excel academically. (260)

Although Goold clearly intended to contrast "academic excellence" with "teacher-training," the examples he chose to include in this statement are quite telling. Underlying his response is an image of the ideal classical scholar disinterestedly pursuing the disembodied life of the mind, answerable only to a standard of excellence that is completely unaffected by considerations of race, sex, or physical ability.[1] This statement, however, belies that image, revealing just how closely the vestments of the ideal classical scholar had been tailored to fit only a certain type of male. The sentence structure indicates that the speaker is introducing categories that range from the unusual to the totally unexpected in order to highlight the inclusiveness of his word "any." But women had been earning a significant proportion of classics doctorates in the United States for a long time—26.5% in the period from 1920 to 1971 (National Research Council 1978, 120). The fact that Goold includes women in his "not only" phrase despite their well-established presence as graduate students in classics demonstrates that he still perceives them as anomalous.

Furthermore, the coupling of categories in this statement suggests that he views both race and sex as forms of disability. By choosing a type of handicap that would make it particularly difficult to complete a Ph.D. in a traditional graduate program, Goold implies that only exceptional individuals in any of these categories could actually "provide evidence of the ability to excel academically." The fact that this version of the "dog walking on its hind legs" argument is presented to demonstrate the *inclusiveness* of the classics profession provides another example of the discipline's lack of reflection on its own heritage. Classics, because its history has been so closely associated with elitist Western religious, social, and political structures, reveals more clearly than other academic disciplines the normative processes that produced the image of the ideal scholar.

TRADITION OF CLASSICAL LEARNING

During the Middle Ages, it was the male clergy who preserved the classical heritage, and in the Renaissance, the male aristocracy made classical learning the core of an education specifically designed to prepare men of rank and social standing (and only such men) for political and civic roles. Latin became "a sexually specialized language, used almost exclusively for communication between male and male" (Ong 1962, 211; see also Ong 1959, in which he discusses training in the Latin language as a male puberty rite).

In their book *From Humanism to the Humanities: Education and the Liberal Arts in Fifteenth- and Sixteenth-Century Europe*, Anthony Grafton and Lisa Jardine carefully study the Western ideal of a humanist liberal arts education in its formative period. The authors vividly demonstrate the implicit standards of sexual, racial, and class suitability underlying such an education by examining what happened to pupils who did not meet these standards, particularly accomplished women humanists like Isotta Nogarola, Cassandra Fedele, and Laura Cereta. The following summary of their conclusions is particularly revealing when juxtaposed with Goold's statement:

> *Ad omne genus hominum*, 'for every type of person', has to be read out as 'for every appropriately well-placed male individual'. 'Opportunity', that is, is a good deal more than having ability, and access to a desirable programme of study. It is also being a good social and political fit for the society's assumptions about the purpose of 'cultivation' as a qualifying requirement for power. (Grafton and Jardine 1986, 44)

The exclusionist role that the study of Latin and Greek has played in the British education system is well known; the connection between a classical education and power (and the gatekeeping function of such an education) is perhaps more direct, open, and long-lived in England than in any other country:

> The classics played such a part in English public life roughly from the mid-eighteenth century to the First World War; they formed an esoteric branch of knowledge, valued for its very uselessness in everyday terms, that regulated entrance to the best schools, the ancient universities, the law, the church and the civil service. Essentially non-vocational, they were the necessary basis of every gentlemanly vocation. (Fowler 1983, 341)

We have access to a significant amount of writing by English women of this period, and many of these women comment explicitly on their exclusion from the study of classics solely on the basis of gender (for most came from "acceptable" ranks of society, and all were intellectually accomplished). Drawing on novels, essays, and diaries, Richard Fowler (1983) traces reactions, ranging from anger to satire, that graphically demonstrate the sense of frustration and untapped potential generated by a system in which the classical languages, especially Latin, "had become not merely a subject which happened to be taught to males, but a genuine male prerogative" (Ong 1962, 215). The following brief and necessarily superficial survey is intended to sketch the way in which this masculinist tradition of classical education interacted with developments particular to the United States to produce unusual opportunities and concomitant problems for women.

WOMEN AND CLASSICAL EDUCATION IN THE UNITED STATES

When the fledgling United States began to seek a suitable form of education for its youth, the English model was naturally influential, but the new country's attitudes toward the European past were highly ambivalent. After the Revolutionary War, this ambivalence crystallized in a series of debates about the role classics should play in American education (Reinhold 1984; Veysey 1979). On the one hand, the classics symbolized civilization and culture;[2] on the other, a classical education appeared antidemocratic, for by long tradition it had "guarded the entrances into the cultivated elite" (Veysey 1979, 53). Most educational reformers were thinking of the sons of farmers and merchants when they inveighed against classical elitism, but Benjamin Rush argued that de-emphasizing the classical languages in American schools would "remove the present immense disparity which subsists between the sexes, in the degrees of their education and knowledge. . . . By ceasing to make Latin and Greek a necessary part of a liberal education, we open the doors for every species of improvement to the female part of society" (Rush [1798] 1988, 26). The democratic ideal of a broadly accessible public education eventually won out, at least at the elementary and secondary levels, but college entrance requirements ensured a place for the classical languages (especially Latin) in the education of upper-class and upwardly mobile American males. Democratic arguments for the education of women, however, centered upon women's role as "mothers of the Republic"[3] rather than as citizens in their own right, and this education did not include classical learning, which was thought to "unsex" women and predispose them toward pride and pedantry (Kerber 1987). Consequently, Benjamin Rush sought to lessen the educational disparity between men and women by de-emphasizing classical languages for males rather than by teaching these languages to females. Accordingly, even the female academies and seminaries offering a full English curriculum did not provide instruction in Latin and Greek, although a few schools, like Miss Porter's School in Connecticut, offered classical languages precisely in order to defy the norm for women.

The social and economic situation of the rapidly expanding United States helped to shape a system of public schooling that proved very different from that of Europe, particularly with regard to the sex of teachers. By the end of the nineteenth century, well over half of all teachers in the United States were women. A national survey of American teachers in 1930 showed a female/male ratio of 19 to 1 in elementary schools and 3 to 1 on the secondary level; in comparison, in Germany at that time, 75% of primary teachers and 71% of secondary teachers were men (Conway 1989, 149). Doubtless the percentage of women teaching Latin in American schools was lower than the overall figures because it was difficult for women to acquire training in the classical languages, but most schoolteachers did not have a rigorous academic preparation in any case, and the early annals of regional classical associations such as the Classical Association of the Atlantic States indicate that a large number of women were teaching Latin by the beginning of the twentieth century (Donlan 1981).[4]

Another unique feature of the educational system in America was the founding of colleges specifically designed to give women a liberal arts education equivalent to that provided by colleges for men. Vassar (1865), Wellesley (1875), and Smith (1875) all offered classics programs, which were essential if these institutions were to fulfill their goal of playing the role for women that Harvard and Yale played for men. Although there were coeducational colleges, the only institutions of higher education where women could be sure that they would be welcomed and taken seriously were the women's colleges (Solomon 1985), particularly with regard to classical learning. For a few determined women, however, even the women's colleges were not serious enough; Abby Leach, for example, went to extraordinary lengths to get classical training equal to that of a man, traveling to Cambridge and making private arrangements to be taught by the classics professors of Harvard. Her arrangements coincided with the efforts of Arthur and Stella Gilman and Mrs. Louis Agassiz to establish an "Annex" in which Harvard professors would give classes for young women (begun in 1879, this arrangement would later evolve into Radcliffe College), and Abby Leach was one of the first to receive a certificate of B.A. equivalency from the Harvard Annex (Briggs forthcoming; Horowitz 1984; Solomon 1985).[5] The first American woman to earn a Ph.D., Helen Magill, did so in Greek from Boston University in 1877, after which she spent three years furthering her classical studies at Cambridge University (Kennedy 1984, 331).

At the same time that women were making inroads into the traditional liberal arts collegiate education, however, higher education in America was moving toward the ideal of the research university along the lines of the Germanic pattern. Patricia Graham argues that American women achieved their greatest gains in higher education during the period of educational diversity and experimentation when the original British standard, "the monolithic ideal of classical education," was breaking up but the new paradigm of the Germanic research university had not yet taken over (Graham 1978, 761). Graham emphasizes "the loss of variety" as a major factor in the subsequent narrowing of educational opportunity for American women, but I maintain that the highly male-identified nature of classics played an important gate-keeping role in this development, as it had in the earlier, monolithic ideal.[6] The movement toward the research university in the United States began with ambitious young men earning doctorates in classics from German universities; when Johns Hopkins was created in 1876 as a research university on the German model, the first professor appointed was Basil Lanneau Gildersleeve, who had received a Ph.D. in classics from the University of Göttingen (Agard 1967; Calder 1992). This German influence helped to perpetuate the maleness of the American professoriate, for the classical profession in nineteenth- and early twentieth-century Germany had a highly masculine, even antifeminine tone (DeJean 1989).[7]

American women seeking to emulate their male compatriots by pursuing advanced classical studies in Germany faced hostility and humiliation. Edith Hamilton and her sister Alice were allowed to attend classes but told they should endeavor to be "invisible"; when Edith petitioned to study classics at the University of Munich, the professors considered putting her in a curtained theater box so she could listen to lectures without being seen but eventually seated her on the side of the lecturer's platform, "where nobody could be contaminated by her" (Ascher 1973, 355; Hallett forthcoming/a). In fact, this kind of hostility to women in the classics profession ironically helped open up a new opportunity for American women to engage in advanced scholarship. When he established Bryn Mawr, Joseph Wright Taylor had intended to found a Quaker college for women along the lines of Smith College, but Bryn Mawr's first dean and second president, the formidable M. Carey Thomas, was determined to pattern the college after the Hopkins model of a research university, a process she began by hiring Paul Shorey, with a recent doctorate from the University of Munich, for the classics program. Thomas's determination stemmed in part from the obstacles she herself had encountered in her pursuit of classical studies. After graduating from Cornell University in 1877, she attempted to enroll in Hopkins' graduate program in classics. She was admitted (possibly because her father was on the board of trustees) and allowed to attend lectures on the condition that she sit behind a black curtain so that she would not be "an unnecessary distraction." However, she was denied access to Gildersleeve's Greek seminar; though she performed very well on the examinations, her year of study was frustrating for her and for Gildersleeve, and he advised her to withdraw (Briggs forthcoming). She then attended lectures and seminars and wrote a thesis at the University of Leipzig but was not granted a degree because of her sex. She continued her studies at the University of Zurich, where despite the numerous obstacles placed in her path, she finally received a doctorate in classical philology summa cum laude in 1882 (Horowitz 1984; 1995).

EARLY WOMEN CLASSICISTS IN THE UNITED STATES

In the face of such obstacles, why did a relatively large number of American women in the late nineteenth and early twentieth centuries choose to study classics? Although similar barriers had confronted Jewish men who aspired to careers in classics,[8] these gradually crumbled, but it proved much harder to diversify the gender and color of "academic man" (note the coupling of women and Blacks in the Goold quotation earlier in this chapter). In describing women who were disadvantaged by race as well as gender, Shelley Haley suggests one possible answer:

> [Frances Jackson] Coppin, [Anna Julia] Cooper, and [Mary Church] Terrell viewed classics as a challenge, a concrete way to disprove the prevailing racist and sexist stereotypes of their times. . . . Each believed that education was the key to overthrowing the disadvantages that Black women and men faced and still face. Since a classical education was the yardstick for intellectual capability, Coppin, Cooper, and Terrell learned classics, that microcosm of their society where Black women were silenced and thought incapable of intellectual endeavor. That learning, in turn, had a symbolic value for them. (Haley 1993a, 25–26)[9]

Paradoxically, as Haley notes, part of the appeal classics had for women may have stemmed from the fact that its tradition excluded them so decisively; demonstrating mastery of the classical languages symbolically represented earning a recognized place in Western culture, a badge of intellectual achievement previously thought possible only for men. In a 1903 speech to the Association of Collegiate Alumnae, M. Carey Thomas triumphantly pointed to "the avidity and rapture with which girls devote themselves to Greek and Latin" as conclusive disproof of the assertion that women are suited only for certain areas of study. She argued that American women had already proven their ability to excel in university examinations and teach high school boys and girls effectively. Although women had not yet demonstrated "the crowning gift of all, the power of original thought and research," this was only because they were still denied the requisite professional conditions for advanced scholarship, which emerges "under the spur of competition for professorships, and of a struggle for livelihood." Furthermore, Thomas argued, women lacked the social support routinely available to their male counterparts, for women scholars "must as a rule deny themselves the companionship of married life" (quoted in Horowitz 1995, 13).

This speech highlights key factors in the situation of women classicists in America. On the one hand, they faced the same elitist and exclusionary masculine tradition as their counterparts in England and on the Continent; on the other hand, they had educational and professional opportunities unavailable to women in other countries. American colleges offered women a classical education earlier in the century and on a more broadly accessible basis than anywhere else in the world. Furthermore, educated American women had respectable ways to use their education beyond the amateur role of the "woman of letters." Many taught Latin on the secondary level, and the network of women's colleges in America offered at least some white women the chance for a professional academic career in classics.

Indeed, we can see what a striking role women's colleges have played in the careers of female classicists in America by glancing at the 11 women who served as presidents of the American Philological Association from its founding in 1869 to 1995 (see table 1 on page 141).[10] With the exception of Gertrude Smith and Helen North, all of these women were educated and/or taught at women's colleges. Seven never married, including all who served before the 1950s. All but Smith and Vermeule were associated primarily with undergraduate colleges (though Bryn Mawr does have a graduate program); in contrast, the vast majority of men elected to the APA presidency taught at research universities with prominent doctoral programs in classics. Gertrude Smith, the only one of these women before the mid 1970s whose career seems to parallel that of distinguished male classicists of her generation, is in some ways the exception that proves the rule. Since she was born and raised in Illinois, attending the coeducational University of Chicago was a more obvious choice than traveling to one of the women's colleges in the Northeast. Once at Chicago, she continued straight through to her doctorate, becoming the star pupil of her dissertation director, Robert J. Bonner, with whom she subsequently coauthored a major, two-volume work on Athenian law. Other women had received doctorates from research universities; what was unprecedented about Smith's career was the fact that the Department of Greek at Chicago immediately offered her a position on its faculty. She subsequently advanced through the academic ranks to full professor and chaired the department for 27 years. As Michael Gagarin points out in a forthcoming article, this position gave her the opportunity to teach and influence many male as well as female students, which made her career unique among female classicists of her era. It seems clear that Smith was not only very talented and determined (qualities that other women classicists similarly possessed) but also extraordinarily lucky—first, to find a male mentor who was willing to work with her on scholarly publications and who doubtless supported her career; and second, to begin her association with Chicago when the university still had a relatively high proportion of women on its faculty.[11] Unlike most other female classicists of the period, Smith did marry, though the circumstances of her marriage were also unusual. Smith married Sam Greenwood when she was 45 years old, retaining her profession and her maiden name. Though Smith's peer in age, Greenwood had received his Ph.D. in classics from the University of Chicago just two years before the marriage; since Greenwood taught at a college in Ohio, the couple had a commuter marriage until both retired and moved to Nashville.

Significantly, not one of these scholars concentrated on women in her research or actively espoused feminist causes within the classics profession, though Leach and Haight advocated women's education in other forums.[12] Haight published 10 books on classical topics (focused particularly on ancient prose fiction) that appealed more to a popular than a scholarly audience; it is obvious that she sought to highlight elements of "romance" and references to women in her sources. Unfortunately, this only contributed to the fear that female classicists would "soften" the classics profession, and classical reviewers criticized her books harshly. One reviewer even derided her treatment of the Greek romances as "potentially dangerous" because readers misled by her "flattering but very imperfect pictures" might dismiss all of Greek literature once they encountered the Greek romances "as they really are" (Rattenbury 1943, 115). Indeed, the only early woman classicist who did focus her research on women in a way analogous to modern scholars of women in antiquity—Grace Harriet Macurdy—was never elected to the APA presidency or accorded any of the other major honors of the classics profession. Educated at Radcliffe and Columbia, Macurdy taught for 44 years at Vassar; when she retired, the president of Vassar, Henry Mac-Cracken, commented on the connection between her commitment to modern women and her scholarship: "Her deep interest in the achievements of women and in their opportunities both for political and for social equality has led her studies of late into the history of Greek women" (quoted in Pomeroy 1994). Her most significant book, *Hellenistic Queens: A Study of Woman-Power in Macedonia, Seleucid Syria, and Ptolemaic Egypt*, first published in 1932, is still used; it was reprinted in 1975 and again in 1977 in the wake of new interest in the study of ancient women. Although Macurdy herself does not explicitly link her sex to that of her subjects, this connection is implicit in her criticism of male scholars' reliance upon feminine stereotypes in their treatment of the Hellenistic queens, illustrated in the following passage about Cleopatra VII:

> [The ancient historian John] Mahaffy finds that she was already false to Antony at Actium and there computed with the utmost care the chances of the rivals, hoping that her charms might still work to secure another great Roman for her own. His views about the psychology of female love, in which he thinks nothing is more frequent than "a strong passion co-existing with selfish ambition, so that a woman embraces with keener transports the lover whom she has betrayed than one whom she has not thought of betraying", must surely have been gathered from an extensive reading of melodrama rather than from an experience of the facts of life. (Macurdy 1932, 221)

It is interesting to speculate about the role that Macurdy's scholarly emphasis on women may have played in the classics profession's failure to confer on her the professional rewards accorded to other women classicists. For example, the contrast with Lily Ross Taylor (discussed later), who focused her work on the masculine sphere, is striking.

Although women were part of the American classics community from the very beginning (the first printed membership list of the APA contains the names of 8 women among the 164 members), the profession responded to their presence in a very ambivalent manner. Some saw them as an embarrassment, an indication of the "softening" of the discipline; most reacted with what we might call "benign neglect," ignoring the sex of the most distinguished women, treating them as honorary men, but not fully acknowledging their contributions. For example, the official history of the first 50 years of the APA consistently refers to members as "men" and "gentlemen" and does not mention women at all, despite the fact that Abby Leach had held the presidency in 1899–1900; the author does, however, refer to "that coy, demure daughter, Simplification" and uses the pronoun "she" for philology (Moore 1919, 12).[13] An accompanying article on "Fifty Years of Classical Studies in America" is also silent about women's contributions, making one disparaging reference to the British classicist Jane Ellen Harrison and including, in the midst of a long list of books referred to by title and author's last name, "Mrs. Wright's *History of Greek Literature*" (Shorey 1919, 49). In a similar vein, a 1953 article surveying classical scholarship in America very briefly mentions only two women, naming a book by the German refugee classicist Margarete Bieber and including Lily Ross Taylor in a list of individuals who "stand out among the modest achievement of our scholars" (Agard 1967, 159).

By the 1960s, the profession was finally ready to take official notice of the presence of women. Early in Lucius Shero's historical sketch of the first 95 years of the APA, he states, "Women members have had a place in the Association from its beginning, and the proportion of them in the total membership has increased. During the course of the years women have taken an active and important part in the affairs of the Association, and from their ranks have come some of the Association's truly distinguished Presidents" (Shero 1963, xx). Herbert Benario points to this passage in support of his claim that "classicists have long since recognized the distinction of many of the women in the field, long before women's liberation began and to an extent which shames the comparable achievement (or lack thereof) of some of our sister disciplines" (Benario 1977, 258); he notes that the APA had nine female presidents by 1977, in comparison with only four in the Modern Language Association and one in the American Historical Association.[14] Such acknowledgment, however, seems rather hollow when we look at it in context. After the passage quoted above, Shero's text does not refer again to any women, either by implication or by name, although many men are extensively discussed (if the female presidents were so distinguished, one wonders, why are none of them discussed or even named?). The only time a woman's name appears in the entire history is among a list of recipients of the Goodwin Award of Merit for a book of outstanding classical scholarship (Lily Ross Taylor had won in 1962). In 1984, when George Kennedy surveyed developments in classics in the United States since the 1828 Yale Report, he included only two female classicists, referring to "the popular scholarship of Edith Hamilton" and mentioning that "new ground was broken by Sarah B. Pomeroy in *Goddesses, Whores, Wives, and Slaves: Women in Classical Antiquity*" (1984, 346–48). However, instead of discussing this new direction in classics any further, he immediately devotes a lengthy paragraph to male homosexuality, "another feature of ancient life which has been allowed to come to the surface" (348). A recent article analyzing "Changing Patterns of Scholarship as Seen from the Center for Hellenic Studies" (Stewart 1990) does not include a single female scholar (although many women had been fellows of the Center), nor does it mention any scholarly trends associated with feminism or the study of women in antiquity.

THE DOUBLE LEGACY FOR WOMEN IN THE AMERICAN CLASSICS COMMUNITY

The unique interaction of classics with the development of educational opportunities for women in the United States has left contemporary women in classics with a double legacy. I can only sketch the broad outlines of this legacy here, but a more detailed study of these issues would profit not only classicists but also historians of women's education in the United States. The many excellent studies produced by the latter largely neglect the significant role played by classics, and the studies of the classical tradition in America pay no attention to women.

The bright side of this double legacy is bluntly summarized by William Calder: "Women scholars first were heard in American classics. . . . Surely the encouragement of women is a proud part of the American achievement" (Calder 1994, xxxvii). Because of the unusual educational and professional opportunities available to them, American women made earlier and more wide-ranging contributions to the discipline and profession of classics than women in other parts of the world.[15] However, I contend that this very success led to the problematic side of the legacy of classics in the United States because it exacerbated the sense of inferiority that American classicists have typically manifested in the face of their European counterparts, particularly the British and the Germans. The general American deference to European culture was compounded in the case of classics by the American classicists' failure to maintain the exclusive masculinity that so marked the history of the profession elsewhere. It was hard to claim the status of male puberty rite for Latin studies when the majority of Latin teachers were women; harder still to hold on to the image of the magisterial, masculine, *wissenschaftlicher* classicist when women were not only publishing scholarly works in the field but even occasionally presiding over meetings of learned societies. Women were undoubtedly *there,* almost from the very beginning, but their presence was construed as a potential embarrassment or even a counterweight keeping American classics from achieving the Olympian heights of European scholarship.

European scholars fueled this sense that the presence of women had trivialized classics in America. After the German professor Eduard Meyer had spent a year as guest professor at Harvard from 1909 to 1910, he commented in a book about the United States that the admission of women to American universities had been disastrous for humanities disciplines, particularly classics, for this led the most brilliant men to dismiss them as *Weiberdisziplinen* and turn instead to the natural sciences (Meyer 1920, 189).[16] A 1955 letter from the British novelist T. H. White crystallizes this attitude; White responded to a gift of Edith Hamilton's *The Greek Way* with the words, "I can't say that I was very much impressed . . . but I am an old-fashioned European reactionary and do not share the American view that women are natural authors, ambassadors, savants. . . . It will be rather fun when the American male eventually revolts" (quoted in Hallett forthcoming/a). A recent anecdote conveyed to me through a personal communication illustrates that this kind of disparaging connection of women and American classicists is still current: when asked to submit his full name for publication, a male classicist responded, "I was taught very early that using first name plus middle initial to style oneself is done only by women and Americans. As I am neither, I would prefer to keep my name as listed [i.e., initials plus last name]."

Faced with such external disparagement and internal insecurity, it is not surprising that male classicists in America attempted to ignore, downplay, or even thwart women in the profession; it is also easy to see why the image of the ideal classical scholar in America had remained so decidedly masculine even as late as 1971, when Goold[17] made the statement quoted earlier in this chapter, despite the undeniable presence and contributions of so many women. Women classicists faced discrimination because of their sex, but they were able to achieve some professional recognition and rewards through a complex gender performance that qualified them as "honorary males."[18]

As an illustration, let us briefly consider the career of Lily Ross Taylor, adduced by Benario (1977) as the prime example of classicists' recognition of women in the profession. From one perspective he is right, and Taylor's career might seem to bear out Goold's contention that the sole criterion for a classical scholar in the United States is academic excellence. For Taylor did receive most of the profession's highest rewards: she was the first woman to win the Goodwin Award of Merit, the third to be elected president of the APA, and the only woman invited to deliver the Sather Lectures at the University of California, Berkeley, in the first 50 years of the lectureship that Benario calls "the most distinguished classical lectureship in this country if not the world." She was the only woman and the only American to be awarded the gold medal of the city of Rome and also the only woman elected honorary member of the Society for the Promotion of Roman Studies (Benario 1977, 259). She is also the only American woman included in the 50 entries in *Classical Scholarship: A Biographical Dictionary* (Briggs and Calder 1990; Broughton 1990); the only other woman in the collection is the British classicist Jane Ellen Harrison. But the very prevalence in this list of the words *first* and *only* should give us pause, for it suggests that Taylor had somehow transcended (and simultaneously suppressed) her sex to achieve these distinctions: one pictures Edith Hamilton sitting on the side of the Munich lecturer's platform in solitary splendor. Taylor's career appears to bear out Rose Coser's observation that a male-dominated system can absorb a few exceptional women, whose "achievement gains salience over their womanhood" (Coser 1973, 472).

A brilliant scholar and teacher, Taylor dressed conservatively and never married. Although her undergraduate degree was from the University of Wisconsin, the bulk of her career was spent at women's colleges. She earned her doctorate at Bryn Mawr and returned there after 15 years at Vassar, ultimately serving as dean of Bryn Mawr's graduate school, which was at that time open only to women. Her numerous publications deal with Roman religious and political institutions; although she made significant contributions to scholarship in these areas, she never attempted to probe beneath the traditionally masculine parameters of these topics in order to discover the role of women. During her lifetime, neither she nor anyone else publicly called attention to her sex;[19] the "memorial minute" read to the APA after her death by her colleague Agnes K. L. Michels (1969) might, if names and pronouns were changed, have applied equally well to a man. However, the trajectory of a similarly gifted man's career would have been very different. A male classicist of comparable distinction would have left Bryn Mawr (as many in fact did) for a position in one of the most prestigious graduate schools and would probably have received far more notice in the official histories of the profession and discipline. Instead of illustrating a gender-free criterion of excellence, therefore, Taylor's career shows how masculine the standard actually was.

Thus, Susan Braley Franklin, who was the first woman to publish an article in *Transactions and Proceedings of the American Philological Association*, was only donning the traditional mantle of the classical scholar by choosing to cloak her sex in the generic masculine pronoun when she wrote about her excitement at attending the first meeting of the Classical Association of the Middle States and Maryland: "To the teacher of Classics wearied by the heated struggle to defend his subject among unbelievers, there comes, like a cool sea breeze on a stifling morning, the consciousness that at last he has entered an assembly where Greek and Latin are in good repute" (Franklin 1908, 98). In order to be accepted as part of that delightful assembly, it seems that American women in the past were willing to submerge their sex, to be—at least as far as the classics profession was concerned—"quiet, tractable, cloistered." As already noted, most of these women were figuratively cloistered in the various women's colleges, and many were literally unmarried.

Ironically, the careers of early women classicists in America would seem to fulfill the dire predictions of early Americans that a classical education would "unsex" women, though not for the reasons advanced by these critics. The reason had nothing to do with women's nature and everything to do with the attitudes of men in the profession. For all the vaunted devotion to "the disembodied life of the mind," it was only women who were required to conform to this ideal, for men's bodies were perceived as perfectly compatible with the mantle of scholarship. For example, classicists did not hesitate to use highly sex-specific language when speaking of their male colleagues: at a retirement dinner for Charles Knapp, who had edited the *Classical World* for 23 years, Moses Hadas stated that this journal "has in a peculiar sense become Professor Knapp's personal organ for the dissemination of sound doctrine."[20] Patricia Graham argues that women have difficulty being viewed as professionals because the construction of womanhood requires eroticism, and "it is difficult to imagine anything more hostile to professionalism than eroticism" (Graham 1978, 771). I maintain, however, that it is erotic *objectification*, not eroticism, that is perceived as incompatible with professionalism. Within the classics profession, male eroticism has been viewed as acceptable and even praiseworthy, from the imagery of courting Philologia to the actual sexual pursuit of female graduate students.[21]

However, the double legacy described above has been even more problematic for female classicists in America than the construction of women as erotic objects, because women themselves have tended to accept the require-ment that they become "honorary males" and internalize it as part of their professional self-definition. Almost from the beginning, American women had some opportunities, however limited, to succeed in the classics profes-sion, but they had to do this without calling attention to their sex, to succeed as "disembodied scholars," because of the pervasive male fear that classics in the United States would be perceived and denigrated as feminine, as *Weiberdisziplinen*. The unique history of education in the United States gave some women entrée into the classics profession, and their achievements made it impossible to discount them. However, the masculinist construction of the profession sought to discipline their performance of gender in accor-dance with male-identified scholarly norms and feminine behavior that would not call attention to their female bodies. The profession rewarded women who were able and willing to perform this complex gender-balancing act, and I do not mean to suggest that women like Lily Ross Taylor perceived their lives as circumscribed. On the contrary, the challenging opportunities offered by the profession were undoubtedly seen as very positive in contrast with conventional female sex roles available at the time. It was not until the advent of modern feminism that some female classicists in the United States began to recognize and protest the inequity of this gender-balancing require-ment, demanding to be taken seriously as scholars, as professional classi-cists, and as women.

FEMINIST NETWORKING AND PROFESSIONAL CHANGE

The year 1972 was a banner year for American women in classics, for it saw the establishment of two significant feminist organizations within the Ameri-can Philological Association: the Committee on the Status of Women and Minority Groups (CSWMG) and the Women's Classical Caucus (WCC).[22] A comparison of the published *Proceedings* of the APA for 1971 and 1972 illustrates the difference.[23] In the 1971 volume, the word *woman/women* does not appear at all; in the 1972 volume, it occurs nine times. In the 1971 volume, an anxious report on the shrinking job market for classicists con-tains the following paragraph:

> The very able, imaginative, highly motivated classicist with a high degree of verbal and some mathematical skill can forge for himself a rewarding career

in many areas of work, and his classical training will have aided him in developing his skills and abilities. He is the very one, however, who can also find a good teaching position in the classics and the one we need to keep in the profession. The classicists who constitute the problem are the more nearly average students who have worked hard to learn the languages and have acquired a good control of their subject which would, until recently, have been more than adequate to ensure them satisfactory and satisfying positions in many educational institutions. These are the ones, however, who will be less likely to get the teaching jobs in the present state of affairs and they are ironically the very ones who will have greatest difficulty adjusting to alternative careers. (Gordan et al. 1971, lvi)

Although this was probably not the intention of the committee, the use of the masculine pronoun for the able classicist, which is highlighted by the switch to plural pronouns for "the classicists who constitute the problem," makes it very difficult for the reader to picture women in the former category. In contrast, although the "generic" masculine is still used rather relentlessly in the 1972 volume, the alternative form unexpectedly appears in the minutes of the board of directors, when *he (she)* and *him (her)* are used in a discussion about selecting an annual meeting and exhibits manager (lxix). Furthermore, the 1972 list of papers delivered at the annual meeting includes the first APA panel ever devoted to women: "Ancient Greek Women and Modern Criticism," chaired by Mary Lefkowitz. The title of one of the papers, referring to the status debate discussed in chapter 1, conveys the sense that this kind of attention to women was long overdue ("Athenian Women: A Reply to Mr. Kitto, At Last," by Virginia Hunter).[24]

This dry official record only hints at the professional ferment underlying these changes. Fired by the various movements for "women's liberation" that emerged in the 1960s, women classicists were beginning to band together and challenge old assumptions on both the professional and the disciplinary fronts (for the latter, see chapter 1). Just as traditional classical scholarship had erased ancient women, so the concept of the individualistic, "disembodied" scholar had concealed the group advantages and gender expectations that automatically favored males. As more women attempted to combine marriage, parenthood, and a professional career in classics (as men in the field had always done), the reality of their lives sharply highlighted the inequities of their situation. For example, Sarah Pomeroy, author of the first modern book-length study of women in antiquity and first chairperson of the WCC, lost a tenure-track position at Hunter College in 1966 because she became pregnant. At that time, the City University of New York had a policy that pregnant women were not allowed to teach; when Pomeroy returned

from this forced leave, she was informed that the tenure-track line on which
she had initially been hired was no longer available and offered only an
adjunct position. She subsequently became a named plaintiff in a major
class-action suit by the Women's Coalition of CUNY that eventually over-
turned this pregnancy policy; though she regained a tenure-track position in
the midseventies, she was never compensated for the years of lost rank and
salary. Experiences like this led women to insist that the classics profession
not only directly acknowledge the presence of women but also recognize the
group disadvantages under which they labored and begin to remove these
obstacles.

Two Feminist Organizations

Under pressure from women classicists, the APA board voted in April of
1972 to establish an ad hoc committee to investigate the status of women in
the classics profession, appropriating the goodly sum of $2,500 for this pur-
pose. On 28 December 1972, a group of classicists who had been meeting to
plan the first journal issue that would focus on the study of women in classical antiquity (*Arethusa* 6.1) founded a more grassroots and activist feminist
organization "open to all individuals, regardless of sex and official occupa-
tional status, concerned with the problems encountered by women involved
in the classics profession" (Pomeroy et al. 1973, 28).[25] By 30 December
1972, the APA board had acknowledged this group as the Women's Caucus
of the American Philological Association and appropriated $150 (later
increased to $300) to support its work.

By the end of the following year, however, the attitude of the APA toward
these two groups had diverged dramatically. The board broadened the mission
of its ad hoc fact-finding committee to include minority groups and established
it as a standing committee of the APA (now called the Committee on the Status
of Women and Minority Groups [CSWMG]) but severed all ties with the more
activist Women's Caucus, curtly instructing the caucus to remove the words "of
the American Philological Association" from its name and transferring appropriated funds to another committee.[26] Making a virtue of necessity, the caucus
changed its name to the Women's Classical Caucus (WCC) and emphasized the
value of "functioning as an autonomous organization committed to the
advancement of women, to meritocratic and democratic standards, and to innovation within the Classics and Archaeological professions" (Pomeroy 1974,
66–67). The first report of the WCC indicates the variety and scope of its
activities: sponsoring a panel on ancient women at the annual meeting whose

papers had been selected through a democratic, anonymous procedure; starting an informal study group to discuss courses on women in antiquity; compiling a roster of women classical scholars; arranging day-care facilities at the APA annual meetings; coordinating with the CSWMG a study of letters of recommendation written for recent female and male doctoral recipients in classics.

The CSWMG was established to ascertain information, not to work for change, but it interpreted its mandate more broadly from the very beginning. Its first report concluded with a series of strongly worded recommendations for improving women's status in the profession; the board subsequently adopted these, agreeing to send out letters to department chairs and journal editors with only a slight toning down of wording (e.g., *must* to *should*). The CSWMG aimed to "present to the Association an authoritative and objective account of the status of women in our profession" (Lefkowitz et al. 1973, 22). Based on a massive mailing of questionnaires to 2,450 individuals in 1972, with a response rate of 36%, the CSWMG reported that 27% of the respondents teaching classics at the college level were women, 73% men. The committee did not hesitate to point out "darker" aspects of this picture: women were disproportionately represented at the lower ranks, in four-year colleges as opposed to universities, and in part-time teaching; women advanced more slowly through the academic ranks and earned consistently lower salaries (the median salary for women was $11,500, for men $13,500, and the gap widened with age). Fewer women than men were married, and the disparity was most apparent at the highest ranks: 70% of women full professors had never married, while this was true of only 14% of men at the same rank. Furthermore, marriage correlated positively with men's publication rates but negatively with women's.

The most disturbing statistic was not published in this report, but it inspired the first successful campaign for change waged by the WCC and the CSWMG: women had delivered only 6.7% of the papers at the 1973 annual meeting of the APA. Since the CSWMG survey had demonstrated that women constituted approximately one-quarter of all professional classicists, this figure was shockingly low and suggested bias in the selection procedures of the Program Committee. The WCC and CSWMG worked hard to convince the board that the Program Committee should review all abstracts anonymously on an experimental basis. In its report, the Program Committee grumbled that anonymity made the selection "more difficult and time-consuming" and doubted whether the results would be much different. Even the doubters, however, were convinced by the statistics—women delivered 13%

of the papers at the 1974 annual meeting and 19.5% in 1975, nearly triple the 1973 rate (Snyder et al. 1977)—and the procedure was made permanent. Armed with these statistics, which dramatically demonstrated the way that even unconscious gender bias could subvert the academic ideal of meritocracy, the CSWMG repeatedly urged journals to institute procedures for anonymous submission and refereeing of articles, and such procedures have been gradually adopted by most classical journals over the years.

The first major struggle that the WCC did *not* win was an effort to persuade the APA to change the venue of its 1980 annual meeting from New Orleans, since Louisiana had not ratified the Equal Rights Amendment. Despite repeated petitions, the APA and the American Institute of Archaeology (AIA), which holds its annual meeting concurrently with the APA, decided that they had to honor their previously existing contract with the Fairmount Hotel. The WCC boycotted the meeting in New Orleans, rescheduling its annual panel and business meeting for the 1981 Berkshire Conference on the History of Women and encouraging members to withhold their APA dues for 1980 and send the money instead to the NOW-ERA fund. In reflecting on the significance of the WCC's actions, Marilyn Skinner, WCC cochair and newsletter editor at the time, underlined the revolutionary nature of what these women were doing:

> When the Caucus finally called a boycott of the 1980 New Orleans meetings, the symbolic force of that act extended far beyond a mere manifestation of support for the ERA. In effect, we asserted that our dignity as women must take precedence over our commitment to the academic order. It was, in retrospect, the only right step—but it was a risky one. . . . [O]ur deliberate non-presence could be interpreted as a rejection of the entire value system of the classical establishment. . . . [W]e know we have made some persons uncomfortable by our determined insistence upon a change of venue. We ask them to try to imagine the frustration we feel at being denied for so long the simple human rights which should have been ours long ago, without question. (Skinner 1980, 1–2)

These two feminist organizations, then, began to make a difference in the profession almost from their inception. Many American women were no longer willing to play the roles of "disembodied scholar" or "honorary man" written for them by men anxious to preserve the masculinity of the category "classicist." They wanted to be recognized as *women* classicists; they wanted professional acknowledgment of their significant presence, of their substantial contributions, of the inequities they faced because of their gender; finally, they wanted the construction of "classicist" to change so that it could encompass female and male, diverse racial and ethnic identities, varying socioeconomic classes and sexual orientations, and a wide range of scholarly interests connected with antiquity. These are sweeping changes, especially for a field with such a long and conservative (some might say "stuffy") tradition, and they are not easily won. Both organizations have functioned, in their varying ways, as a hardworking "loyal opposition" within the APA. The CSWMG has attacked the issues through gathering information, drawing conclusions, and making recommendations; the WCC has played a more activist, gadfly role by challenging assumptions, protesting inequities, and proposing solutions. The struggle has been difficult and at times acrimonious, but important changes have been effected. Let me summarize a few of the more significant changes, using a thematic rather than a strictly chronological format.

Some Key Areas of Professional Change

The first area involves changes in the nature and organization of the program at the APA annual meeting, the central gathering place of American classicists. In keeping with its commitment to promote scholarship on ancient women and feminist approaches to all aspects of classical antiquity, the WCC has regularly presented a panel at the APA annual meeting.[27] These panels were unusual not only for their innovative subject matter and approaches, but also for their open calls for papers and democratic selection processes, and they garnered large audiences. By the end of 1973, the WCC had become one of the "affiliated groups" that met and presented panels at the annual meeting but had no organizational ties with the APA; the APA listed the panels presented by these groups in its program, but their structure and content had always been determined by the groups themselves. However, in the 1980s, the Program Committee of the APA began to assert gatekeeping authority over the content and methods of affiliated group panels, and in 1985, the committee rejected as "not up to the mark" two papers in the proposed WCC panel entitled "Reappropriating Male Texts: The Case of Ovid." The WCC strongly protested this decision, and the panel developed into a cause célèbre within the APA, drawing a large and enthusiastic audience. One of the papers, "Decentering the Text: The Case of Ovid" (Culham 1990), later became the focus of a special journal issue (*Helios* 17.2). Reflecting on the significance of this event, the panel organizer, Mary-Kay Gamel, mused:

When the question is one of methodologies and what constitutes knowledge, when a subject is controversial, dismissal of work with "insufficient quality" as the sole explanation is indistinguishable from sheer prejudice against the approach. I would read the 1985 events as a sign that feminist interpretation of important literary texts, at least in the particular form in which they were presented to the program committee, were [sic] deemed sufficiently threatening to cause an institutional overreaction. I might even suggest that while the APA was content to accept work on "women in antiquity" as a contribution to the established fund of knowledge (note the financial metaphor), a feminist attempt to re-appropriate the cultural capital required calling the thought police. (Gamel 1990, 173)[28]

The ultimate fallout from this event has been quite far-reaching, since the WCC protests led to formal reevaluation and ultimately reform of program policies.[29]

The second area involves the increasing democratization of the APA. Although officers and directors of the APA were elected by the membership, the process was only marginally democratic: candidates (usually from major universities) were selected by an appointed Nominating Committee, some positions were unopposed, and candidates' names were accompanied by brief lists of degrees, institutional affiliations, and publications. In the 1970s, the WCC began working to inform the electorate and to encourage candidate responsibility by sending out questionnaires to candidates and publishing the responses in the *WCC Newsletter*. The questionnaires became quite popular with the voters (though not necessarily with the candidates), especially after the WCC raised enough money in 1988 and 1989 to mail the responses to all members of the association.

By 1990, the APA had agreed to take over the questionnaires, now designed by a committee that included representatives of the WCC and CSWMG, and print the responses along with candidates' names and vitae. The caucus also pressed for more contested elections, and by 1991, vice presidents were no longer running unopposed. Furthermore, in 1992, the APA made a commitment to seek a balance in its slate of candidates with regard to geographical region, type of institution, and professional rank as well as sex, printing a form for members to submit who wished to be included in the pool of nominees, a process the WCC had advocated as early as 1979.

Ironically, it was a measure designed to promote voter participation in the APA (the provision for adding a candidate to the official slate of nominees through a petition signed by at least 20 members)[30] that created the opportunity for the most blatant protest against women's increasing recognition and influence in the history of the APA. After the election of Helen North in 1973, no woman was elected to the APA presidency until 1982, when one of the two male candidates selected by the Nominating Committee withdrew. The Nominating Committee insisted that it could not find another candidate, so the executive committee of the board asked Helen Bacon to run, and she was subsequently elected. No more female candidates were nominated until after the members of the Nominating Committee began to be elected instead of appointed (starting in 1985); however, the women nominated in 1988 and 1990 both lost to male candidates. Hence, the 1991 slate of candidates seemed at long last to accord modern feminists a place in the APA hierarchy, for *both* nominees for president were women (the first time this had happened in 123 years), as were four of the five official nominees for two positions on the board of directors.[31] Both of the presidential nominees (Helene P. Foley and Marilyn Arthur Katz) and most of the women nominated for director had also made substantial contributions to feminist classical scholarship, and all were longtime members of the WCC. However, such an affirmation of women and feminism in the profession was apparently too much for some APA members to stomach. Soon after the slate was announced, Richard F. Thomas of Harvard organized a petition to nominate Ludwig Koenen (then serving as APA vice president for research and chair of the classics department at the University of Michigan) for president, and Thomas himself was added by petition to the slate of candidates for director.

This invocation of a rarely used provision of the bylaws seemed to many a high-handed rejection of feminist women in the profession. The WCC sent out mailings explaining the circumstances surrounding the election, but when the votes were tallied, Koenen had been elected president and Thomas had been elected to the board of directors along with the lone man proposed by the Nominating Committee. At the annual business meeting of the APA, the WCC presented a trenchant statement maintaining that "the petition process has been used to marginalize and silence strong women candidates who earned nomination through their scholarly productivity and service to the APA," which will now be "perceived to have repudiated the modest advances that women have made in our profession." The statement closed with a call for the officers of the association to "demonstrate that this election does not signal the closing off of the APA to feminist perspectives on the study of classical antiquity and to contributions of its women members" (*APA Newsletter* 15.1 [1992]: 3). Further resolutions urged publication of the vote tallies and institution of a system of preferential balloting whenever more than two candidates are running for the same office. Indeed, when the vote tallies of the 1991 election were finally revealed, it became evident that the women candidates had split the majority vote (together they received 59.4% of votes cast), and Koenen had won by a plurality, as had both Thomas and the other man elected to the board of directors.

The entire altercation caught the attention of the national academic press, spawning articles and follow-up letters in the journal *Lingua Franca* as well as in the *Chronicle of Higher Education*.[32] When the dust had finally settled, everyone was still standing, and the wounds were painful but not permanent. Parties on all sides were surprised at the fervor of the reactions. On the one hand, feminists had not expected such a potent fear that they were somehow "taking over" the APA; after all, the vast majority of past elections had presented slates of candidates who were all men, mostly drawn from research universities and often very similar to each other. One election composed primarily of feminist women did not seem like such a revolution, but perhaps it was this very "mirror image" quality that appeared so threatening to more conservative elements. On the other hand, some of the petitioners seemed genuinely puzzled by the depth of the outrage aroused by their intervention in the election: why should this be perceived as a repudiation of feminism or women, when all they had wanted was to give voters more choice in this particular election?[33] Those in office at the time of the election were embarrassed by all of the events; they had not anticipated and did not welcome the nominations by petition, but neither did they want to alienate senior members of the profession or to be regarded as revolutionary themselves. In the end, many of the men made conciliatory speeches and gestures (notably Ludwig Koenen), several changes were made in electoral procedures (including automatic publication of vote tallies and preferential balloting), and a breakfast meeting between the leadership of the APA and the WCC was instituted as a regular feature of the annual meeting.

Professional ethics is a third area of concern for which the WCC has fought many battles, leading ultimately to the adoption within the APA of a Code of Professional Ethics in 1989[34] and the formation of a Division of Professional Matters with its own elected vice president in 1992. By constantly raising social and ethical issues—from the ERA to AIDS, from child care to personal safety at conventions, from editorial responsibility to equitable interviewing practices—the WCC and CSWMG pushed the APA to recognize that its self-image as a "learned society" devoted solely to disinterested scholarship was no longer tenable and to take on the functions of a full professional association (for the distinction, see Goodstein 1988).

Let me briefly cite a few instances where the WCC mobilized opinion against unfair practices in the profession. In 1986, the *Classical Journal* published a review article on women in antiquity research that attacked and derided feminist scholarship (Fleming 1986a). The author, Thomas Fleming, had no record of scholarly expertise or previous publications in the field of women in antiquity but had a well-established record of hostility toward feminism, having previously published an article entitled "Old Adam, New Eve: Lies, Damn Lies, and Feminist Scholarship" in a journal of conservative opinion (Fleming 1986b). Marilyn Skinner later published a feminist response to the Fleming review (Skinner 1987a), but the incident still resonates in a line from the Code of Professional Ethics: "In sending out publications for review, editors should make every effort to ensure that those solicited for reviews are qualified scholars who can provide fair, accurate, and informed assessments." When the *American Journal of Philology* established a new editorial board consisting of ten men and one woman and published an editorial manifesto that seemed to dismiss contemporary approaches as having less scholarly validity than traditional philology (AJP Today 1987), Amy Richlin organized the WCC, the CSWMG, and other professional groups to sponsor a major public forum at the APA annual meeting to debate the issue.[35] By the following year, the journal had named a new editor and had reconstituted its editorial board to include several women, among them feminists.

Sexual discrimination and sexual harassment have proved to be the most thorny ethical issues engaged by the WCC. Because of legal ramifications and concerns about confidentiality and privacy rights, the caucus has had to deploy its most effective procedures—publicity, open discussion and debate, rallying of opinion—with great caution. But the WCC has provided individuals fighting sexual discrimination and harassment with advice, emotional support, letters of recommendation and protest, and even financial support through an equity fund established in 1990 (see Gutzwiller 1989 for a description of cases that ultimately wound up in the law courts). In order to raise professional consciousness about the problem of sexual harassment, the WCC devoted an issue of its 1988 newsletter to the theme of "survival," anonymously presenting poignant stories of discrimination and harassment submitted by WCC members. Inspired by this issue, the CSWMG issued a call for anonymous testimony in preparation for a panel on sexual harassment at the 1992 APA annual meeting. Plans for this panel were fraught with difficulties as the APA scrambled to obtain legal counsel, liability insurance, and protection against all possible repercussions. As a consequence, when the panel was finally presented to a standing-room-only audience, the legal restrictions were so stringent as to prohibit all spontaneous questions and discussion. Nevertheless, the panel served an important educational function, since it set testimony from classics faculty and students in the context of broader theoretical and legal perspectives about sexual harassment; in the words of the organizers, "We are ... strengthened by our sense that our labors have instilled a greater awareness about sexual harassment in at least some of our colleagues and that we have paved the way for future efforts to combat and avoid sexual harassment" (Gold 1993a, 19).[36] This has, in fact, been the case, since experts in sexual harassment issues presented a panel and workshop at the 1995 APA annual meeting on concrete techniques for dealing with and preventing sexual harassment.

As is clear from these brief descriptions, the changes instigated by the WCC and CSWMG have benefited many sectors of the profession, not just women. This fact has not escaped the notice of male classicists seeking an overview of the profession. Writing in *The Encyclopedia of the American Left*, David Konstan credited the WCC with inspiring a new critical perspective on ancient civilization and providing "the most important stimulus to reevaluate the classical heritage" (Konstan 1990, 141–42). Lowell Edmunds singled out the caucus as an exemplar of "how organization and the mobilization of opinion can effect change in the profession" (Edmunds 1989, xvi). Significantly, Ludwig Koenen, the man whose candidacy by petition prevented the election of a feminist APA president in 1991, later paid one of the most apt tributes to the broadly beneficial professional changes instigated by the WCC: "Within the profession, much of what was first thought of in the Women's Caucus has now become common procedure, safeguarding our mutual respect in our professional and human relations, and we can no longer imagine any other way" (Koenen 1994, 22).

STATISTICAL PROFILES

Although many aspects of the professional climate have improved for women in the last 20 years, women are still proportionately underrepresented in academic employment in classics. Figure 1 (see page 155), based on information reported to the CSWMG by United States and Canadian colleges and universities, graphically demonstrates that women's overall representation in the classics faculty has increased by only six percentage points since 1975 (to 30%), lagging behind general statistics for the United States, which indicate that women comprised

31.75% of the total faculty in fall 1991 (National Center for Education Statistics 1994, 230). The most optimistic aspect of the picture for women classicists is the fact that the entire proportionate increase occurred in the *tenured* ranks. Indeed, women have enjoyed a high rate of success in tenure decisions, outpacing men's success rate by 9% since 1983, when the CSWMG began to tabulate this figure (mean percentages of 89.5 versus 80.5).

However, the slow rate of overall growth contrasts sharply with women's proportion of earned doctorates in classics, which grew from 33% in 1975 to slightly over 50% in 1994 (see fig. 2 on page 156; the 1988–95 mean was 44%).[37] The increase in classical doctoral degrees awarded to women has been much more rapid than the growth in women's representation on the classics faculty, as figure 3 demonstrates (see page 156). Since the late sixties, most women with doctorates have been seeking academic employment; figures from the APA Placement Service indicate that women have represented well over 30% of all registered candidates for academic positions since at least 1978 (see fig. 4 on page 157). In addition, women constitute approximately 36% of the individual membership of the APA.[38]

Although women have apparently been obtaining appointments at a rate close to or higher than their representation in the candidate pool since at least 1981, as figure 4 indicates,[39] the nature of the job market has made it difficult to increase significantly their overall presence on classics faculties. Women began seeking classics positions in large numbers in the early seventies, just at the point when the job market was tightening; by the mideighties, more and more appointments in classics were nontenure-track or temporary positions (in 1993, only 50% of the 118 vacancies listed with the Placement Service were tenured or tenure-track positions).[40] Under these conditions, women would have to obtain new appointments, especially tenure-track positions, at a much higher rate than men in order for substantial growth in their overall proportion of the classics faculty to occur, but this has not been happening. In fact, men have obtained over half (mean: 58%) of the appointments announced between 1989 and 1994. Figure 5 (see page 157) shows a comparative percentage breakdown of the rank of these appointments (means were used to compensate for annual fluctuations). While the general proportions are quite similar, men obtained a significantly higher percentage of the tenured or tenure-track positions that were available; only in the lowest ranking positions were the male and female percentages nearly equal.[41]

Figure 6 (see page 158) vividly illustrates the consequences of these hiring patterns, using mean figures from 1986 to 1994 CSWMG department surveys to compensate for variations in annual response rates. The percentage breakdown of different segments of the classics faculty indicates that women constitute 48% of nontenure-track faculty but only 22.5% of tenured faculty. Since classics faculties are heavily tenured (mean: 68%) and women's share of this large chunk of the pie is so small, women would have to far outnumber men on the tenure track in order to increase their share. However, women are still not even half of the tenure-track faculty (39%). Women's higher tenure success rate cannot compensate for the fact that men continue to outnumber women in tenure decisions (an average of 60.5% of tenure decisions from 1983 to 1994 involved men).

When faculties are analyzed according to level of degrees granted (see fig. 7, page 159), it is obvious that women continue to be more heavily clustered in undergraduate departments (35% total faculty) than in the more prestigious and influential graduate programs (26% total faculty). However, the historical trends illustrated in these charts reveal an interesting phenomenon: although women have made slow but steady gains in the faculty of graduate programs, including the tenured ranks, they actually lost ground in undergraduate programs in the early eighties and have barely returned to 1975 levels in recent years. So the increase in women's overall representation in the classics faculty has apparently occurred at the expense of their proportion of the faculty in undergraduate departments. Moreover, despite their gains in graduate programs, women still represent a small proportion of senior faculty in these institutions (women currently represent 20% of tenured faculty in graduate programs). This is particularly evident in the dissertation statistics (see fig. 2): in the last eight years, women have directed a tiny proportion of the dissertations reported to the APA (mean: 15%, representing only 48 individual women directing dissertations).

National statistics indicate that the salaries of doctoral recipients in classics are among the lowest in the humanities (only slightly higher than music), with men earning an average of $3,500 more than women (Brown and Mitchell 1994, 20–21). American Philological Association surveys in 1972 and 1979 showed that median salaries for male classicists were approximately 15% higher than the salaries of their female colleagues (Cole 1983, 13). Although the APA has not gathered more recent salary information from the general membership, CSWMG figures for new appointments suggest that this gender salary gap cannot be explained solely by the fact than men tend to hold higher-ranking positions than women. For example, according to responses to the 1991 CSWMG placement survey, women's average starting salary was more than $2,000 lower than men's despite the fact that the jobs were at similar levels.

CONCLUSIONS

At the end of chapter 1, I asked whether the advent of modern feminism has led the discipline and profession of classics in America to cross a "rational frontier." On the professional front, at least, the answer must be a qualified "yes." Certainly increasing numbers of men and women are recognizing the professional presence and contributions of female classicists. The old, unspoken requirement that women must become "disembodied scholars" is relaxing its hold on the profession, though it still exerts a largely uncon-scious influence on many women as well as men. Some classicists are even beginning to take pride in the prominent role played by women in American classics, claiming this as a distinctive and positive feature of our national professional culture.

Moreover, the prodding of feminist organizations has steered the APA in more democratic and inclusive directions. The academic job market has proved more recalcitrant than the APA, probably reflecting negative demo-graphic and economic trends even more than gender bias, but women have made noticeable gains in the classics faculty, particularly with regard to tenure. For ethnic minority groups, however, there have been no statistical gains at all; the latest mean figure of 1.6% of the total classics faculty is the same as the percentage reported in 1975, and minorities barely appear in the doctorate statistics (one in 1991–92 and three in 1993–94).[42]

The American classics community has clearly embarked on the course of redefining its professional boundaries. We now resume the story begun in chapter 1, turning to contemporary classical scholarship to examine how intellectual currents in the discipline have shifted in response to feminism.

3

CLASSICAL
SCHOLARSHIP:
SINGING IN ANSWER

In Euripides' *Medea*, the playwright imagines his female chorus longing for
the divine power of the lyre so that they can frame a song of their own in
answer to men's version of history (lines 410–30). We have already seen
how feminist classicists took hold of the lyre—"rescued" (Skinner 1986) or
even "hijacked" it (Richlin 1990)—but we must now consider the nature of
the song they have composed. Answering the question posed at the end of
chapter 1, whether the feminist ferment of the 1970s has led to a significant
redirection of the discipline of classics in America, requires some effort to
assess changes in the content and approach of classical scholarship. Is this
song a monody chanted by adepts in one corner of the temple, a harmony in
which all feminist individuality has been lost in the blending with traditional
voices, or a complex polyphony of contrapuntal melodic lines?

It is certainly no longer possible to deny the *existence* of the song, but
some classicists hear it as a monody with little impact on the rest of the disci-

pline. For example, James Redfield asserts that the influence of contemporary theory in classics "is not diffuse but intense within a kind of subculture which tends to function politically as a faction" (Redfield 1991, 11–12).[1] However, this type of assertion, based on the reading and experience of the asserter rather than on any form of systematic investigation, may tell us something about individual perceptions but cannot be relied upon as an overview of the discipline. Many of the earlier assessments of feminism and classics shared this characteristic (Gutzwiller and Michelini 1991; Hallett 1983, 1985; Lefkowitz 1985, 1989; Padel 1990; Rabinowitz 1993b; Richlin 1990; Skinner 1985, 1986, 1987a). While all of these articles made important contributions to our knowledge about the relationship between feminism and classics, none attempted to document their assertions. A substantial portion of my efforts for this volume, therefore, has been directed toward investigating the broader picture in a more systematic fashion and providing some statistical documentation to supplement impressions and experience. I do not claim scientific precision for any of my studies; I am no statistician, and the accessible information is in any case too unreliable for that kind of claim. Nevertheless, I do believe that the data I have gathered present a more credible overview than anything heretofore available. Because reading this material is so demanding, I have provided tables and charts whenever feasible. In chapter 2, I discussed some statistical information about the position of women in the classics profession; here I will begin my analysis of contemporary classical scholarship with a look at the numbers before turning back to the nature of the feminist "song in answer."

OVERVIEW:
WHAT THE NUMBERS SHOW

The results of several studies that I conducted involving books, articles, and dissertations indicate certain patterns and trends occurring in classical scholarship published in English. The clearest trend involves the recent explosion of book-length publications dealing with ancient Greek and Roman women and related issues (e.g., family, sexuality, gender studies). Classical journals in the United States and Canada have also increased the number of articles dealing with these issues, though the growth is less dramatic, and these journals also demonstrate an increased involvement of women as authors, referees, and editors. My study of journals also revealed changes in scholarly approach as well as content. Finally, if dissertation titles reveal anything about content and approach, these show the least feminist influence of all forms of classical scholarship, though some change is also apparent.

Books

In August 1995, I searched the Library of Congress's on-line database of books acquired since 1968. Using Boolean combinations of *Greece* or *Rome* plus variants of a number of keywords (e.g., *women, family, gender, sexuality*, etc.), I searched the subject fields and then manually eliminated all irrelevant items and classified the books according to language, gender of author, type of focus, and culture (Greece, Rome, or both). I included modern translations of ancient works when relevant (e.g., Rayor 1991) as well as translations of contemporary scholarship or reprints of older scholarship, since the very fact of translation or reissue indicates an interest in the topic. This search strategy produced a manageable list of 293 books that I believe accurately represents publishing trends in the field, though it is by no means a comprehensive bibliography because of keyword limitations and inconsistencies in subject fields. For example, books on literary works or individuals that do not include the keywords, such as *The Homeric Hymn to Demeter* (Foley 1994), *Antonia Augusta* (Kokkinos 1992), or *Feminist Interpretations of Plato* (Tuana 1994) are not included in the list.

Table 2 (page 142) presents a summary of my results, and they clearly indicate the magnitude of the growth in such books since 1970. Close to 40% of all the books on the list were published since 1990; this percentage is even greater (49%) when we count only books published in English (including works translated into English). Indeed, over half (55%) of all the books are in English, followed by German (17%), Italian (12%), and French (8%). When we consider the books published in English, a number of patterns are immediately obvious. The percentage of books dealing with Roman civilization (25%) is less than half that of books dealing with Greek civilization (53%). Significantly more women than men have published books on these topics, and the percentage of women authors is particularly striking (64%) in the books that treat both Greek and Roman civilizations. When I classified the books according to the primary focus or approach (insofar as this could be determined from the full record and my own knowledge of many of the books), I found that the majority employed a social/historical focus (broadly defined), with a literary approach also prominent. It is interesting to note that the percentages for these two approaches were nearly identical in the books dealing with Greek culture but quite disproportionate in the books dealing with both civilizations, of which 80% employed a social/historical approach. The dearth of books whose primary focus is art historical or archaeological is also noteworthy, though many of the collections include at least one article featuring art and/or archaeology, and the most recent women in antiquity text has thoroughly integrated visual materials (Fantham et al. 1994). None of these trends will surprise anyone who has read widely in these topics, but this study, limited as it is, goes beyond anecdotal evidence to provide some statistical support for these prevalent impressions.

Articles

A new bibliographic tool on CD-ROM—*The Database of Classical Bibliography (DCB*, released June 1995)—has made it possible to search volumes 47–58 (1976–87) of *L'Année Philologique (APh)*, the major international index to classical publications (Clayman 1995). Table 3 (page 143) presents a summary of the results of *DCB* full-text searches of publications in English using keywords connected with variants of *women, gender, feminism, family, marriage,* and *sexuality*. By reading the full record (including abstracts when available), I manually eliminated all irrelevant items and included only those pieces that I judged would interest a classicist researching some aspect of gender studies. This process yielded a list of 614 scholarly works published between 1976 and 1987. Over 80% of these works are articles (70.7% in journals and 13% in collections), since the major growth in book-length publications did not occur until after the period covered by the *DCB*. It was not possible to classify the authors of these works by sex, because most of the authors are identified only by first initials. However, an analysis of the *APh* rubrics under which these pieces are classified indicates their range and diversity of content.

Figure 8 (page 160) shows the percentage of pieces included under each of 12 general rubrics, with the number of different categories represented in each (a total of 143 different categories).[2] Still, it is obvious that the majority of these works employ a broadly defined social/historical or literary approach; only a tiny percentage emphasize art or archaeology. Indeed, most of the articles dealing with visual materials that initially turned up in the search had to be eliminated because they represented an art-historical approach of the "female bust in the such-and-such collection" type. Hence, the *DCB* study supports the same general trends that appeared in my Library of Congress study: a large number and variety of works that favor Greece over Rome and a social/historical or literary approach over an artistic/archaeological focus.

The one trend that does not emerge as clearly in this study because of the brief chronological span of the *DCB* is the increasing growth in the number of gender-related classical articles. However, this is amply demonstrated in a study I conducted of 15 major classical journals, selected to be representative of various aspects of the discipline in the United States and Canada. The journals included two from Canada—*Phoenix* and *Echos du monde classique/Classical Views (EMC)*, both sponsored by the Classical Association of Canada; two art-historical/archaeological journals—*American Journal of Archaeology (AJA)*, sponsored by the American Institute of Archaeology, and *Hesperia*, sponsored by the American School of Classical Studies at Athens; two dedicated to contemporary theoretical approaches to classics that have published special issues on women in antiquity—*Arethusa* and *Helios*; four sponsored by large classical associations in the United States—*Transactions of the American Philological Association (TAPA)*, the *Classical Journal (CJ)*, the *Classical World (CW)*, and *Vergilius*. The remaining journals are all connected with major U.S. universities—*American Journal of Philology (AJP*, Johns Hopkins University); *Classical Antiquity (CA*, University of California); *Classical Philology (CP*, University of Chicago); *Illinois Classical Studies (ICS*, University of Illinois); *Harvard Studies in Classical Philology (HSCP*, Harvard University).

For this study I skimmed all the articles published in these journals during the calendar years of 1971 (*ICS* and the new series of *Helios* were not published at that time), 1981, and 1991, tracking the gender of the authors and the content and approach of the articles. Table 4 (pages 144, 145) summarizes the results of this study, demonstrating a slow but steady growth in the percentage of women authors (17%, 20%, and 28%) and a more dramatic increase in the proportion of articles relevant to some aspect of classical gender studies (5%, 9%, and 23%). By 1991, over half of the articles in *Arethusa* and *Helios* were related to gender studies, and every one of the 15 journals was publishing some relevant articles, including those with the most conservative of philological traditions (e.g, *AJP*—14%; *CP*—13%; *HSCP*—18%). Interestingly, men authored 57% of all the gender-related articles in this study, although women wrote 57% of those that I have classified as feminist (i.e., the articles in categories 3 and 4 in table 4).

As part of my work on the APA's Committee on the Status of Women and Minority Groups, I recently interpreted longitudinal data supplied by the editors of 14 classical journals, many of which were the same as the journals included in my three-decade study. The full report, published in the December 1995 issue of the *American Philological Association Newsletter*, concludes that the increasing participation of women in all aspects of journal publication marks a significant development in the classics profession. In 1977, when the CSWMG began to track submissions and acceptances instead of published articles, women accounted for 16% of all submissions and 18% of acceptances. Ten years later, in 1987, women were responsible for 25% of submissions and 22% of acceptances, and by 1993 these figures had risen to 32% and 34%, respectively. In 1977, only 4 journals required anonymous refereeing; this figure had risen to 7 by 1987, and 11 by 1989. In 1981, women comprised 16% of journal referees and 18% of editorial boards; by 1993, 34% of referees and 33% of editorial boards were women. Most striking, perhaps, is the fact that by 1996, women served as editor in chief of five of these journals *(Arethusa, CP, Hesperia, Phoenix,* and *TAPA).*[3] Figure 9 shows the growth in the aggregate percentages for women's submissions, acceptances, refereeing, and service on editorial boards from 1981 to 1993, clearly demonstrating that women's participation in journal publication has now outstripped their representation in classics faculties, which stands at 30%, according to the most recent CSWMG figures.

There has also been a significant increase in conference papers devoted to issues of ancient gender; in fact, it is difficult to find a classics conference today that does not include some presentations on this subject. A comparison between the programs of the 1971 and the 1994 APA annual meeting will illustrate the change. The 1971 program included only four papers whose titles indicated any relevance at all for gender studies (5% of the program), and these appeared to be fairly traditional literary studies; in 1994, however, six panels, comprising 26 papers, employed a strong feminist/gender focus, and 34 additional papers on gender-related topics were dispersed throughout the conference (together these papers constituted 18% of the program). Though 18% is still a small proportion in absolute terms (considerably below the representation of women in the profession, for example), it marks a dramatic improvement over conferences with no gender-related panels and a few scattered papers. In fact, the Program Committee put together nine individually submitted abstracts to constitute a three-hour paper session on "Gender in Literature and Society." The varied topics of the six organized panels testify to the diversity of their subject matter: "Women and Slaves in Classical Studies" (the WCC panel), "Power, Politics and Discourse: Augustan Elegy and Beyond," "Violence, Language, and Culture in Rome," "The Personal Voice in Classical Scholarship," "Constructing the Family in Late Antiquity," and "Constructions of Gender and Genre in Roman Comedy and Elegy."

In addition to the noteworthy increase in papers and panels, several U.S. classical associations or universities have sponsored whole conferences devoted to studies of ancient women, sexuality, or other gender-related topics, and at least two of these conferences have been explicitly feminist: "Feminism and Classics: A Symposium" (University of Cincinnati, November 5–7, 1992) and "Feminism and Classics: Framing the Research Agenda" (Princeton University, November 7–10, 1996). Moreover, classical scholars have been frequent speakers at the triennial Berkshire Conference on the History of Women, and papers presented at the 1987 conference form the core of a book on *Women's History and Ancient History* (Pomeroy 1991b).

Dissertations

Judging by the titles of completed dissertations published in the *APA Newsletter* since 1988, this area of classical scholarship shows the least change in response to feminist influence, although women have been earning a steadily increasing percentage of doctorates in classics (see fig. 2). As table 5 (page 146) demonstrates, women now account for nearly half of the doctorates listed in the *Newsletter* (eight-year mean, 44%). When I considered the dissertation topics, however, I deemed only 48 (9%) relevant to classical gender studies. This does not represent a significant advance over the 34 dissertation titles that emerged in the 1976–87 *DCB* search, particularly in light of the large increases in scholarship on gender studies in other forms of classical publications. Indeed, I included some dissertations in the gender-related category on the basis of content alone, since the title did not depart from disciplinary convention: for example, "Tradition and Innovation in Apollonius' Characterization of Medea in the *Argonautika*" (Alan Huston Rawn, University of Washington, 1993–94).[4] On the other hand, the most recent dissertation lists show a small but promising increase in the number of relevant topics and also in the nature of the titles themselves. Titles that pay explicit attention to gender issues can be found not only in studies of women—"Gender, Genre, and Power: The Depiction of Women in Livy's *Ab Urbe Condita*" (Davina McClain, Indiana University, 1993–94)—but also in other areas not obviously connected with gender—"Too Intimate Commerce: Exchange, Gender and Subjectivity in Greek Tragedy" (Victoria J. Wohl, University of California, Berkeley, 1993–94), "Altered States: Gender and the Theater of Civic Identity in Euripides' Political Plays" (Daniel Mendelsohn, Princeton University, 1993–94). When we note that these last three dissertations were all directed by women (Eleanor Winsor Leach, Leslie V. Kurke, and Froma I.

Zeitlin, respectively), it is hard not to connect the lag in feminist influence on dissertations with the dearth of women professors in graduate programs: between 1987 and 1995, 48 women directed a total of 84 classical dissertations, representing only 15% of the 543 dissertations listed as completed in that period.

OVERVIEW: CHANGES IN SCHOLARLY APPROACH AND PERSPECTIVES

All of these statistical studies amply demonstrate that a striking expansion in the content of classical scholarship, comprising major new emphases on ancient women, family, sexuality, and other gender-related issues, has occurred since the advent of modern feminism in the profession, most notably in the last five years. However, changes in scholarly approach are much more difficult to document and quantify. In my journals study, I attempted to confront this issue directly by skimming all of the articles from the included journals published in 1971, 1981, and 1991, and reading more carefully any that appeared relevant. Though extremely time-consuming, the process was also very enlightening, leaving me with a strong sense of positive change. For one thing, I found a much broader range of topics and approaches in the later journals, whose articles also struck me as more interesting, nuanced, and generally better written than the earlier articles even when they were not related to the study of gender. I am sure that this reaction stems in part from my own current attitudes and approach to the discipline, but it cannot be attributed to my age, since I was already teaching in 1971 and remember reading some of the early articles with approbation when they were first published. Indeed, as I read the old articles "with new eyes," I was led to reflect on the profound impact feminism has had on my own approach to the discipline.

When I began this study I expected to find only minimal progress in journals other than *Arethusa* or *Helios*, especially after reading Sarah Pomeroy's description of her comparison of the table of contents page of 45 classical journals (Pomeroy 1991a), which suggested few feminist inroads in journal publication. My study, however, differed from hers in three important ways: it included primarily journals published in the United States (plus two from Canada); it involved actually reading the articles; and it included comparison with earlier volumes of the same journals. Even though the absolute number of gender-related articles in 1991 was not huge, I did perceive very substantial differences from earlier journal articles. So the study convinced *me*, but how was I to convey these differences to others? I decided to classify the articles according to a somewhat artificial scheme based on patterns I observed: category 1 includes articles that treat women, feminism, or gender studies in a flippant or hostile manner; category 2 articles treat topics relevant to some aspect of ancient gender studies but do not employ a feminist approach; category 3 articles employ a feminist, gender-conscious analysis in studying topics directly connected with women or gender; and category 4 articles show significant feminist influence on the treatment of topics not obviously related to the study of ancient women, family, or sexuality. This method of classification enabled me, at least to some degree, to quantify and communicate the unquantifiable (see table 4), but I believe that discussion of some concrete examples will best illustrate and support my findings.

Category 1

Donald Richter's article on "The Position of Women in Classical Athens" (1971), discussed in chapter 1, is obviously a category 1 article, as is a study of the fifth book of the *Aeneid* by Stephen Bertram, who dismisses another critic's argument that the Trojan women set fire to Aeneas's ships because they had suffered long hardships with no chance for the glory and honor that the men would earn. Instead, Bertram argues, the women's action is consonant with "Vergil's view of women as either potential obstructionists prone to hysteria . . . or vapid instrumentalities" (Bertram 1971, 12 n. 4). But category 1 articles were not confined to the earliest volumes I examined. The 1992 volume of *Harvard Studies in Classical Philology* (no volume was published in 1991) contains three such articles: Goold (1992), Skutsch (1992; discussed briefly in chapter 2), and Wijsman (1992). The last of these, with the promising title "Female Power in *Georgics* 3. 269/270," analyzes two geographical references in a passage from Vergil that describes "mares in the grip of love's passion." He associates the mountain Gargara with the story of Hera's seduction of Zeus and the river Ascanius with Heracles' boy-companion Hylas, ravished by nymphs, and concludes that a common thread links the references: "women on heat, singly (Hera) or collectively (the nymphs) are too much for the strongest God or the strongest of men; and this in the context of a herd of mares raging after lust" (Wijsman 1992, 259, 261). It is not the content of Wijsman's conclusion that led me to classify this article in category 1 but rather his manner and attitude, for he seems to accept this ancient construction of female sexuality at face value, even linking it with "women" (although only animals and mythological beings are found in the literary references) and terming it "female power."

In a somewhat similar vein, George Goold's article, written to justify some of the textual changes in his new Loeb edition of Propertius, relies on unstated assumptions about male-female relationships and particularly about women's nature and behavior to explain his readings of the text. For example, he has changed the line "Cynthia, forma potens: Cynthia, verba levis" (2.5.28) to "*verna* levis," translating it "Cynthia, mighty beauty . . . flighty slut." Propertius intended the poem, Goold says, as a "savage denunciation of Cynthia's conduct: she is behaving like a common tramp" (Goold 1992, 295–96). Again, it is not so much the specific reading that I find problematic, although I do feel that the image of capriciousness or lightness in speech (conveyed by the original wording, *verba levis*) makes sense in the context of a poem about the power of the poetic word. What Goold has done here, under the cloak of philological objectivity (for he frequently makes statements like "the solution is simple and certain," 311), is to present his unexamined assumptions as logical justifications. For example, he takes for granted the idea that the word *verna*, meaning a home-bred slave and by extension a vulgar, town-bred person, would automatically mean "slut" when applied to a woman.[5]

However, of the five category 1 articles I found in the most recent volumes of the journals studied, only one manifested outright hostility to feminism, an antitheoretical attack on the role of social constructionism in recent studies of Greek sexuality (Thornton 1991). Unsurprisingly, all of the articles in category 1 were written by men.

Characteristics of a Feminist Approach

I classified in the second and third categories articles whose subject matter would interest a classical scholar researching some aspect of ancient gender studies: extensive discussions of literary, mythological, or historical females, ancient sexual concepts or behaviors, studies of marriage or the family, sex/gender divisions in society, and many related topics. Although these topics are not totally new to classical scholarship, they have come into increasing prominence in the last 20 years, as demonstrated above. But for this journals study, I attempted to differentiate between a feminist and a nonfeminist treatment of these subjects, so some explanation of my differentiating criteria is necessary.

I have never found a thoroughly satisfying "definition" of feminism in print, and in any case, I believe that feminism is plural and dialogic rather than monolithic. I do think, however, that one can identify a sine qua non for feminism, and the following characteristics represent my criteria for distinguishing a feminist scholarly approach:

1. Feminist scholars differentiate sex from gender and view the latter as a socially/culturally constructed category. Gender is learned and performed; it involves the myriad and often normative *meanings* given to sexual difference by various cultures. Feminists may differ in the importance they assign to sex, which is a biologically based category, but the idea that gender norms can be changed is central to feminist theory.

2. Although sex/gender systems differ cross-culturally, most known societies have used and still use sex/gender as a key structural principle organizing their actual and conceptual worlds, usually to the disadvantage of women. Thus, feminist scholars argue that gender is a crucial category of analysis and that modes of knowledge that do not take gender into account are partial and incomplete.

3. Feminist scholars also seek to question and transform androcentric systems of thought that posit the male as the norm. In practice, this means not only revealing and critiquing androcentric biases but also attempting to examine beliefs and practices from the viewpoint of the "other," treating women and other marginalized groups as subjects, not merely objects.

4. Feminists believe that existing inequalities between dominant and marginalized groups can and should be removed. Therefore, feminist scholarship has an acknowledged and accepted political dimension, as opposed to the hidden political dimension of scholarship that claims to be "neutral" and "objective." Although the commitment to feminist politics and organized feminist movements will not be equally stressed in all pieces of scholarship, it will never be denied or criticized (if it is, the approach is not feminist no matter what the author may claim). With regard to scholarship, the political goal of feminist work is broader than simply a stronger emphasis on women, though that is an important part of it; the goal is to revise our way of considering history, society, literature, and so on, so that neither male nor female is taken as normative, but both are seen as equally conditioned by the gender constructions of their culture (as indeed we, the observers, are).

A scholarly focus on ancient women does not in itself make an approach feminist, since scholars can and do study women without accepting these premises. When I classify an approach as "nonfeminist," I do not mean to imply that the scholarship is not valid or valuable; however, as a feminist who does accept the premises listed above, I will by definition see such scholarship as preliminary and incomplete. Let me refer to some of the articles from my journals study to illustrate how I used these criteria to differentiate articles in the second and third categories.

Category 2

An article by Elizabeth Clark and Diane Hatch that analyzes a late antique poem by a woman poet, Faltonia Betitia Proba, provides an easy example of category 2 because the authors explicitly state that they will concentrate only on the form of the poem even though they recognize that the gender of the poet is an issue (Clark and Hatch 1981, 31). A more complex case is Christina Kraus's discussion of Livy's story about Fabia Minor (*Ab Urbe Condita* 6.34.5–35.1), which she presents as a comic variant of the "Lucretia story" in which an outrage against a woman provides the catalyst for significant political change in Rome (in this case the granting to plebeians of the right to serve as consul). Kraus's interesting and well-developed analysis sets the story of Fabia in the context of other such stories in Livy (Lucretia, Verginia), recognizes the reliance on feminine stereotypes in the story, and ultimately concludes that it is the very insignificance of Fabia as a woman that prompts Livy to use the story as part of a narrative movement toward a "new, less heroic Rome" (Kraus 1991, 325). But Kraus pays attention to gender only as Livy does, as a factor to be manipulated in narrative; she does not seek to analyze the effects of this kind of social mythologizing on the Roman men and women who heard these stories, on the Roman concept of the state, or on the modern men and women who read Livy. The difference is obvious when this article is compared with two feminist analyses of this type of story (Joplin 1990; Joshel 1992). Claiming that feminist scholarship "has made it impossible to read Livy from Livy's point of view," Patricia Joplin seeks to take the viewpoint of the victim in these stories: "The struggle to lay hands on Verginia's neverpenetrated body represents the struggle to determine who will control the body politic. . . . But no one in the story or in the act of interpreting it seems to notice that the mute victim the crowd backs away from and allows to be taken finally has no rights to self-determination at all" (Joplin 1990, 52, 63).

In the appendix to his study of Roman concubinage, Thomas McGinn notes his topic's "resonance . . . for such areas of contemporary concern as sexuality, marriage, and the status of women," and he explicitly recognizes that his sources treat the question of respectability "exclusively from the (upper class) male's point of view" (McGinn 1991, 373, 350). Nevertheless, I have classified this article in the second category because McGinn himself cannot seem to break free from this male point of view. His long and detailed discussion of the Roman jurists is peppered with phrases like "the *lex Iulia et Papia* permitted women to be taken as concubines . . ." (347) and "a freeborn prostitute . . . enjoyed immunity from *stuprum*" (361), where the content objectifies the women even as the sentence structure apparently makes them subjects. The two questions McGinn uses to sum up the thrust of his article also reveal the pervasive male viewpoint: "What concubines were preferable in terms of upper-class practice? . . . Who made the best concubines with respect to criminal liability?" (370).

Elise Garrison's article on "Attitudes toward Suicide in Ancient Greece" in the same volume of *TAPA* is classified in the second category for a somewhat different reason—the fact that she denies the relevance of gender to her argument. Applying a framework developed by Emile Durkheim, she maintains that the Greeks viewed suicide primarily as a response to social pressures and did not treat the corpses of suicides as abnormal. The bulk of her article deals with tragedy, and while she recognizes that figures like Antigone and Deianeira face different types of pressure than Ajax, she does not see the value in analyzing these differences in terms of gender distinctions and dismissively observes that Nicole Loraux (1987) "overstates" the importance of gender (Garrison 1991, 33 n. 124). Interestingly, despite her claim to include "a wide variety of sources" (33), Garrison never considers a relevant medical source, the Hippocratic treatise *Peri Partheniôn*, discussed by feminist scholars before Garrison's article (King 1983), which states that young, unmarried girls were prone to suicide because of the pressure of the blood that could not flow out because they had not yet been "opened" by intercourse.

As I read the articles in category 2, one of my strongest impressions was a sense of missed opportunities. For example, Diane Juffras presents an intriguing hypothesis, based on a close philological analysis of the passage in Sophocles' *Electra* (973–85) where Electra asks Chrysothemis to help her murder Aegisthus and thus win public glory: "I suggest that the image Sophocles evokes here is of a public statue commemorating Electra and

Chrysothemis, on a parallel with the paired statues of Harmodius and Aris-
togeiton that stood in the Agora from the fifth century on" (Juffras 1991,
103). Juffras does not, however, explore the implications of the cognitive
dissonance that such an image would immediately provoke because of its
violation of gender ideology and cultural norms. Harmodius and Aristo-
geiton were honored as tyrannicides because their act fit the heroic code for
males; in contrast, the male chorus of Aeschylus's tragedy *Agamemnon* is
particularly horrified when they hear about Clytemnestra's murder of the
king because it was a *woman* who performed the deed. When such deeds are
evaluated, gender clearly matters. Although Juffras's idea is fascinating and
her analysis persuasive, I was left with a sense of incompleteness, as though
she had stopped just short of the most significant applications of her argument.

Juffras at least recognizes that gender has a bearing on her topic, but I
encountered many articles where the author paid no attention at all to issues
of gender even when these should have been prominent features of the topic
(I did not count such pieces among the gender-related articles). For example, when David Bright (1981) compares passages of Ovid and Apuleius
that purport to discuss the elegiac poets' use of pseudonyms to represent the
"real" names of their mistresses, his interest centers only on the question of
which author is more "reliable"; his article shows no recognition of the significant questions that can be raised about the attitude toward women in
these passages or their relevance for our understanding of Roman gender
ideology.

Category 3

It is easier to explain the choice of category 3 articles because one can point
to what *is* present rather than what is not. For example, Mary Boatwright
(1991) reinterprets evidence for the lives of imperial women of the Trajanic
and Hadrianic eras to demonstrate that women connected with these two
emperors were publicly presented in domestic and submissive roles that
downplayed their financial resources, connections, and lineage, the major
sources of prestige and influence for elite Roman women. By attempting to
view the evidence from the perspective of the women themselves and placing their situation in the context of political and social changes occurring
during this period, Boatwright concludes that these women had little personal power or autonomy despite their high status; in fact it was because of

that status that they were so constrained by the emperors' efforts to revive certain threatened aspects of the Roman sex/gender system.

On a very different topic, Alan Shapiro (1991) interprets "The Iconography of Mourning in Athenian Art" as a manifestation of religious and social changes occurring in Athens during the sixth and fifth centuries B.C.E. Shapiro not only employs gender differences as a key factor in his analysis of the iconography, but he also ties these to social practices and conceptualizations relating to both men and women. He speculates that the increasing democratization and emphasis on public funerals for the war dead must have been experienced by women as a double deprivation: not only was their traditional prerogative of family mourning greatly diminished, but they could no longer be buried with their menfolk because women were excluded from the state burial grounds.

Lauren Taaffe is quite explicit about the feminist nature of her study of Aristophanes: "A feminist viewpoint, informed by performance theory, leads to these questions: What was Aristophanes' purpose in playing with gender roles and the ideology of the city in *Ecclesiazusae*, and what are we, as twentieth-century American readers, to make of this transvestite play?" (Taaffe 1991, 91). She makes the sex/gender system of Athens central to her analysis, arguing that Athenian gender ideology demarcated the roles of men and women so clearly that "metaphors of gender were often used to illustrate power relations" (105). Since all elements of the play are seen to be under the control of men (male playwright, male chorus, male actors), Aristophanes was free to play with the idea of gender role reversal without ever seriously challenging Athenian power structures and could use the restoration of proper clothing and language at the end of the play to reaffirm traditional values (107).

On a related topic, Jeffrey Henderson (1991) asks whether women attended Athenian dramatic festivals. While previous studies had concentrated on debating the significance of conflicting pieces of evidence, Henderson opens up the question in a feminist way, examining how the evidence fits into the pervasive sex/gender ideology of classical Athens. He distinguishes between the notional audience, conceptualized and addressed as the male citizenry, and the actual audience, which also included foreigners, resident aliens, and most probably citizen women as well. Henderson then makes the women playgoers the subjects of his analyses, as he speculates about how they might have responded to various aspects of the dramas (including their notional invisibility) and how their presence might have influenced the playwrights, particularly in the presentation of female characters. He concludes, "Thus the female spectators, if such there were, at once counted and didn't count, a situation reflecting their overall role from the point of view of the polis, and reflecting also the dual role of the theater as exclusively political and inclusively festive" (147).

Category 4

The feminist articles discussed above have been classified in the third category because they all deal with topics immediately relevant to the study of ancient women. My last category, articles with strong feminist elements on topics not obviously related to such a study, is in some ways the most notable, since it indicates that feminist influence is not confined to a limited number of subjects or "ghettoized in a subfield." My first example of a category 4 article was published in *Classical Philology*, one of the more traditional classical journals. In this article, Anne Pippin Burnett sets out to analyze "cases in which an early poet clearly depicts a consciousness that collides with an unknown aspect of the self" (Burnett 1991, 275). While gender plays a role in all three of the cases discussed by Burnett (from the *Iliad*, *Oresteia*, and *Iphigeneia among the Taurians*), I will concentrate on Homer, where her gender-conscious analysis is both unexpected and effective.

Burnett discusses the monologue in which Hector, at first compared to a poisonous snake, debates whether to meet and negotiate with Achilles or to stand and fight; although he decides on the latter course, his muscles do not obey his mind and he turns and runs like a dove pursued by a hawk (*Iliad* 22.96–143). Gender is profoundly implicated in the "unauthorized part of the self" that has risen unbidden in Hector's mind to imagine a peacemaking scheme:

> [Homer] makes the Trojan prince unconsciously figure himself as a girl because that is the most efficient way of saying that this man for a moment longs to be his own opposite. Hector knows himself to be one of the greatest warriors on this field, but just now his wish is to be the reverse: to be one whose only weapons are words, whose mode is not violence but yielding and soft persuasion. He would like to renounce his martial science, and since the emblem for one who knows nothing of war is Woman . . . he sees himself now in that guise. (Burnett 1991, 287)

Rejecting readings that would eroticize this scene or draw on feminine stereotypes to view Hector's behavior here as cowardly, Burnett's analysis reveals how the understanding of a cultural gender schema can illuminate even the interpretation of a brief passage in a pervasively masculine epic.

Lillian Doherty's analysis of Odysseus' tale of his underworld adventures in *Odyssey* 11 (1991) is a thoroughgoing feminist treatment of an aspect of the poem not previously connected with gender studies: the auditors of the tale within the epic and its implied external audience. Doherty demonstrates how Odysseus' Phaeacian auditors are "marked for gender" (146) through the structure and content of the tale and its narrative frame, and how the narrative implies the presence of women in its external audience, whether or not we can actually prove they were historically present at any performance. A key element of Doherty's analysis is her emphasis on female subjectivity, both in terms of subject positions within the epic (which she reads as subtly manipulated within the poem to reinforce prevailing gender ideology) and of ancient and modern audience response. Doherty argues that women are included in the implied audience of the *Odyssey* but not the *Iliad;* this method of differentiating the two epics provides an interesting complement to the Burnett article and offers a welcome contrast to the conventional (and stereotypical) distinctions based on content.

The other articles from my journals study that I classified in the fourth category treat very diverse topics. Christopher Faraone (1991) discusses binding magic in the ancient world from a social history perspective, paying close attention to gender differences and interpreting their possible significance. Judith Hallett and Lee Pearcy (1991) both consider issues of gender relating to the history of the classics profession in America as they set the context for the reminiscences of a panel of seven classical scholars who taught in America between the two world wars. In the light of my analysis of the profession in chapter 2, it is noteworthy that the three women panelists all describe the way their sex affected their careers, but the four male panelists do not deal with this issue.

Brent Shaw (1991) discusses the resurgence of interest in Athenian democracy in the context of a review article on recent books about the subject. Despite the fact that the books he is reviewing do not raise this issue, Shaw, citing the feminist historian Joan Wallach Scott, relates this resurgence to "the ever more urgent problem of gender equality": "How on earth are the measures that will be necessary to enforce greater equality of opportunity, and of actual sharing in the powers and resources of our societies, to be squared with the claims of the prior 'natural equality' of all the members of the same society" (206). Although Shaw does not treat this question in detail, the very fact that he raises it as a significant issue for the study of Athenian democracy testifies to the strength of feminist influence in classics.

Similarly, feminist influence is very prominent in two of the three trends that Craig Kallendorf characterizes as "the most promising trends in recent Vergilian scholarship" (Kallendorf 1991, 74). Indeed, feminist work was the origin and source of both trends—the emphasis on multiple and even subversive points of view provided by various characters, particularly the women, and the reflexive attention to the scholar's own experience and its effect on his or her study of the epic. Although he notes how these approaches diverge from that of traditional philology, Kallendorf treats them in a very positive manner: "This is the history of classical scholarship as it should be: vital, fully engaged in the changing ideological matrix of civilization, and fully worth a central place in the *Vergilius* annual bibliography" (80).

OVERVIEW: SUMMARY

I have described the journals study in some detail because it constitutes a viable way to combine quantitative data with qualitative assessment. Once the criteria for and nature of my classification of articles have been understood through the above illustrations, table 4 can be read as providing three "snapshots" of classical scholarship taken at 10-year intervals. As with all photographs, these views are partial, due to structural limitations imposed by the camera lens and the subjective choices made by the photographer, but the snapshots are directly comparable because they are taken of the same scene, with the same camera, and by the same photographer. Besides the fact that there are progressively more women in the pictures, the most obvious difference is that the number of gender-related articles more than quadrupled in 20 years. While barely noticeable at 5% in 1971, such articles constituted a conspicuous 23% of the picture in 1991. In 1971, feminist colors were nowhere to be seen; in 1981, they were barely visible; but in 1991, 10 of the 15 journals sported some feminist hues, including several peeking out of unexpected places.

Taken together, all these bibliographical studies indicate something of the nature of feminist influence on classical scholarship. With regard to the question of *what* classicists write about, my studies point to a dramatic increase in the number of gender-related topics since the advent of modern feminism, especially in the last five years. And, contra Redfield, this expansion of content has indeed been diffuse, reaching into almost every area of classical scholarship, as demonstrated by the *DCB* study, in which only 1 of the 10 broad *APh* rubrics *(Les études classiques)* had no gender-related articles. When I broke down the gender-related articles in my journals study using rubrics like those employed by *APh*, the results were very similar (see fig. 10, page 161), with 10 different areas represented. The books and the journals studies also show that men as well as women are actively producing gender-related scholarship.

On the other hand, despite the striking growth in content relevant to gender studies, the majority of classical scholarship still deals with traditional topics; this is no "feminist takeover," although some classicists, influenced by the nearly total lack of serious scholarly attention to these topics in earlier eras, may exaggerate the amount of current interest. My journals study demonstrates this most clearly, because there, the gender-related pieces can be measured against the total number of articles in the 15 journals studied, constituting slightly less than one-fourth of the whole in 1991. Although a study of the 1995 volumes of these same journals would reveal heightened growth, I suspect that the total percentage would still not be more than one-third. Book-length studies, more sensitive to the commercial marketplace than any other form of scholarship, seem to show the most rapid proliferation, but there is no reasonable and efficient way to measure the proportion of gender-related studies to all classical titles. What we can be sure of is that gender studies sell, for otherwise publishers would not be accepting so many of them.[6] Dissertations, the area of classical scholarship most controlled by the profession and least involved in the open marketplace (the marketplace of ideas as well as the commercial marketplace), show the least amount of change in response to feminism.

If we consider *how* classicists approach their research and writing, we can also see feminist influence, though less marked than the impact on content. Here again, the journals study is most revealing, showing an increase in pieces with a feminist approach from none in 1971 to 7% of all articles published in the 1991 volumes of the 15 journals. Since 32% of those feminist articles are on topics not obviously connected with gender, this study offers further support to the contention that feminist influence is not confined to a single subfield but instead is becoming more diffused. Furthermore, these figures represent the most conservative assessment of feminist influence, for I also found a great deal more attention to other forms of contemporary theory in many of the 1991 articles not classified as feminist. Until feminist classicists mounted a concerted challenge to disciplinary epistemology and methodology in the 1970s, classics had remained largely impervious to the

radical theories emerging from Europe and greatly affecting other humanities disciplines (Peradotto 1989), except for isolated individuals in the discipline. Since it was largely under the banner of feminism that European theories began to breach the barricades of traditional philology (Skinner 1989;
Konstan 1990), employment of other contemporary theoretical approaches in
these articles can be at least partially attributed to feminist influence.[7]

Thus, my studies suggest that the feminist "song in answer" is not a
monody, chanted by a select few on a single topic; nor are the voices all
female. Neither is it a harmony in which feminist voices blend so well with
the dominant strains that their distinctiveness can no longer be perceived.
Instead, the feminist counterpoint, while still faint in relation to the whole,
can be heard more and more distinctly, producing a polyphony whose
melodic lines sound together euphoniously but do not merge. In order to hear
this counterpoint more clearly, let us now consider its dominant strain, examining some of the characteristics of current feminist scholarship on women in
classical antiquity. Here, because of the sheer volume of material that has
been published, I will not attempt to present a comprehensive overview but
rather will point out some notable trends that highlight the distinctiveness of
the feminist song.

CURRENT SCHOLARSHIP ON WOMEN IN CLASSICAL ANTIQUITY

In the 1970s, feminist-inspired classical scholarship focused almost entirely
on ancient women, but more recent work has emphasized the way that gender ideology and sex/gender systems pervaded the cultures of Greece and
Rome, affecting males as well as females, public as well as private life, and
institutional as well as intellectual constructs. A comparison of the titles of
the special issues of American journals devoted to ancient gender studies
gives a glimpse of this changing focus (I include here only those special
issues in which gender is the dominant topic).

The earliest special issues all had some variant of "Women in Antiquity"
for titles—*Arethusa* 6.1 (1973) and 11.1–2 (1978); *Women's Studies* 8.1–2
(1981). Subsequently, *Helios* published "Rescuing Creusa: New Methodological Approaches to Women in Antiquity," 13.2 (1986) and "Studies on
Roman Women," 16.1–2 (1989), after which the word *women* practically
disappeared from the titles: "Sexuality in Greek and Roman Society," *differences* 2.1 (1990); "Decentering the Text," *Helios* 17.2 (1990); "Documenting

Gender: Women and Men in Non-Literary Classical Texts," *Helios* 19.1–2 (1992); "Rethinking the Classical Canon," *Arethusa* 27.1 (1994). Despite the change in titles, however, women still feature prominently in the articles (least so in the *differences* volume, which is somewhat typical of studies of ancient sexuality, especially those inspired by Foucault; see Richlin 1991). And in all of my computerized bibliographic searches, I retrieved far more "hits" on the word *women* than on any of my other search terms. Thus, although ancient gender studies has moved from a simple focus on women to broader and more complex frameworks, all these studies were initiated by an interest in ancient women, and this is still the driving force in the majority of gender-related classical scholarship.[8]

While most classical studies of women still exhibit the six methodological principles that I noted in chapter 1 as hallmarks of the new scholarly approach to this topic, I will here organize my discussion of trends in contemporary classical scholarship on women according to the four features that I outlined earlier in this chapter as the sine qua non of feminist scholarship. While this scholarship employs many different theories and methodologies, these four feminist principles do provide a unifying framework for much of this work and contradict the charge of incoherence stated in Sally Humphreys' introduction to her second edition of *The Family, Women and Death*: "Though much has been published on women in antiquity since these essays were written [1983], the field seems to be still incoherent, a patchwork of structuralism, literary criticism, and Anglo-Saxon common sense. Incoherence in the aims of the feminist movement and in the conceptualization of gender in our own culture may well be responsible for our inability to find anything disconcerting in ancient conceptions and treatment of women" (Humphreys 1993, xxv).[9]

Gender as Socially/Culturally Constructed

In 1981, Helene Foley divided scholarship on ancient women into two lines of research: the first, dealing mainly with ancient literature, emphasized "the larger cognitive and symbolic systems," while the second, dealing mainly with the realities of women's lives, emphasized "methodological problems" encountered in the effort to recover information about women (Foley 1981, xii). Current studies of women, however, are increasingly merging these two strains as scholars ask what were the ancient gender constructions, how were they created, what was their influence on the lives and behavior of ancient men and women, and how do we know? The introduction to Sue Blundell's recent book on *Women in Ancient Greece* emphasizes the need to begin with the cultural ideology of gender: "By examining the roles which men constructed for women, and the system of gender differences into which they were incorporated, we gain an insight into the cultural dynamics of a male-dominated society" (Blundell 1995, 11). Although she notes that we have little or no evidence about how women themselves viewed this gender ideology, she feels that we can recapture something of the "social reality" of women's lives, including the fact that these ideological constructs were a part of women's lived experience. So her book begins and ends with cognitive and symbolic systems but in between draws on many diverse types of evidence from the social, political, legal, economic, and medical spheres, noting all the while how these were shaped by the ideological constructs.

Collaborative work. In seeking answers to the above questions, feminist scholars recognize the simultaneous need for highly specialized information and skills (in order to locate and interpret evidence that is fragmentary, uncontextualized, and often hidden in documents intended for quite different purposes) and for broad interdisciplinary knowledge, theoretical sophistication, and synthetic abilities (in order to fit all these tiny pieces of evidence together into a more or less coherent picture). From its inception, therefore, scholarship on ancient Greek and Roman women has emphasized *collaboration,* particularly in the form of the panel or collection of articles that brings together scholars from many different subspecialities of classics (Skinner 1986, 1).[10] Indeed, my Library of Congress search yielded 18 such collections in English since 1981, 8 of which had multiple editors (and this does not count any of the journal special issues listed above).

One of the problems with anthologizing articles by scholars from different specialities is that the task of synthesis is often left up to the reader, as Skinner pointed out, noting the need for feminist methodology and theory to bring more coherence to the study of ancient women. Indeed, Skinner sketched out a formidable challenge: "To gain theoretical scope without sacrificing due fidelity to the historical context and rigorous documentation of scholarly claims is the challenge presently facing the postclassicist feminist researcher" (Skinner 1986, 4). In an effort to meet this challenge, feminists are seeking to bring together the researchers, not just the fruits of their research. Many of these collections began as panels or seminars, and some ask authors to comment on each other's work (e.g., Pomeroy 1991b, using pairs of articles).

Amy Richlin describes the effect of the more extensive collaboration undertaken in *Pornography and Representation in Greece and Rome:* "to an extent unusual in Classics, we wrote this book together; a collective made up of the six original panelists read all the papers, and rewriting took place in the context of group discussion and with much pooling of bibliography and ideas. Whatever effect we will have on our field, the experience has certainly transformed us as a group" (Richlin 1992b, xi). The reader can perceive the results of this collaborative effort throughout the book—in the provision of a time line, the use of a single bibliography, and especially in Richlin's highly synthetic and explicitly feminist introduction to the collection.

Collaborative scholarship on ancient women has recently led to an entirely new phenomenon in classics, a book jointly authored by five specialists from different areas on *Women in the Classical World: Image and Text* (Fantham et al. 1994).[11] With the exception of two discrete chapters written by invited experts, these scholars worked together on the whole book, which is also unusual in its efforts to give equal prominence to the visual and textual evidence about Greek and Roman women.

Newly emphasized sources in new configurations. Like archaeologists seeking to reconstruct an ancient mosaic from myriad tiny, disconnected fragments, classicists studying ancient women have had to pay attention to every scrap they can find, putting these together in various configurations until a possible picture emerges, riddled with blank spaces to be sure, but giving an impression of the content and contours of the original. Feminist theory, particularly feminist anthropology, provides overall frameworks and suggestions for testing the position of individual pieces, but the researchers are still limited by the number and nature of the fragments they find.

In the 1970s, scholars started with the larger, readily available pieces provided by canonical literary and historical texts; by interrogating and arranging these in nontraditional ways, they could see the outlines of a new picture of women emerging. However, it was obvious that this picture would never be coherent without filling in as many of the smaller pieces as possible. Therefore, a major thrust of modern feminist work in classics has involved bringing together and making accessible new sources—noncanonical literature, nonliterary texts (inscriptions, papyri, medical and legal texts, economic documents, magical spells, etc.), and material evidence (vases, paintings, sculpture, reliefs, coins, remains of private homes, etc.).[12] Most of these sources had been studied before, by specialists working in relative isolation and interpreting them for purposes that had nothing to do with women (e.g., vases for dating, establishing schools of painters, art-historical styles, etc.). The feminist movement galvanized specialists not only to find and interrogate relevant materials in their areas but also to present these in a way that would be meaningful to specialists in other areas who were also working on women.

As these scholars encountered the work of other specialists in the numerous panels and anthologies that resulted from these efforts, they discovered new possibilities in their own areas. Even if all the work was not directly collaborative, it had a spiraling, mutually reinforcing effect. Many materials formerly available only to specialists were translated, contextualized, reinterpreted, and brought together in easily accessible form: to give just a few examples, a source book containing translations of many different types of documents (Lefkowitz and Fant 1982); images, particularly vase paintings (Keuls 1985); legal documents (Gardner 1986); extant works of women poets (Snyder 1989). The fact that so many of these sources are now available makes it much easier to attempt synthetic studies or indeed to teach various types of courses relating to ancient women. To return to the mosaic analogy, the more pieces that are laid side by side, the easier it is to envision how they might fit together.

Oddly enough, classical archaeologists have been among the last specialists to become involved in this effort to assemble and interpret evidence relating specifically to women and to ancient gender constructions, despite the fact that material remains would seem to offer some of the most crucial pieces of the puzzle. As noted above, my various on-line searches turned up only a small number of works whose primary focus was on such remains. Recognizing the need for visual evidence as a primary source (not merely as illustration for textual materials), organizers of panels and anthologies sought to include analyses by specialists that would focus on relating these materials to women and gender (e.g., McNally 1978; Walker 1983; D. Williams 1983). The effort to incorporate visual evidence has become increasingly prominent (e.g., Richlin 1992c; Fantham et al. 1994; Cohen 1995), though it is seldom the major concern of the study. However, a new collection edited by Natalie Kampen (1996) somewhat reverses the emphasis of earlier collections; here it is the visual evidence that provides the focusing lens through which other forms of cultural discourse are examined (morality, religion, politics, etc.).[13] The lavish catalogue of the art exhibition *Pandora's Box: Women in Classical Greece* by Ellen Reeder (1995) also includes a number of essays approaching the topic of Athenian women from various perspectives; the catalogue itself follows the metaphoric/symbolic structure of the exhibit. In both the early and more recent studies, the art-historical emphasis has been more prominent than the archaeological.[14]

Shelby Brown (1993) explores a number of complex, interrelated professional and disciplinary reasons for the unresponsiveness of archaeology in general and classical archaeology in particular to feminist concerns (see also Morris 1994, who is more concerned with the general "depeopling" of classical archaeology than with the scarcity of gender analysis). Certainly the lack of attention to gender issues that characterizes both classical art history and classical archaeology can be at least partly attributed to self-definitions that primarily involve aesthetics and extant material remains instead of the ancient social context. For example, Natalie Kampen's 1976 dissertation (Brown University) was classified under the *APh* rubric *Archéologie romaine* when it was entitled *Images and Statues of Roman Working Women: Second and Third Century Reliefs from Ostia* but was reclassified under *Civilisation romaine* when it became a book entitled *Image and Status: Roman Working Women in Ostia* (Kampen 1981).

There are promising signs that this situation is changing, however; in 1994, the call for papers of the American Institute of Archaeology (AIA) Program Committee for the Annual Meeting included a specific statement of interest in colloquia on gender studies, although this resulted in only one panel—"Body Image and Gender Symbolism: Women, Dress, and Undress"— and a few scattered papers. In the same year, some 22 years after the establishment of the APA Committee on the Status of Women and Minority Groups, the AIA instituted a subcommittee on Women in Archaeology under the aegis of the Committee on Professional Responsibilities. Besides Kampen (1996), another feminist anthology of articles on ancient gender is currently in preparation: *Naked Truths: Women, Sexuality, and Gender in Classical Art and Archaeology* (Koloski-Ostrow and Lyons in press).

For approximately the last 20 years, scholars from various classical specialities have been working together more or less collaboratively to piece together evidence about Greek and Roman gender constructions and the women and men whose lives these affected. According to Eva Stehle, a feminist approach to the study of ancient women is cognizant of both of these threads:

> Culturally shared images are part of a whole web of conceptualizations of the world, a web within which the construction of gender categories takes place and into which women and men are born. Images, therefore, both provide women's own self-definition and influence the material conditions of women's existence.... This statement is not the same as the claim that everything is text; it implies a Foucauldian view of power as diffused in discourse throughout a system, the more insidious for being without an apparent

origin. Study of women's activity and of images that articulate their place in the power structure should complement one another to produce a three-dimensional view of women's lives and possibilities. (Stehle 1989a, 115)

While I agree with the general thrust of this statement, "a three-dimensional view" is more than we can reasonably expect, given the state of the evidence. I prefer my earlier analogy of a reconstructed mosaic: flat and two-dimensional, full of blank areas where the pieces are missing, but containing a few striking areas where many small pieces have been successfully fitted together and set in an overall framework of ancient gender ideology that helps to orient the modern viewer and hint at the contours of the picture. The third dimension, substantial ancient evidence from women themselves, is forever lost to us.

The Difference Gender Makes

Cultures map gender constructions onto a vast cognitive grid that serves to structure not only modes of thinking but also life patterns and societal institutions within their civilizations. This grid is frequently invisible to members of the culture unless thinkers explicitly draw attention to it, as for example Athenian dramatists did or contemporary theorists seek to do today. The concept of enculturated lenses provides a useful analogy (Bem 1993, 2). When we simply look *through* gender lenses, they will structure and condition everything we see without our realizing it. We may not be able to see anything without their help, but we must look *at* the lenses, consciously examine how they affect what we see, if we are to sharpen our vision of the world. Thus, it is crucial that we analyze specific phenomena within a civilization with an awareness of how gender operates and a knowledge of the specific gender constructions and prevalent gender ideologies within that culture. Prefeminist classical scholarship studied ancient civilizations wearing an androcentric lens. Looking at ancient males, classicists saw human beings ("the Greeks," "the Romans"); they did not notice gender at all, or identified it solely with women, who were relegated to a tiny subtopic considered peripheral at best to the study of ancient civilizations. It was feminists who first called attention to the lenses of gender, initially decrying their androcentric bias and effacement of women, but later, aided by various poststructuralist theories, examining the lenses themselves (both ancient and modern) and seeking to explain their effects.

Gender as a category of analysis. One of the main tenets of feminist approaches is that gender is an indispensable category of analysis when studying any aspect of a culture, whether associated predominantly with men or with women. Feminist studies of individual phenomena therefore seek to demonstrate the difference it makes when gender is taken into account, particularly insofar as cultural sex/gender systems structurally disadvantage women (which is not at all the same thing as treating women as "victims"). I will present here just a few of the many possible examples to illustrate how this principle is being implemented in current classical scholarship.

By paying attention to gender while studying one type of ancient medical treatment ("excrement therapy," the use of animal feces as a therapeutic remedy), Heinrich von Stadten noticed something that all earlier commentators had apparently missed—the Hippocratic texts prescribe this type of treatment only for the gynecological ailments of women. He was able to illuminate the intersection of practice and conceptualization by linking the Hippocratic treatments to a more general Greek construction of women as "exceptionally susceptible to impurity and dirt" (von Stadten 1992, 13).

Examining the same medical writings for a different purpose, Lesley Dean-Jones presents a detailed and complex analysis of the functional model of female sexuality presented in the Hippocratic gynecological treatises. She convincingly demonstrates (pace Foucault) that this model was significantly different from the medical conception of male sexuality, which constructed the male as a desiring subject who maintained health through the virtues of continence and self-mastery. For women, sexual desire was neither important nor necessary; according to the Hippocratics, a woman's need for intercourse was physiological and completely outside her conscious control: "The functional model of the Hippocratics does not allow for a woman to be a moral agent in her own sex life" (Dean-Jones 1992, 83). Dean-Jones emphasizes the underlying political dimension of the medical model of female sexuality, explaining how it validated existing social practices that subordinated women but also speculating about how women might have been able to use it to get sexual attention from their husbands.

Similarly, Susan Cole perceives gender-based differences in religious rules posted outside Greek sanctuaries. She points out that certain Greek phrases, meaning "it is not sanctioned by custom" and "it is not sanctioned by divine law," were used only in restrictions imposed on women or foreigners: "In other words, the privileged group defined itself by exclusion of others" (Cole 1992, 106). Cole relates these and other ritual restrictions to pervasive cultural tendencies to map gender onto the categories of the sacred and polluted.

My last example, Judith Evans-Grubbs's (1993) study of monogamous sexual relationships between freeborn Roman women and lower-class males (either freedmen or slaves), can be profitably compared with McGinn (1991). Although McGinn is aware of the importance of gender for his study of Roman laws relating to concubinage, his article fairly consistently posits only the male as subject and actor. Evans-Grubbs, on the other hand, concentrates on the flip side of the question, on relationships in which women must be viewed as subjects and actors because of the unfree status of their male partners. In the process, she clearly reveals the structural disadvantage that the laws imposed on women; unions that were tolerated or respectable for men were disreputable and even punishable for women. For example, after 52 C.E., a free woman who cohabited with someone else's slave could be enslaved herself, and a freeborn woman could not free her own slave in order to marry him before he reached the age of 30, even though men could free their slave women for this purpose when the women were much younger. Nevertheless, Evans-Grubbs adduces evidence that such unions did occur and even that some Romans themselves misunderstood the gender differentiation (e.g., a case where the owner of a female slave thought he could enslave the free man who was cohabiting with her).

Cross-cultural study of ancient sex/gender systems.   Cross-cultural studies of sex/gender systems help to make their outlines more vivid and demystify their power as universals. Although feminist classical scholars frequently juxtapose and compare the gender norms and ideologies of Greek and Roman civilizations, there has been relatively little work done on the other ancient Mediterranean cultures that were interrelated with what we still persist in calling the "classical" civilizations. This insularity is at least now recognized as a problem (Haley 1993a; Richlin 1993; Zweig 1993), both in terms of how it limits our understanding of the cultures we do study and in terms of its exclusionary impact on modern students. British collections (Cameron and Kuhrt 1983; Archer et al. 1994) have in the past included more articles on other ancient cultures than American anthologies; however, the most recent such work, although entitled *Women in Antiquity: New Assessments* (Hawley and Levick 1995), announces in the preface that papers on other cultures "had to be excluded in order to give the volume its Classical focus" (xiv). Most recently, the collection edited by Kampen (1996) includes articles on ancient Mesopotamia, Egypt, Iran, and Etruria, but even these are cross-cultural in content rather than approach, since they do not explicitly compare the material from different cultures (see Zweig 1993 for an example of a more cross-cultural approach).

Much of the reluctance to undertake cross-cultural work is caused by the history and self-definition of the classics profession and particularly by the powerful socialization to "standards" that require mastery of the language and masses of empirical evidence before one can make any claims about a culture. Classicists hesitate to discuss any culture for which they do not have the kind of skills and knowledge that they have acquired for Greece and Rome. Perhaps the desire for a more complete and inclusive cross-cultural understanding of ancient sex/gender systems will prompt feminist classicists to break out of their disciplinary isolation and initiate the kind of collaborations with feminist scholars working on other ancient Mediterranean civilizations that they have already established so successfully with specialists from various areas within the discipline of classics. Speaking particularly of the incorporation of Black feminist thought, Shelley Haley envisions how such cross-cultural collaboration would affect the discipline: "Through Black feminist thought, classics can be radically transformed from a discipline into a multiracial, multicultural, multivalent field which better reflects the ancient world it studies" (Haley 1993a, 38).

Deconstruction and Reconstruction

Critiquing the androcentric norm. Part of any feminist enterprise involves making androcentric bias visible and revealing the partiality and inequity it fosters. In feminist classical scholarship, this process has required a double critique: of the pervasive ancient conceptualization of the male as the universal human norm and of the patriarchal content and methods of classical scholarship. The double nature of this critique can be seen very clearly, for example, in Eva Keuls's introduction to *The Reign of the Phallus,* when she says that she seeks to reveal both "the phallic rule at the root of Western civilization" and the story of its suppression "as a result of the near-monopoly that men have held in the field of Classics" (Keuls 1985, 1). The necessity for such deconstruction has influenced some critics to see only negativism in feminist classical scholarship, to equate feminism with "indignation": "[F]eminist indignation is out of place in the study of ancient Greece. The Greeks may have been at fault in their treatment of women. . . . But it is too late to correct those faults" (Sealey 1990, 168).

But Keuls herself indicates that her critique has a positive dimension: she is not seeking to disparage Athenian culture but to enrich and deepen our understanding of it. One of the values of studying a civilization "from the outside" is that one can gain an understanding of the cultural lenses through which individuals living in that civilization view the world, lenses that are frequently invisible to those individuals. If we simply adopt those cultural lenses ourselves, we will miss an entire dimension of the civilization; when we remove those cultural lenses, we can better discern the ideological scaffolding that supports the whole. Martha Nussbaum pointedly demonstrates this when she employs Aristotle's own method to reveal the flaws in his concept of women; in the process, she illuminates "the tremendous power of sexual convention and sexual prejudice in shaping a view of the world. It was the one area of life in which [Aristotle] was so deeply immersed that he could not compensate for bias or partiality, he could not even follow his own method" (Nussbaum 1986, 371).

Of course we, the observers, are still wearing our modern cultural lenses, without which we could not see at all, but theories like feminism have helped us become aware of those lenses and learn to compensate to some extent for their effects. Keith Bradley, defending his own scholarly focus on Roman slavery, also feels that present concerns can lead to a deepened understanding of the past:

> I submit that it is an utterly false approach quietly to set aside those aspects of the past that strike us as unpalatable while blithely searching for the admirable—how can "truth" possibly be captured from that methodological point of departure?—and I suggest that if presentist concerns actually lead to a more comprehensive view of the past, then engagement between the present and the past is not to be resisted but positively encouraged. Distorted vision may be imperfect vision, but it is preferable to no vision at all. (Bradley 1992, 134)

The purpose of deconstructing ancient androcentrism is not merely to provide a more comprehensive view of the past, however; it is also to gain a greater understanding of how gender ideology operates in the present. The indignation that Sealey decries is not directed at the ancient Greeks or Romans but rather at the social injustices and inequities in modern cultures. In this respect, the study of classical antiquity can be very illuminating. Not only were the gender ideologies of ancient Greece and Rome more open and pronounced than they are today, but the distance and strangeness of these cultures help us to view and evaluate with unusual clarity the way gender constructs affect many different aspects of a civilization. This is very useful for teaching purposes—Daniel Tompkins, for example, points out how Nussbaum's critique of Aristotle's concept of women can be used in the classroom (Tompkins 1994, 20–31)—but it also can make a significant contribution to the contemporary feminist enterprise.[15]

Presenting the other side. Although its critics rarely acknowledge this, feminist scholarship puts at least as much emphasis on reconstruction as it does on deconstruction and critique (epitomized in the commonly used phrases "making women visible" and "recovering women's voices"). Because of the nature of the evidence, this is more difficult for ancient cultures than it is for more recent ones; there is virtually no chance of recovering a Zora Neale Hurston or a Kate Chopin from antiquity. Feminist classicists have, however, developed a number of interrelated strategies for presenting ancient women as subjects.

The first and most obvious involves highlighting the few women's voices that have survived, a project that has received increasing attention. For example, my Library of Congress study yielded 26 books on Sappho in various languages (9% of the total); 13 were translations of her poetry and 17 were published since 1980. Snyder (1989) presents an overview of ancient women writers, translating many of the often fragmentary surviving works as well as providing commentary and context. Before the 1970s, none of these writers but Sappho was taken seriously in classical scholarship (Skinner 1987a, 185), but we now have many insightful studies that seek to explicate the ways that these writers present female subjectivity, work with or against patriarchal traditions and male literary conventions, address themselves to the general public or to a specifically female audience, and provide an alternative perspective on classical culture.

For example, Marilyn Skinner uses the poetry of Sappho to counter the claim, based on French theory, that "it is impossible to find any hint of authentic female reality in the Greek signifier 'woman'" (Skinner 1993, 128). She argues that Sappho's poetry constituted the poetic discourse of a desiring female subject speaking to and among other women, organizing female experience around a different pole than patriarchal culture, and conjectures that its ultimate purpose was "to encode strategies for perpetuating women's culture" (135). Both Judith Hallett (1992b) and Amy Richlin (1992d) discuss a Latin poet named Sulpicia who wrote in the late first century C.E. (a different person than the Augustan elegist Sulpicia), whose work survives in a two-line fragment but who is discussed in the poetry of her contemporary Martial. In varying ways, both scholars attempt to turn this Sulpicia from an object to a subject. Hallett uses the words of Martial to reconstruct a Sulpicia who herself appropriates the poetic language and erotic scenario of the earlier male elegist Propertius in order to challenge social norms for women (Hallett 1992b, 120–22). Richlin, on the other hand, concentrates not only on the few words of Sulpicia herself that are extant but also on the later reception of her work in order to reconstruct a satirist who articulated the perspective of a strong and even angry woman, who wrote with "transgressive force" (Richlin 1992d, 138). All of these articles are of necessity speculative, but they do make use of what little evidence remains to posit a female subjectivity.

A related strategy involves reconstructing the lives and accomplishments of historical women with more attention to the women's own possible perspectives on their lives: for example, Fulvia (Delia 1991), Antonia Augusta (Kokkinos 1992), and Hypatia (Dzielska 1995). Because there is often very little actual evidence for such a project, some scholars have taken a different tack, concentrating on the "afterlife" of these historical women and exploring the varying ways their names and lives have been appropriated by writers and scholars throughout history (e.g., Sappho [DeJean 1989] and Aspasia [Henry 1995]). This is more closely allied with the deconstructive project of feminism, for it means primarily writing about men, as Madeleine Henry points out. However, there are moments in the story when women seek to appropriate the subjectivity of their ancient forbearer (for Aspasia, Heloise and the eighteenth-century French painter Marie-Genoviève Bouliar), and an alert scholar can use these moments to "begin to place Aspasia in the history of feminist epistemology" (Henry 1995, 128).

Another strategy feminist classicists use in seeking to reconstruct the women's side of history is to flip existing evidence over and examine its underside, deriving information from what is *not* said. A small but telling example can be found in *Women in the Classical World* (Fantham et al. 1994, 265–67), when the authors read Livy's account of the life of the second-century B.C.E. centurion Spurius Ligustinus for information about his unnamed wife. Livy states only that the wife was dowerless and overly fertile, bearing Ligustinus eight surviving children. The authors ask us to imagine what that wife's life might have been like as she struggled to raise eight children in Ligustinus's small hut during the 22 years when he was mostly away on military service, and as she tilled his acre of land before the children were old enough to help. Livy praises Ligustinus for volunteering for further service in Macedonia after he had completed his term of military duty. However, it is not hard to conjecture that his wife's reaction would have been far less positive, particularly when we juxtapose the actual words written by another ancient woman to her husband in an analogous situation (Isias to Hephaistion, 168 B.C.E., from a Hellenistic papyrus):

> [A]bout your not coming home, when all the others who had been secluded there have come, I am ill-pleased, because after having piloted myself and your child through such bad times and been driven to every extremity owing

to the price of wheat, I thought that now at least, with you at home, I should enjoy some respite, whereas you have not even thought of coming home nor given any regard to our circumstances. (Fantham et al. 1994, 160)

Similarly, Helen King probes the Hippocratic Corpus to discover opportunities for the agency of women patients—"strategies women used within the system" (King 1995, 141).

Feminist scholars have also begun to study extant material remains from the subject position and perspective of the women who used, viewed, and inhabited them. This involves a radical departure from the traditional art-historical reliance on the male gaze. Robin Osborne (1994) makes an important statement simply by posing the question "Does the Sculpted Girl Speak to Women Too?" Since his answer is ultimately "no" with respect to classical sculpture such as the Aphrodite of Knidos, the article ends up paying more attention to the dynamics of viewing for the male spectator than for the female, but his analysis of the archaic *korai* (statues of aristocratic young women) does suggest that these statues may have spoken to women of the period about their own value and even potential agency. He posits that the artistic move away from the *kore*-type statue may be related to changing attitudes toward marriage and religious traditions that circumscribed the role of aristocratic families (and hence women) in Athens.

Eva Stehle and Amy Day (1996) treat the concept of a female gaze even more directly as they analyze the pedimental sculptures of the Temple of Zeus at Olympia from the "local, gendered perspective" of a hypothetical Elean woman. Using the framework of women's rituals in the Elean community, they propose that this female viewer might first see in the sculptures positive messages related to her ritual experiences, though these would be increasingly contradicted by the ideology of the sculptural group as a whole. Understanding this tension, they argue, is significant not only for envisioning the distinctive features of a woman's perspective but also for gaining a better sense of the complexity of messages for male viewers.

Molly Myerowitz (1992) considers erotic wall paintings in Roman houses from the viewpoints of both the women and the men who saw them on a daily basis; after setting these paintings in the context of related cultural discourses (particularly erotic poetry), she ultimately concludes that these paintings objectify men as well as women: "These paintings serve as a stylized frame that accomplishes and underlies the transformation of the biological into the cultural, a mirror for identification and alienation" (154).

Cross-cultural material from more recent societies, when employed cautiously and buttressed with ancient evidence, can also be helpful in the effort to view beliefs and practices from the standpoint of women. In an earlier study (McManus 1990), I showed how anthropological reports about the attitudes of modern Greek women, coupled with ancient visual and textual evidence, can help us to reconstruct how the young upper-class Athenian bride might have viewed her own wedding. Keith Bradley (1992; 1994) has also employed cross-cultural evidence (American slave narratives) to good effect in his efforts to examine Roman slavery from the slave's point of view, and it is reasonable to assume that Bradley and other contemporary scholars who are seeking to reconstruct the perspectives of various marginalized groups in antiquity have been influenced by feminist theory and methodology. Indeed, Bradley himself indirectly credits feminism, calling classicists' interest in women's history "perhaps the most striking example" of how present concerns have considerably broadened the focus of classical studies (Bradley 1992, 133).

Acknowledged Political Goals

Feminist scholarship openly acknowledges its political impulse—the desire to reveal and transform existing social inequalities. From its inception, the feminist study of ancient Greek and Roman women presented itself as politically engaged: "The story of the women of antiquity should be told now, not only because it is a legitimate aspect of social history, but because the past illuminates contemporary problems in relationships between men and women" (Pomeroy 1975, xii). Although feminists in classics, as elsewhere, emphasize a variety of political agendas ranging from a primary focus on transforming the discipline and the academy to a radical dedication to eliminating sexism, racism, and other forms of discrimination in society, they all share a commitment to greater equality and a willingness to acknowledge this commitment openly (Rabinowitz 1993b provides a good overview of the political dimension of feminism in classics). The Women's Classical Caucus and the Committee on the Status of Women and Minority Groups, both overtly political organizations, bear witness to the union of scholarship and activism, for the CSWMG occasionally sponsors panels and the WCC regularly does so, besides offering annual awards for feminist research. The openly political dimension of feminist scholarship has been the focus of much of the criticism it has attracted in the discipline of classics, which has prided itself on its "scientific" (i.e., neutral and detached) approach to antiquity, as already described in chapter 1. Mary Lefkowitz, for example, who has herself published a great deal about ancient women, finds the political dimension of feminist work especially problematic: "I would suggest that if the history of women in antiquity is not yet regarded as a fully respectable subject by some traditional scholars, it is because of the persistent, subjective anachronism that drew attention to the subject in the first place, but that makes it all the harder to separate what we would like to see from what is really there" (Lefkowitz 1989, 251–52).

The engaged politics of feminist scholarship is based on the conviction that all scholarship has a political dimension, although this is frequently hidden in the guise of "neutral facts" or "universal truths." Such a disguise enables both authors and readers to avoid doing the hard intellectual work of directly grappling with these political ideas, whether to defend or critique them.[16] For example, Florence Dupont's *Daily Life in Ancient Rome* (1992) presents itself as neutral and apolitical; those who criticize feminist scholarship for being openly political would very likely view this book as an objective attempt to analyze "what was really there." But the subtext of this book is that only men were "really there" in ancient Rome, or rather that theirs was the only significant presence. Despite the book's title and the wall painting of six women reproduced on the cover of the English paperback edition, the text almost totally elides women (for a pertinent review, see Richlin 1994). For example, the section on "The Roman Body" begins, "The body is the man" (239), and only the male body—in health and illness, naked and dressed, bathing and eating—is discussed. In this whole section, women appear only fleetingly and dismissively, as the recipients of men's "outpourings of sensuality of little consequence" at banquets (284). Dupont's almost exclusive focus on the elite Roman male is not accidental but rather programmatic; it is a statement about what is considered important and worthy of scholarly attention. As such, it is highly political, and its political stance is all the more insidious for being unrecognized and unacknowledged.

ENGENDERING POLITICS

The fact that a book originally written in the late 1980s can purport to analyze "daily life" while hardly noticing women should prevent us from being too sanguine about the extent of feminist influence on classical scholarship. My journals study suggests that feminist influence can be perceived most strongly in studies that deal more or less directly with ancient women, although it is beginning to be felt in other areas of classical scholarship as well. I would like to conclude this chapter by looking briefly at one area that is *not* directly connected with ancient women, political history, which has in its mainstream work taken little cognizance of the feminist principles discussed above. Jennifer Roberts's assessment of the "state of the question" with regard to scholarship about democracy in classical Athens remains generally true of other areas of classical political history:

> The way in which people have written about the dynamics of the Athenian state makes resoundingly clear that for most people writing about politics has meant writing about people who exercise political power.... Even among those who would not dream of disputing the value of studying Athenian women and Athenian slaves, the belief remains common that this study is discrete from the study of politics: though contemporary interest in social history has led more and more scholars to focus their research on Athenian residents who did not vote (women, slaves, the resident aliens known as "metics"), it is not unusual for those who have taken up the mission of describing the dynamics of Athenian political life to limit themselves to voters—that is, free adult males. (Roberts 1994, 19)

Without attempting a comprehensive overview of the scholarship in classical political history, I will raise a few issues where I see a current lack of mainstream influence yet a potential for significant feminist contributions to the study of Greek and Roman politics.

Athenian Democracy

Few scholars today would be as open and blunt in dismissing consideration of women's exclusion from Athenian government as Malcolm McGregor was in his 1970 presidential address to the American Philological Association on "Democracy: Its Admirers and Its Critics": "If we wish to be strict, or if we have the emotions of the suffragette, this was an undemocratic element in the Athenian way of life. Since it does not disturb me and since it is not my purpose to defend or advocate democracy, I do not propose to linger over it" (McGregor 1971, 54). Nevertheless, Josiah Ober's *Mass and Elite in Democratic Athens: Rhetoric, Ideology, and the Power of the People*, which received in 1989 the APA's highest scholarly honor, the Goodwin Award of Merit, makes essentially the same point in more polite language:

> The exclusion of women, slaves, and foreigners from political rights must be faced by anyone who hopes to gain a fair understanding of classical Greek civilization. . . . The limitation of the franchise to freeborn males is certainly undemocratic by current standards, but to deny the name democracy to Athens' government, on the grounds that the Athenians did not recognize rights that most western nations have granted only quite recently, is ahistorical. We may deplore the Athenians' exclusivist attitude, but moral censure

should not obscure our appreciation of the fundamental importance of the new democratic political order. (Ober 1989, 6).

Ober, like Raphael Sealey, has missed the point of feminist scholarly principles—not moral censure but recognition of the deep and fundamental role played by gender constructions in all arenas of life, including (perhaps especially) politics. Of course, it would be ahistorical to expect enfranchisement of women in any ancient society, however democratic. But it is crucial to call attention to the highly gendered nature of the form that democracy took in classical Athens, not only to understand the historical Athens better but also to comprehend the role gender constructions play in the political life of modern democracies that do enfranchise women.

Most current scholars writing about Athenian democracy do indeed include the requisite statement "deploring" the complete exclusion of Athenian women from politics, but they see that as the end of the matter. Not only are women omitted from further discussion, but so are males, as "the Athenian" and "the citizen" become gender-neutral, universal categories of discourse; contrast the practice of Jennifer Roberts (1994), who frequently reminds her readers that she is referring only to males when using these terms. Ober's book not only says very little about women (for 339 pages of text, the index cites only 5 pages referring to women) but also thoroughly elides discussion of gender, despite the great stress laid on the role of ideology, inclusion of theater as a forum for political debate, and a frontispiece that depicts Demokratia in female form crowning Demos in male form (from an Athenian public document relief on which was inscribed the Law against Tyranny).[17] This is not to deny the many merits of Ober's book; indeed, it is because of its scholarly significance that the book provides such a good example of a work that would produce a richer texture by incorporating the contrapuntal voices of feminism.

Brent Shaw, whose review article of recent work on Athenian democracy was quoted earlier, describes Ober's book as "a giant stride towards a much better understanding of the real world of Athenian democracy" and hopes that it will "suggest ways of reconsidering" urgent modern problems such as the lack of gender equality (Shaw 1991, 209, 206). But how can Athenian strategies for mediating the differences between mass and elite classes speak to our situation if we fail to recognize that all of these strategies were predicated upon shared conceptions of "manhood" constructed through definitive exclusion of women, no matter what their class?[18] How can we understand the exclusivist side of Athenian democracy if we continue to link together all groups without political rights—women, slaves, foreigners—

as though the nature of their exclusion were the same? How can we appreciate the differences between excluded groups if we fail to study the complex ideological stratagems by which women were rendered both insiders and outsiders in the *polis,* as simultaneously citizens and noncitizens, as necessary genetic transmitters of citizenship to sons who yet claimed a common autochthonous descent from the Athenian land (see Patterson 1986 and Loraux 1993)?[19] Feminist scholarship has a great deal to contribute to our understanding of Athenian democracy, but its influence on traditional classical studies of this topic has been very limited. Even Roberts's book (1994), which makes a strong case for the significance of gender studies in this area, might be viewed by some classicists as "outside the mainstream" because of her emphasis on postclassical interpretations of Athenian democracy.

Roman Politics

At first glance, Roman politics appears to offer far more scope for studies of women's political roles, and indeed one can compile a much longer bibliography of political history that pays some attention to women, including whole books such as *War, Women and Children in Ancient Rome* (Evans 1991) and *Women and Politics in Ancient Rome* (Bauman 1992). The highly class-conscious nature of Roman politics, coupled with the greater economic capacities and social freedom of elite Roman women as compared with their Athenian counterparts, gave some individual women scope for political influence even in the Republic, and the virtual identification of the state with the imperial family in the Empire gave a few women even more opportunities. Consequently, named Roman women have figured in classical political history from the beginning, though modern historians have frequently adopted without question the bias and hostility of their ancient sources.

One can see this even in the works of noted historians such as Ronald Syme, who, in his famous study *The Roman Revolution,* makes statements like "Influences more secret and more sinister were quietly at work all the time—women and freedmen" and refers to the "deep and devious" private activities of Livia, wife of Augustus (Syme 1939, 384, 385). In a much later work, *The Augustan Aristocracy*, Syme describes women's "uses for the historian. They offer relief from warfare, legislation, and the history of ideas" (Syme 1986, 168). Although this may have been intended as a joke, the very fact that he could proffer such a jest in 1986 testifies to the strength of the traditional separation of women from the serious business of mainstream history.

Although Evans criticizes "the tendency to treat the history of women in antiquity as a discrete topic, or to put it another way, the failure to integrate women's history into the broader fabric of Ancient History at large" (Evans 1991, x), both his book and Bauman's, as monographs that treat women as a special topic, must be viewed as preliminary to the task of full integration. The existence of both books testifies to the influence of modern feminism,[20] though neither work is informed by feminist theory. Both authors approach their topics in the manner of traditional classicists, with a heavy emphasis on textual material and a positivist mode of demonstration. This is unlikely to convince traditional classicists of the merit of studying women, however, since this approach does not work well with the types of evidence available for Roman women, and both authors end up relying on problematic information from ancient historians and biographers.[21] This approach, combined with a lack of attention to cultural gender constructions and ideology, seriously limits these books' potential for providing a viable model for the integration of women into political history.

Feminist scholars have, however, developed a framework that has this potential. Judith Hallett has demonstrated how, in the hierarchical class structure of Roman society, elite women were constructed as both "same" and "other" by their male blood kin (Hallett 1984; 1989a). As "same," women were conceived as sharing in valued qualities and traits that distinguished men of prominent families from other elite families and from the lower ranks of society; thus, elite women could not only cement political alliances through marriage but even represent their kin publicly in various ways. As "other," elite women simultaneously carried the feminine gender constructions that set all women apart from all men, no matter what their family or class. This paradoxical ideological construction created a much more complex situation and hence more opportunities for elite Roman women than for their Athenian counterparts, since the egalitarian male ethos of Athenian democracy was in part predicated upon a consistent "othering" of women. The complexity of Roman gender constructions for elite women has provided a productive framework for studying many of the contradictions and discrepancies between conceptualization and practice that marked the lives of Roman women (e.g., Gardner 1986 on law; Dixon 1988 on the *matrona;* and Stehle 1989b on female sexuality).

Here, as an illustration of the possibilities that this approach offers for the integration of women into Roman political history, I will concentrate on two articles by Phyllis Culham that explore the internal contradictions of the imperial ideology crafted by Augustus with regard to gender: "Did Roman

Women Have an Empire?" (1996) and "Imperial Ideology and Perceptions of Women's Roles" (1992). Culham argues that several of the major planks in the imperial platform constructed by Augustus simultaneously excluded and included women, or included them in contradictory ways. For example, Augustus controlled the old Republican competition for political rank and status by channeling it into a more orderly, step-by-step advancement through reconfigured or newly created offices. However, because he did not include women in these orderly ranks, he had no mechanism to control their competition for status. Since he attempted to link these publicly assigned ranks to concepts of elite *family* honor, however, elite women were perforce included in the system; indeed, his efforts to merge respectable behavior with high rank led him to insert the concept of "senatorial daughters" into some of his legislation, which paved the way for women to begin directly claiming political rank (a process that culminated in various formal titles and juristic disputes in the second and third centuries C.E.). Furthermore, Augustus's encouragement of acts of public beneficence, such as building projects on the part of men of rank, also led wealthy women to take up this practice in their efforts to achieve status (see Fantham et al. 1994 for evidence and interpretation of the way elite women used this option in various parts of the Empire). In this way, as Culham concludes, "Augustus' political and legal formalization of rank and status gave women new weapons to use in claiming status and constructing a public role" (Culham 1996, 196).

Similarly, when Augustus concentrated the power of the state in the imperial household, the women of the imperial family were inevitably drawn into the circle of power and patronage, despite the fact that he attempted to project for them a public image of old-fashioned domesticity. His public message was that they were members of his household but excluded from its rank; yet he had earlier conferred the sacrosanctity of the tribune's office on his wife and sister, and in his will he adopted Livia into his lineage, giving her the title Julia Augusta.[22] As Culham points out, this paradoxical situation continued throughout the Empire: "The public presentation of the women of the imperial household undermined the ideological content of the message about women's roles it was intended to convey. . . . The emperors were utterly unable to render the women of their family popular, respected, revered, and yet known to be without influence" (Culham 1992). The example set by the imperial women affected the perceptions and conduct of elite women in various parts of the Empire and even, as Culham indicates, had some impact on women outside the elite ranks. Technically speaking, the political rights of women did not change in the transition from Republic to

Empire (as "other," women were still excluded from voting and holding state office), but the simultaneous construction of women as "same" in certain contexts gave women new political opportunities in this period and even a measure of political rank.

Although this brief summary cannot do justice to the complexity and detailed argumentation of Culham's two articles, I hope it will convey some sense of the potential of this type of approach. Culham graphically demonstrates how feminist theoretical frameworks can help the ancient historian present a more complete view of Roman politics, one that includes women as well as men, one that helps us understand not only how women functioned in Roman politics but also how Roman politics functioned.

CONCLUSIONS

Modern feminism has affected not only the constitution and structure of the profession of classics in America (as demonstrated in chapter 2) but also the nature and focus of classical scholarship. I would term the change in scholarship radical but not revolutionary: the content of classical scholarship—*what* classicists consider worthy of study—has expanded greatly, but the approach—*how* they study it—is only beginning to change in most areas, particularly those not directly connected with ancient women.[23] Still, any change is remarkable in a discipline whose traditions are as deeply entrenched and resistant to innovation as classics. Feminism is not the only force working for change in classics; other contemporary theories are also beginning to make a mark, and changing demographic, economic, and political conditions that have imperilled the once-secure position of classics in academe have imparted their own urgency to the situation. But feminism, as the first large-scale challenge to the discipline and still the only organized one, has certainly provided the major impetus for disciplinary transformation.

I have envisioned the feminist song as a complex polyphony of contrapuntal melodic lines, and this counterpoint occurs within feminism as well as outside it, for there are many different scholarly methods and emphases within the feminist perspective, a fact I have been unable to demonstrate here because of the scope of this book. Counterpoint produces more difficult and complex (but to my mind more beautiful) music than either monody or harmony. Some will of course prefer the Gregorian chant that earlier characterized the discipline, because of its stronger (and more masculine?)

melodic line, but the polyphony that I have described here fits well with the effect envisioned by Euripides' female chorus in *Medea* as they imagined women singing of history in concert with men: "The long span of time has many things to say about the lot of men, and many things about our lot" (lines 429–30).

4

TRANSGENDERED
MOMENTS: REVISITING
VERGIL'S *AENEID*

Up to this point, I have been speaking with the voice of a surveyor, presenting an assessment of the overall impact of modern feminism on the discipline and profession of classics in the United States. In this chapter, however,
I want to speak in a more specific and personal voice, focusing on a single
text in order to provide a concrete illustration of how feminist theory has
transformed and enriched my own perspectives as a classicist. In the process,
I hope to suggest another way to approach texts that seem most hopelessly
entangled in patriarchal values and masculinist readings.

I have chosen Vergil's *Aeneid* for this demonstration for a number of reasons. It would be hard to find a text that has been more closely associated
with normative masculine cultural values for a longer time than this epic.
Indeed, T. S. Eliot (1945) argued that the *Aeneid* is the quintessential "classic" of European culture, and Theodore Ziolkowski's survey of *Virgil and the
Moderns* (1993) amply testifies to the patriarchal nature of twentieth-century

responses to Vergil in Europe and America. Furthermore, the *Aeneid* has
been a canonical text in the education of elite Western males since Roman
antiquity; Marilynn Desmond points out how this long tradition has constructed the reader of Vergil as typically masculine (Desmond 1994, 1–13).
The *Aeneid* still plays an important role in the teaching of Latin, not only on
the university level but also in secondary schools, where it is the most commonly offered Advanced Placement course in Latin;[1] though Homer's epics
may take precedence over Vergil's poem in general humanities courses, the
Aeneid is arguably the most frequently translated of all ancient texts in the
contemporary United States.

Despite this ubiquity, the *Aeneid* has not attracted nearly as many feminist readings as most other canonical texts from classical antiquity,[2] so there
is obviously a need to analyze the performance of gender in this text. However, when I told a noted feminist classical scholar about my plan to focus on
this epic, she responded that the dearth of feminist work on the *Aeneid* may
stem from a lack of complexity regarding gender in the text itself. Although
she had not examined the issue carefully, she said, it was her impression that
gender in the *Aeneid* never "slips and becomes a liminal staging area for
other concerns" as it does in works by Catullus or Ovid: "Aeneas is never put
into 'feminized' space." Since it is likely that many contemporary classicists
share her impression, I took this comment as a challenge and used it to frame
my investigation of the epic.

My final reason for choosing the *Aeneid*, however, is more personal; this
epic was my first great love in classics and the subject of my first major
scholarly efforts in the field. My 1976 dissertation, "*Inreparabile Tempus*: A
Study of Time in Virgil's *Aeneid*," was highly formalistic in approach, in
keeping with the fact that I was a passionate, card-carrying New Critic when
I conceived the project. Although I would not now repudiate any of the conclusions I reached in the dissertation,[3] as I reread my work, I was surprised
by how totally oblivious I had been to matters of gender, even to the point of
writing the following sentence with no apparent sense of its phallic, let alone
seminal, imagery: "If a man does not actively thrust himself into the future,
the inexorable movement of life toward death will pull him into the past, and
he will leave no lasting imprint upon time" (McManus 1976, 97).[4] Throughout the dissertation, I employed the so-called generic masculine pronoun
when speaking of the reader; in fact, I am struck by my earlier self's resem-
blance to Judith Fetterley's profile of the "immasculated" reader, a woman
who has so completely absorbed masculine practices of reading and norms
of scholarship that she does not even notice their dissonance with her own

gender (Fetterley 1978, xx–xxiv). By 1983, when I worked on *Women in Classical Antiquity: Four Curricular Modules*, produced by Sarah Pomeroy's NEH Institute on Women in Classical Antiquity, I was at least able to perceive how many of the polarities in the epic are mapped onto the grid of gender, although at the time I thought that this could best be understood through a structuralist analysis of "woman as mythic symbol" in the *Aeneid*. I never undertook such a study, however, because my own burgeoning interest in feminist theory and the study of ancient Greek and Roman women led me far away from Vergilian scholarship. As I revisit the *Aeneid* now, the difference in my reading is therefore a sign, in miniature, of the kind of changes I see taking place across the discipline.

The following reading of the *Aeneid* represents a personal return to a text that I have long neglected and that has only recently begun to engage other feminist scholars in the discipline. It is not intended to supplant or contradict other readings, but rather to suggest how new questions and a changed angle of vision can enrich our perception of a text that many regard as highly patriarchal, if not misogynistic. I have not tried to present an exhaustive compilation of other critics' interpretations, whether they concur or contrast with my own, though I do point out those that have most influenced my own thinking. I present these reflections on certain aspects of gender performance in Vergil's epic both as an index of my own development as a feminist reader and as a signpost for others who may want to pursue the topic further.

TRANSGENDERED MOMENTS

As I noted earlier, it is not at all unusual for modern male intellectuals to indicate that the *Aeneid* has significantly influenced their lives or work (T. S. Eliot and Allen Tate are only two of many possible examples), although similar testimony from a sports celebrity is striking enough to warrant attention from scholars whose pages would normally not include such a figure. Both Theodore Ziolkowski (1993, 154) and Karl Galinsky (1992b, 158) refer with approval to the autobiography of Penn State football coach Joe Paterno, in which Paterno testifies to his "deep relationship" with Vergil: "The adventures of Aeneas seeped into far corners of my mind, into my feelings about what is true and honorable and important. They helped shape everything I have since become" (Paterno 1989, 42). Galinsky, in fact, tries to undercut what he sees as a criticism of Aeneas's masculinity by Thomas Van Nortwick

(1992) through referring to the admiration for Aeneas expressed by Paterno, "who has excelled in a very male profession" (Galinsky 1992b, 158).

A similar statement from a female intellectual, however, *is* unusual; if women do not read Vergil from an "immasculated" perspective, they are expected to identify with Dido.[5] So I was quite surprised to hear the following words from Madeleine Blais, a Pulitzer Prize–winning journalist, when she returned to the College of New Rochelle in 1988 to deliver an honors convocation address:

> Speaking of role models, I remember my class with Dr. Barbara McManus well. She had studied at Harvard, was recently married, newly pregnant, and a Vergil genius. This class with her was a wonderful gift, especially for a scholarship student. As a journalist, I have interviewed many people, the most notable being Tennessee Williams and the Boston Red Sox. Along with another woman, I was the first of my gender to cover a game. I think about those interviews and I think of my life as a mother. During those moments, for some reason, my mind makes a quick and unconscious leap back to that hour when it was my hardest job in life to revel in those sheerly elegant rhythms of Vergil's poetry, and inevitably the opening lines, stately and grand, bidden now, like a mantra, enter my mind, music across the vale of centuries: "Arma uirumque cano, Troiae qui primus ab oris / Italiam fato profugus." The words are perfect for that ancient warrior buffeted by circumstances and for me. "Fato profugus." Fate tossed! Me and Aeneas.

What Blais describes here is much more complex than either a "female-identified" or "male-identified" perception of the *Aeneid*'s influence on her life. In her senior year, I had offered to meet with her to study Vergil on a tutorial basis, because she could not fit the course into her schedule. I was recently out of graduate school and certainly no "Vergil genius"; at that time, as my dissertation attests, I did not have any awareness of issues of gender. Yet somehow Madeleine Blais escaped "immasculation." Perhaps it was simply the fact that I represented such apparently incongruous elements—on the one hand, Harvard and Vergil; on the other, female, married, and pregnant (if so, this would support arguments that diversity on a faculty, in and of itself, has a positive influence on students). In any case, Blais describes herself as thinking of Vergil particularly when she is behaving in a very gender-appropriate way (being a mother) as well as in a gender-transgressive way (being one of the first women to cover a Red Sox game); her identification is with Aeneas, the warrior driven by fate, but she identifies with this male hero *as a woman*.

Blais's statement can be interpreted through the concept of what Georgia Duerst-Lahti and Rita Mae Kelly call the "transgendered"(1995a, 6; 1995b,

28, 33). Transgendered moments, traits, or behaviors are those that have come to be considered appropriate for both men and women but that are still affected by gender expectations and gender power differentials; in other words, these moments or behaviors are interpreted and evaluated differently when performed by different sexes. The authors distinguish transgendered moments from "sex-role crossovers" (when a member of one sex is perceived as inappropriately taking over a role considered to belong to the opposite sex and hence seeking to "become" that sex) as well as from hypothetically "gender-neutral" moments, where gendered prescriptions would not come into play at all. They deny, however, that the latter situation is currently possible: "Given the climate for gender today, *traits and behaviors cannot be neutral* [italics original]; they can at best be understood as transgendered" (Duerst-Lahti and Kelly 1995b, 28).

In fact, Madeleine Blais's most recent book, *In These Girls, Hope Is a Muscle* (1995), which follows one year in the life of a high school girls' basketball team, is a study of transgendered moments (for example, at the commencement of the game for the state championship, Blais says: "To the world, they were a bunch of teenage girls; inside their heads, they were commandos," 250). The process of transgendering in this book can be seen most clearly in the story of the team's forward, Kathleen Poe, a natural athlete whose play is inhibited by gender prescriptions; she is just too *nice*. She learns to circumvent these prescriptions by role playing on the court—not taking on the role of a boy but rather that of a twin with the nongendered name of "Skippy." Her realization of what she has learned at the end of the season is a good illustration of the meaning of a transgendered moment: "Be nice when it's time to be nice and when others are nice to you. But niceness has no place on the court because the other team wants you to lose. The court is where you can be all those things we're not supposed to be: aggressive, cocky, strong" (228–29).

Although contemporary societies offer some transgendered possibilities, it is much harder to find anything comparable in ancient civilizations. Certainly ancient Roman ideological discourse advocated distinct roles and traits for men and women; on the ideological level, at least, the transgendered was precluded, for any blurring of these distinctions was censured as a sex-role crossover in which the offender was conceptualized as simulating the opposite sex. The frequency with which elite Roman males used charges of "effeminacy" to criticize a whole range of traits or behaviors that had little connection with sexuality testifies to the strength of this ideology, as has been amply demonstrated by such studies as Richlin (1983), Edwards (1993) and Gleason (1995). One can also trace its influence in Juvenal's sixth satire when he says that a female who wants to be seen as learned and eloquent ought to cinch her tunic up to her calves, sacrifice a pig to the god Silvanus, and frequent the cheap public baths: that is, dress and act like a man (6.445–47).[6]

However, on the level of behavior as opposed to ideology, the situation appears more complex, and we can find traces of negotiations for transgendered public moments particularly around some elite Roman women (see my comments on women in Roman politics in chapter 3). During the lifetime of Vergil, for example, the figure of Fulvia, who attempted to strengthen her husband Mark Antony's position against Octavian when Antony was away from Italy (even participating to some extent in a military campaign), represents the failure of such negotiations. Whatever the reality of her life (see Delia 1991 for an attempt to disentangle the life from the rhetoric), the public rhetoric surrounding Fulvia trapped her image in the sex-role-crossover mode. During and after her lifetime, she was repeatedly portrayed as a virago whose only feminine characteristic was her body, and the sling-bullets from the Perusine War inscribed "I aim at the cunt of Fulvia" can be understood as an attempt to nullify her sex-role crossover by reducing her to a penetrable body (Hallett 1977, 154–55, 160–63; Wyke 1992, 110–11).

On the other hand, I believe that the public role so painstakingly constructed for Augustus's wife Livia can be seen as transgendered, at least during her own lifetime, primarily because her special legal status, civic honors, statues, dedications, and public acts and patronage (all traditionally male prerogatives) were carefully crafted within the discourse and imagery of femininity (Culham 1992; Flory 1993; Purcell 1986). During this same period, male poets like Catullus, Propertius, Tibullus, and Ovid were also exploiting transgendered possibilities within the conventions and situations of elegiac poetry. Thus, transgendered moments, however elusive and contested, did exist in the political and poetic climate within which the *Aeneid* was composed, and the concept of the transgendered offers a fruitful way to explore some of the tensions and ambiguities within the epic.

GENDER AND THE FIGURATIVE LEVEL OF THE *AENEID*

Susanne Wofford has recently investigated the figurative dimension of the epic genre, including not only actual tropes and rhetorical figures such as simile and apostrophe but also metanarrative elements such as divine agency and mythic symbolism; she maintains that this figurative level "can be distinguished imaginatively and epistemologically" from the naturalistic level of action, which is narrated within the limits of what the human characters can know and do (Wofford 1992, 8).[7] It is crucial to distinguish these two levels in the *Aeneid* when analyzing gender, for the ideological discourse of gender is relatively clear-cut on the figurative level and problematized primarily on the level of action. In the figures, a whole complex of positively charged ideological and cultural values are regularly and repeatedly associated with males and masculinity (order, rationality, *fatum*, *pietas*, *imperium*, Rome, Jupiter) while their negatively charged contraries are associated with females and femininity (disorder, irrational emotion, *furor*, *impietas*, defeat/submission, Carthage, Juno). It is thus easy to see why readers who identify the "meaning" of the poem with the figurative argument view the epic as misogynistic (if they pay any attention to gender at all; some simply view this kind of polarity as "natural").

The opening scene of the epic presents a succinct portrayal of the way the epic figures link gender with these ideological polarities. By the fourth line of the poem, Juno is mentioned as the cause of Aeneas's difficult journey: "saeuae memorem Iunonis ob iram" [on account of the remembering wrath of fierce Juno], 1.4.[8] The first word of this passage will become her primary epithet, *saeua*, bringing together suggestions of fierceness, harshness, cruelty, and savagery (note also "saeuique dolores" [her savage sorrows], 1.25). In the first 33 lines, Juno is associated with anger three times (1.4, 11, 25), as well as with lack of respect for *pietas*, since she persecutes a man who is renowned for this characteristic ("insignem pietate uirum" 1.10). The reasons given for her behavior combine hostility to fate (her favorite city, Carthage, is destined to be conquered by the Romans) with emotions typically gendered as feminine—a slight to her beauty (in the Judgment of Paris) as well as sexual jealousy (Jupiter's ravishing of Ganymede). Her disruptive actions are motivated by both political and erotic concerns, but the erotic increasingly takes center stage as the poem progresses, thus eliding the problematic aspects of Roman imperialism by emphasizing women and sexuality as the primary obstacles to destiny.[9] Her first action in the epic is emblematic of all her future deeds: she unleashes the forces of disorder and destruction in the form of a terrible storm at sea, and she achieves this through sexual means, by promising Aeolus a beautiful nymph if he will release the winds from their caves. As figure, Juno is not only female but also strikingly (and negatively) gendered as feminine.

Almost immediately, the epic presents a contrasting series of male/masculine figures whose increasingly positive values construct the ideological framework of the figurative argument. In contrast to Juno, whose interference with the winds is illicit, Aeolus rules the winds with lawful authority ("imperio premit" 1.54) given to him by Jupiter himself ("pater omnipotens" 1.60) and tamps down emotion instead of stirring it up ("mollitque animos et temperat iras" [he soothes their spirits and tempers their anger], 1.57). Although Aeolus is suborned by Juno, the resulting storm is subsequently calmed by Neptune, who, in the act of restoring order to wind and sea, is compared to the ideal Augustan orator/statesman, a man dignified by *pietas* and meritorious service ("pietate grauem ac meritis . . . uirum" 1.151), who is able to calm a seditious, rioting mob merely through the authority of his presence and words. The comparison with the storm unleashed by Juno, the use of the verb *saeuit* (1.149), and the suggestion of animality (the erstwhile rioters listen "arrectisque auribus" [with ears pricked up], 1.152) all associate the mob with "feminine" qualities.

The opening scene explicitly ends ("Et iam finis erat" 1.223) with the figure of Jupiter, the apex of masculine imagery in the poem, looking down from the heights of Olympus. He is characterized as supremely potent ("hominum sator atque deorum" [the begetter of men and gods], 1.254), the epitome of reason and order (his very countenance calms storms), and the master of fate. He not only knows but also wills the contents of the scroll of fate and has the power to give unlimited empire to the Romans, bring Juno into submission, and forever confine the forces of disorder:

> his ego nec metas rerum nec tempora pono:
> imperium sine fine dedi. quin aspera Iuno,
> quae mare nunc terrasque metu caelumque fatigat,
> consilia in melius referet, mecumque fouebit
> Romanos, rerum dominos gentemque togatam.
> . . . .
> claudentur Belli portae; Furor impius intus
> saeua sedens super arma et centum uinctus aënis
> post tergum nodis fremet horridus ore cruento. (1.278–82; 294–96)

[On the Romans I place limits neither of space nor of time; I have given them empire without end. In fact, raging Juno, who now in her fear exhausts sea, lands, and sky, will retreat into better counsel, and with me will foster the Romans, the toga-wearing race, masters of the world. . . . The gates of war will be closed; inside, sitting on the savage weapons, arms bound back with a hundred bonds of bronze, *Furor impius*, ghastly, will roar with bloodstained mouth.]

In the long speech that legitimizes Roman power, Jupiter leapfrogs through history, from the Italian war that takes place in the second half of the epic, to the establishment of Lavinium, Alba Longa, and Rome, to the conquest of Greece by the Romans and the Caesar who will bring back the golden age and definitively close the gates of war (i.e., Augustus). All that is positive here is emphatically masculine, even to the characterization of Romans as "the race who wear the toga" (a garment that could be worn only by male citizens), while the passion and disorder that will be defeated bear the stamp of the feminine. *Furor impius*, though not explicitly gendered, is associated with Juno through the proximity of the passages, the references to rage and savagery, and the undertones of monstrous animality.

All this is well known, and I do not want to belabor the point here. This gendered ideological polarity is developed, even magnified, throughout the rest of the epic, as Juno enlists other female figures in the service of disorder and passion, including Venus, Juturna, and the hellish Fury Allecto. Even when Juno is forced to submit and abandon her stormy campaign ("mentem . . . retorsit / . . . nubemque relinquit" [she wrenched her heart away and left the cloud], 12.841–42), the feminine figuration of *furor* does not cease. For Jupiter himself keeps two snaky Furies ("Dirae" 12.845) beside his throne, whom he dispatches when the divine plan needs to stir up some disorder (death, pestilence, or war) in the service of ultimate order (12.851–52); it is noteworthy that even disorder that is justified by fate ("meritas" 12.852) must be represented through female figures.[10]

On the figurative level, therefore, gender is strongly polarized and ideologically charged as positive/masculine and negative/feminine. If we seek transgendered moments in the *Aeneid*, we will not find them here but rather on the narrative level of action and character, which is both distinct from the figures and in tension with them.

THE NARRATIVE LEVEL: FEMALE CHARACTERS

Two of the female characters in the *Aeneid* achieve transgendered moments in traditionally masculine spheres—Dido in the realm of politics and Camilla in the military sphere. The situations of both characters exhibit the two major features of the transgendered: (1) their positions and actions in these spheres are accepted and positively valued by the other humans in the epic (i.e., on the narrative level, not necessarily on the figurative level); (2) their positions and actions in these spheres are still seen as feminine and interpreted through the lenses of gender (i.e., these women are neither constructed as "masculine" nor evaluated in the same way as men in similar positions).

Dido's transgendered moment extends through most of book 1, from the first introduction of her story to the commencement of Venus's plot to ensnare her (1.340–656). The first line of this section stresses Dido's position as legitimate ruler through the redundancy of *imperium* and *regit*: "imperium Dido . . . regit" [Dido reigns over the sovereignty], 1.340. Yet her feminine gender is also stressed; she was wife to Sychaeus, whom she deeply loved ("magno miserae dilectus amore" 1.344). After her brother, Pygmalion, had deceived his sister and treacherously murdered Sychaeus, Dido organized all dissidents in Pygmalion's kingdom and led an escape, stealing away from Pygmalion the treasure he had killed Sychaeus to acquire. The famous phrase that concludes this narrative—"dux femina facti" [a woman was leader of this exploit], 1.364—provides an epitome of a transgendered moment. The action is traditionally masculine (*dux* can designate either a political or a military leader), the actor is female and recognized as such (*femina*), the tone is positive, but the amazed and wondering nature of the admiration distinguish it from the approbation that would be accorded a male actor (one cannot imagine a Roman saying "dux uir facti" in similar circumstances, for *uir* was already implied in *dux*). The construction of the city of Carthage, with its huge walls and rising citadel (1.365–66), offers an emblem of Dido's achievement; although one might be tempted to read phallic imagery in the repeated references to these erections, it is important to note that Dido herself is never described as manly or characterized by masculine imagery.[11]

It is instructive to analyze Dido's own actions during this transgendered moment according to the framework of traditional codes defining the concept of "authority," as summarized by Kathleen Jones (1993, 103–4):

> [A]n authority is someone who is *official* (occupies a public, professionalized role recognized as having the capacity to issue rules), *knowledgeable* (has knowledge that meets certain epistemic criteria for issuing rules), *decisive* (possesses singularity of will and judges dispassionately so that the rules will be enforced), and *compelling* (constructs political obedience to the rules ordering public life through institutionalized hierarchy). (italics original)

Throughout this section of the *Aeneid*, Dido manifests an authority that is constructed according to these codes (office, knowledge, judgment, and command). She is clearly the publicly recognized ruler of Carthage; besides the emphatic use of *imperium regit* noted above, she is called *regina* five times in this section, and she herself refers to Carthage as her kingdom ("regni" 1.563). She proceeds to the temple of Juno with a large crowd of attendants and sits on a high throne surrounded by armed men. All these details emphasize her official status. Moreover, her actions are described as both knowledgeable and decisive:

> iura dabat legesque uiris, operumque laborem
> partibus aequabat iustis aut sorte trahebat. (1.507–8)

[She issued ordinances and laws to the men; she apportioned the labor with just division of the tasks or assigned them by lot.]

Finally, her orders command obedience; Ilioneus addresses the request for asylum directly to her, and she grants it in her own name, with a series of emphatic first-person statements culminating in her majestic offer to share her city with the Trojans: "urbem quam statuo, uestra est" [the city which I am establishing is yours], 1.573.

Richard Monti (1981, 1–29) has demonstrated that Roman political terminology and concepts in book 1 of the *Aeneid* establish the association between Dido and Aeneas as that of *hospitium*, an alliance between peoples initiated by the hospitality of one party and incurring an obligation of gratitude and repayment on the other, based on a mutual *fides* (trustworthiness and reliability). Although Monti argues convincingly that Dido's "typical mode of behavior is that of a political person" (32), he pays no attention to the difference it makes when a political person is female.[12] His approach is gender neutral while that of the epic narrative is, I maintain, transgendered. Throughout this section Dido is presented as a *woman* who rules; both her beauty and her physical presence are emphasized ("forma pulcherrima Dido" 1.496), and the text hints at the unconventional nature of her position through the emphasis on *uiris* in line 507 ("she issues laws *for men*"). However, while her gender affects her rule, it does not delegitimize her authority. Compassion is presented as the hallmark of her response to the Trojans:

> me quoque per multos similis fortuna labores
> iactatam hac demum uoluit consistere terra;
> non ignara mali miseris succurrere disco. (1.628–30)

[A similar fortune has also willed that I, tossed about by many troubles, at last come to rest in this land; not unaware of suffering myself, I am learning to help the unfortunate.]

Indeed, the transgendered authority presented in this section of the epic is strikingly similar to what Kathleen Jones envisions as "compassionate authority," authority reconceptualized to include that which is gendered as feminine and based on an imaginative assumption of the standpoint of a concrete other instead of on traditionally neutral, dispassionate judgment (Jones 1993, 143–56).[13]

But Dido is not allowed to remain in this transgendered position, and Vergil marks the change with a dramatic intrusion of the epic figures into the level of narrative action. Venus schemes with her son Cupid to take the shape of Aeneas's son, Ascanius, and overwhelm Dido with passion for Aeneas: Cupid is to capture the queen with an ambush and surround her with fire ("capere ante dolis et cingere flamma / reginam" 1.673–74, a metaphor based on the siege of a city). The scene combines such military terms with amatory and maternal imagery, troping a city ruled by a woman with the physical penetrability of a woman's body and the emotional vulnerability of a mother ("insidat" 1.719, simultaneously suggests that "he occupies" the city, "he penetrates" her body, and "he sits on" her lap). After this action, the narrator immediately describes Dido as "praecipue infelix, pesti deuota futurae" [especially unlucky, doomed to future ruin], 1.712, where *infelix* also suggests "unhappy" and "barren," while *deuota* indicates something consecrated or sacrificed to the infernal gods. Although Dido herself, on the level of action, has no awareness of this ("inscia" 1.718), her story has been "contaminated" by the polarized gender ideology that marks the figurative argument of the epic.

Terming such scenes "symbolic distortions," Susanne Wofford explains how they work throughout the *Aeneid* (1992, 97–211). The mythic symbolism of the epic, figured through the actions of divine beings, forms an alternative plot that works both with and against the action. This alternative plot, of which the reader is fully cognizant, presents its own ideology and seeks to impose closure on the action. Since the characters are for the most part unaware of this plot, however, different meanings may emerge from the level of action. Of the various rhetorical devices that work to connect figure and action, "symbolic distortion" is the most violent, for the figures literally "touch" the action and become narrative events, affecting the reader's interpretation, but not that of the characters. Since such figurative incursions in the *Aeneid* are almost always proleptic, they appear to cause the subsequent actions and hence generate "allegories of compulsion":

> Virgil uses this scheme politically to legitimize Aeneas's venture because it suggests that the forces of history are beyond individual control, and that they shape and direct even the most private emotional involvements. This

vision of the historical shape of emotion poses a moral dilemma, however, as it denies to the individual the possibility of making ethical decisions. (Wofford 1992, 140)

The most powerful allegories of compulsion occur when the figures intervene directly in the action (usually without the knowledge or understanding of the characters being controlled); such scenes do not simply reveal the outcome but actually consummate it. Dido's fate is overdetermined by such figurative interventions (not only the assault of Cupid but also the collusion of Juno and Venus to precipitate the supernatural storm and "marriage" with Aeneas in the cave), and Vergil's insistence on such highly visible divine interference should caution against any simplistic reading of Dido's story as misogynistic or the gods as a "Trope for Human Motivation" (G. Williams 1983, 20). Those who read book 4, either with or without approbation, as an essentialist portrayal of women's unfitness to rule or excessive susceptibility to passion ignore the way that the divine figures take control of Dido's emotions and actions and hence disempower her as an ethical agent. The only comment in the epic that seeks to generalize Dido's behavior in this way comes not from the narrator but from Mercury in a dream designed to hasten Aeneas's departure from Carthage: "uarium et mutabile semper / femina" [a women is always a fickle and changeable thing], 4.569–70. Despite this phrase's subsequent history as an oft-quoted apothegm, it carries little force in context, being more applicable to the behavior of Aeneas than of Dido, who has been single-minded in her efforts to persuade Aeneas to stay with her in Carthage.

It is true, however, that Dido's actions, marked off from book 1 by Aeneas's long tale of the fall of Troy and his wanderings, are no longer transgendered; indeed, the "symbolic distortion" has gendered her as excessively feminine in the most emotional, disorderly, and subjugated sense. Vergil graphically represents her loss of the qualities of office, knowledge, judgment, and command by the total cessation of building in Carthage (4.86–89); her "feminine" subjugation is summed up in Juno's bitter statement, "liceat Phrygio seruire marito / dotalisque tuae Tyrios permittere dextrae" [let her wait on a Phrygian husband and hand over her Tyrian people into your hand as a dowry], 4.103–4. It is only now that the Libyan king Iarbas, her overlord and rejected suitor, prompted by the incursion of another female figure (Fama), can contemptuously dismiss her as a mere woman to whom he sold land for a "tiny city" ("urbem / exiguam" 4.211–12) and who has accepted Aeneas as her "master" ("dominum" 4.214). Vergil gives us one final glimpse of Dido as the transgendered leader, however, when she pronounces her own epitaph just before her suicide:

uixi et quem dederat cursum Fortuna peregi,
et nunc magna mei sub terras ibit imago.
urbem praeclaram statui, mea moenia uidi,
ulta uirum poenas inimico a fratre recepi. (4.653–56)

[I have lived my life, I have completed the course that Fortune had given me, and now I shall go beneath the earth as a mighty apparition. I founded a distinguished city, saw my walls rise, avenged my husband, and took revenge on my hostile brother.]

These words resemble the kind of life courses typically inscribed on the tombstones of elite Roman politicians (Monti 1981, 69), and they also evoke the Dido of book 1, living out a transgendered moment that the Roman imperial ideology of the *Aeneid*'s figurative register could not allow to stand.

Only one other female character in the *Aeneid*, Camilla, is presented in such a transgendered context. Although Camilla's sphere is war, an area that would appear even more resistant to transgendering than politics, she is not decisively displaced from her transgendered moment as Dido is. Although Camilla is sacrificed to the demands of the epic's figurative argument, she dies as a heroic warrior-maiden and has, as it were, the last word in the epic, since the protesting cry with which her life departs (11.831) finds an exact echo in the cry of Turnus that closes the *Aeneid* (12.952). Camilla is apparently Vergil's own creation; both the prominence and manner of her presentation are all the more striking because of the lack of epic precedent.

Camilla is constructed in accordance with the features (discussed above) that characterize transgendered moments: her role as a warrior is both accepted and positively valued but still gendered as feminine and colored by this interpretation. Her first appearance, at the end of the Italian catalogue (7.803–17), illustrates these features well. She is described as leading her cavalry, as accustomed to endure the hard toils of battle, as a superb runner, as armed with spear and arrows, and as clothed in a mantle of royal purple ("regius ... honos," 7.814–15, where *honos* also connotes the dignity of public office). The public acceptance and admiration for her role are emphasized by the lines that describe the crowd, including both youths and mothers, who have come out of their houses to see her pass (7.812–14). But her feminine gender is also strongly marked: she is termed "bellatrix" (7.805) and "uirgo" (7.806). In fact, Vergil calls her *uirgo* 13 times (plus two other uses of cognate terms), but never *uirago*,[14] which is used only once in the epic (12.468, applied to Juturna, who belongs to the figurative register). Her hands, though accustomed to battle rather than spinning and weaving, are still called "womanly" ("femineas" 7.806), and the royal mantle covers shoulders described as "smooth" ("leuis" 7.815). The difference that gender makes is stressed not only by her placement at the end of the catalogue, even after Turnus, but also by the degree of admiration she excites. The crowd is described as "attonitus inhians" [awestruck and openmouthed], 7.814; in fact, Camilla is the only leader in the catalogue for whom we are able to observe the people's response.

This transgendered pattern is continued throughout Camilla's battle exploits in book 11. Although some Italians have been less than whole-hearted in their support of Turnus, Camilla volunteers to lead the charge against the Trojans while he protects the city (11.502–6); the words *audeo, solaque,* and *prima* highlight her courage. Turnus eagerly accepts her offer, though charging her with the city's defense as he sets up an ambush for Aeneas; in effect, he makes her co-commander of the Italian forces ("ducis et tu concipe curam" [you also take on the responsibility of general], 11.519). The unusual adjective *horrenda,* used to characterize Turnus's opinion of Camilla ("horrenda in uirgine" 11.507), stresses the difference that gender makes; courage that would be admirable in a man is "awe-inspiring" in a woman.

At this point, the narrative action is interrupted by the figurative register, as the goddess Diana relates Camilla's history to the nymph Opis and com-mands her to avenge Camilla's impending death (once again, the figures pro-leptically determine the action). The fantastic story of the baby girl tied to a spear, thrown across a river, and dedicated to the virgin huntress Diana serves as a confirming trope for Camilla's role; as figure, it does not negate the heroic nature of the subsequent battle scenes. Although this passage links Camilla's virginity and her martial nature ("aeternum telorum et uirginitatis amorem" [her unending passion for weapons and for virginity], 11.583), this does not ungender her, since many mothers view her as a desirable daughter-in-law (11.581–82). This reference to hopeful (if thwarted) mothers-in-law sits rather oddly with the rest of the passage; its very oddity calls attention to the fact that the human actors in the epic do *not* view Camilla as "a woman who is not a woman," as Brooks Otis describes her (1964, 364 n. 1).

Camilla's *aristeia* begins at 11.648, where she is called an Amazon and described as going into battle with one breast uncovered; this recalls the description of Penthesilea on the frieze of Dido's temple, and Penthesilea is mentioned in the simile that compares Camilla and her followers to Amazons (11.659–63).[15] The descriptions of battle that follow emphasize her courage, skill, strength, and ferocity but also highlight her gender. As she slays one

Etruscan, she boasts that Etruscan threats have been refuted with "muliebribus armis" [womanly arms], 11.687, and she is enraged when another enemy speaks scornfully of her sex (11.705–20).

Camilla's final scene (11.768–831) is the most difficult to interpret according to the transgendered paradigm. Attracted by the dazzling armor of the Trojan Chloreus and intent upon acquiring it, Camilla is caught unawares by the spear of Arruns, which pierces her beneath her naked breast and kills her. In the line "femineo praedae et spoliorum ardebat amore" [she burned with a feminine passion for booty and spoils], 11.782, many commentators take the adjective *femineo* as the key that unlocks the reason for her death: Camilla "is finally betrayed by her woman's love for finery" (Otis 1964, 364; see also Wiltshire 1989, 64; Suzuki 1989, 140). In context, however, this passage is more complex. The text gives two possible reasons for Camilla's desire to capture the armor of Chloreus, either in order to set it up as a military trophy in front of the temples or to wear it herself (11.778–79). The first alternative is praiseworthy according to the code of military behavior; the second is a motivation that some male warriors also share (e.g., Hector, Euryalus, Turnus). Nor can *praedae* in this context be translated as "finery"; its primary meaning of "military booty, plunder" is strongly reinforced by its juxtaposition with *spoliorum* (military spoils). One way to read this passage, of course, is to say that her feminine nature contaminates the otherwise masculine desire for spoils;[16] another, more transgendered reading is to recognize that her gender complicates her ability to function effectively in a male-defined sphere (in a fashion similar to the way that Dido's political relationship with her overlord Iarbas is complicated by the fact that he is a rejected suitor). It is certainly true that the passage presents Camilla's desire for Chloreus's armor as unwise, but this in itself would not differentiate her behavior from that of Hector, Euryalus, or Turnus, whose deaths are also related to plundered armor. In any case, Camilla dies a hero, and her final words fulfill her commission as military commander, summoning Turnus to return to the defense of the now unprotected city.

No matter what our interpretation of *femineo* here, Camilla's portrait is still predominantly positive and transgendered; unlike Dido, she is never touched directly by the epic figures and thus is not contaminated by the symbolic distortion imposed upon Dido by the figurative register. She escapes such contamination for several reasons: (1) her story never comes into direct contact with that of Aeneas and so need not be tainted by Juno/*furor*; (2) being consecrated to virginity, she can be completely set apart from sexuality (she is "intemerata" [unstained, undefiled], 11.583);[17] (3) although appearing in the narrative register of action and character, she has an aura of fantasy that distinguishes her from legendary/historical women like Dido, Lavinia, and Amata.

It is tempting to speculate about why Vergil gave such prominence to two women whose presence was not required by the legends he was relating, and why they appear in luminous transgendered moments even though the gender ideology of the figurative level is so polarized and the feminine symbolism so relentlessly dark and destructive. Perhaps that very contrast with the figurative argument is a partial answer; as many critics have pointed out, there are numerous currents in the narrative action that run counter to the poem's dominant ideology, and these transgendered moments may be seen as part of that creative tension. Moreover, as noted above, when Vergil was composing the *Aeneid,* contemporary Roman politics and elegiac poetry were already sites of negotiation for transgendered spaces. The most conflicted of these negotiations, that involving Cleopatra VII, makes an oblique appearance in the figurative register of the poem (in the *ekphrasis* of Aeneas's shield). The fact that a real queen from the east, sexually linked with a Roman commander, for a time posed a literal threat to Roman imperial hegemony casts a long shadow over Dido and certainly contributes to the compulsive violence with which the figurative argument rends her transgendered portrayal.[18] Finally, these depictions of female characters in transgendered contexts should be read in relation to the representation of Aeneas in the epic.

THE NARRATIVE LEVEL: AENEAS

Before considering whether the character of Aeneas is ever put into "feminized" space, it is important to recognize that negotiation of the transgendered is even more complex and conflicted for males in a patriarchal society than it is for females. Women seeking to transgender a "masculine" space may be seen as potentially dangerous contaminators of that space, but at least they are viewed as reaching for what is powerful, valued, superior. Men in an analogous position risk the perception of self-contamination; they hazard charges of sex-role crossover into what is weak, devalued, inferior. Such a risk would be particularly potent in a highly competitive society such as that of elite males in late Republican Rome, where any form of social, political, or moral weakness could be gendered as female and provoke charges of "effeminacy." Edwards (1993) and Richlin (1983) demonstrate how common such charges were; for example, Suetonius says that Pompey accused Augustus of effeminacy, that Mark Antony claimed Augustus had secured his adoption by fornicating with Julius Caesar, and that Antony's brother accused Augustus of self-prostitution (*Divus Augustus* 68). To put Aeneas in a feminized space, therefore, was to risk such self-contamination; Vergil had to ensure that Aeneas would be perceived as transgendered rather than as a sex-role crossover.[19]

The characterization of Aeneas has long been a problem for commentators, who have frequently asserted that Vergil is struggling to define a new kind of heroism for Aeneas. I had originally conceived of this new heroism as end-determined rather than self-determined; the plot of the *Aeneid* demanded "a subordination of his past and his present in the service of a future goal that was not of his own choosing" (McManus 1976, 74). As I examine Aeneas now, I see the gendered dimensions of this concept.[20] Especially in the context of Roman discourse, where autonomy and self-assertion were highly valued marks of manliness, subordination and submission could easily be perceived as feminine. Augustus himself had to deal with this dilemma, finding a way to reconfigure the dominant discourse in order to curb the aristocratic drive for self-aggrandizement and ensure submission to his own power; hence paradoxical slogans like *primus inter pares* [first among equals]. Paul Zanker (1988) presents ample evidence of the subtle and ingenious Augustan deployment of all forms of public imagery to achieve this complex task. This project involved a campaign to elevate and masculinize the traditional concept of *pietas*, for its meaning of "dutifulness" to family, fatherland, and gods implied a kind of submission; Zanker says *pietas* became "one of the most important leitmotifs of the Augustan era" (102). Augustus conspicuously identified himself with this quality. For example, it was prominently engraved on the golden honorary shield awarded to Augustus in 27 B.C.E. when he "restored the Republic" and "returned power to the Senate and Roman people." Traditionally, the "shield of valor" *(clipeus uirtutis)* celebrated the achievements and noble qualities of the person being honored; inscribed on the shield awarded to Augustus were clemency, justice, and *pietas* toward gods and fatherland. The military and "manly" connotations of the shield (*uir* is the root of *uirtus*) lent an aura of masculinity to the virtues stressed by Augustus. He would later use an image of Aeneas in a similar way, as a masculine emblem of *pietas*, proleptically depicted in Roman armor, holding his son by the hand and carrying his father and the *penates*.[21]

Vergil's characterization of Aeneas should be understood in this context.[22] The opening lines of the epic epitomize the contested grounds of gender that mark Aeneas's role. On the one hand, the first words, *arma uirumque,*" are emphatically masculine, as are his projected foundation of a city and introduction of his gods to Latium, actions that will ultimately lead to the lofty walls of Rome. On the other hand, the words used to describe Aeneas's actions suggest a remarkable passivity. He is "exiled" or "fugitive" on account of fate ("profugus" 1.2). His *Odyssey* is conveyed by "iactatus" ("greatly tossed about on land and sea" 1.3), and his *Iliad* by "passus" ("enduring many things in war" 1.5). His most distinguishing quality is *pietas* (1.10). The Trojans as a group are "driven by the fates" ("acti fatis" 1.32); they are the "leavings" of the Greeks ("reliquias" 1.30). The text seeks to divert all of these "feminine" resonances away from Aeneas by displacing them onto an epic figure, Juno, who will serve as a lightning rod for the negative feminine energy that surges through the poem. However, this strategy does not totally distance Aeneas from the feminine, since he appears dominated by the female deity who "drove him to submit to so many hardships" ("tot adire labores / impulerit" 1.10–11).

Aeneas's own sense of himself is highlighted by a perception of powerlessness and forced submission to a will not his own. When describing his last night in Troy, he appears to be defending himself against some inner accusation of cowardice and lack of manliness:

> Iliaci cineres et flamma extrema meorum,
> testor, in occasu uestro nec tela nec ullas
> uitauisse uices, Danaum et, si fata fuissent
> ut caderem, meruisse manu. (2.431–34)

[Oh ashes of Troy and final conflagration of my people, I call you to witness, at your fall I did nót avoid any weapons or any hazards from the Greeks, and, had the fates been that I should die, by my hand I earned death!]

It takes repeated interventions from the figurative register, including a vision provided by Venus and a meeting with the ghost of Creusa, to force him to leave Troy, and his last word, *cessi* (2.804, meaning both "I left" and "I gave up"), bitterly underlines his sense of compulsion. Aeneas is touched by the figurative level more often than any other character in the epic, and he is also given more awareness of these interventions (although he rarely understands them fully). On the ideological level, this is part of the strategy that legitimizes and justifies Aeneas's actions; on the psychological level, this is the way that Aeneas is motivated to reach Italy and establish a settlement there.

But ironically, a device that gives him ideological power makes him *feel* powerless (Wofford 1992, 117). He frequently speaks of himself as unwilling: "Italiam non sponte sequor" [I do not seek Italy of my own will], 4.361; "invitus, regina, tuo de litore cessi" [unwillingly, O queen, did I leave your shore], 6.460. He also describes himself as carried along by forces beyond his control: "feror exsul in altum / cum sociis natoque penatibus et magnis dis" [I am carried over the deep, an exile with my companions and my son, with the *penates* and the great gods], 3.11–12; "nos alias hinc ad lacrimas eadem horrida belli / fata uocant" [the same dread fates call us from these to other griefs], 11.96–97.

Thus, both the ideology and the narrative structure of the *Aeneid* put Aeneas in a feminized space, and the poem employs a number of strategies to ensure that Aeneas retains his masculinity while moving in this space (i.e., that his actions are characterized as transgendered). In fact, the text underlines the risk that Aeneas will be perceived as a sex-role crossover by having both Iarbas and Turnus contemptuously call him effeminate:

> et nunc ille Paris cum semiuiro comitatu,
> Maeonia mentum mitra crinemque madentem
> subnexus, rapto potitur. (4.215–17)

[And now this "Paris" with his effeminate retinue, his oily hair and chin beribboned in a Phrygian headdress, possesses the plunder (i.e., Dido and her kingdom).]

> da sternere corpus
> loricamque manu ualida lacerare reuulsam
> semiuiri Phrygis et foedare in puluere crinis
> uibratos calido ferro murraque madentis. (12.97–100)

[Grant that I may lay his body low, and tear off and pull apart with my strong hand the breastplate of that effeminate Phrygian, and foul in the dust that hair curled with hot irons and dripping with perfume.]

However, the hyperbole in their language and their obviously personal reasons for belittling Aeneas undercut the reliability of their perceptions.

One of the major strategies Vergil uses to emphasize Aeneas's masculinity is to concentrate all the negative energies that oppose the founding of Rome in female deities and feminine symbolism on the figurative level, which then contaminates female characters on the level of action. By gendering the forces that hinder Aeneas as so conspicuously feminine, the text tends to elide the feminized aspects of his own role and thus highlight his maleness. Indeed, this may be one of the reasons why the epic's ideology displaces blame onto the female so tangibly. Significantly, the female figures never contaminate Aeneas the way they do so many other characters (e.g., Allecto, Juturna, and the *Dira* infect Turnus); the figures that "touch" Aeneas are almost all male, and when Venus contacts Aeneas directly, her interventions are positive (as when she heals his wound). In fact, one of the figures actually uses the threat of effeminacy to motivate Aeneas to leave Carthage. When Mercury flies down to Libya, we see Aeneas through his eyes (i.e., through the dominant ideology of the poem). Although Aeneas is directing the construction of the city, the gaze of the god lingers on the hilt of his sword, starred with yellow jasper, and the cloak across his shoulders, made by Dido and glowing with Tyrian purple and golden embroidery (4.260–64); the commentator T. E. Page is only putting the god's sentiments into words when he says that Aeneas's magnificent apparel "indicates a woman's wanton . . . rather than a warrior" (Page 1900, 365). Mercury's speech to Aeneas is described as an "attack" ("inuadit" 4.265). He contemptuously terms Aeneas "uxorius" (4.266), which indicates either a person who is excessively attached to a wife or something that belongs to a wife, and he criticizes Aeneas's dereliction of duty to Jupiter, his fated kingdom in Italy, and his son. This speech serves to link manhood and *pietas* and has a pronounced impact on Aeneas, as his hair stands on end and his voice sticks in his throat: "attonitus tanto monitu imperioque deorum" [he was thunderstruck by the mighty warning and the authority of the gods], 4.283. Although Vergil hints at the emotional price Aeneas pays for leaving Dido, the subsequent scenes stress the contrast between the passionate violence of Dido's feelings and the repressive emotional control of Aeneas.

Another strategy the epic uses to put Aeneas in a transgendered context involves explicit praise for his masculinity. A prominent example can be found in three related passages that compare Aeneas to Hector. The first two of these lend authority to the comparison because the speakers are themselves Homeric characters who saw Hector in action, while the third is Aeneas himself. Andromache expresses the hope that Ascanius will be inspired by the heroic example of Aeneas and Hector: "ecquid in antiquam uirtutem animosque uirilis / et pater Aeneas et auunculus excitat Hector?" [Does his father Aeneas and his uncle Hector arouse him toward ancestral valor and manly courage?], 3.342–43. Diomedes, who would have killed Aeneas in battle had not Venus intervened (*Iliad* 5.297–317), refuses to aid the Latins because of his respect for the gods and for the fighting ability of Aeneas, whom he compares with Hector: "ambo animis, ambo insignes praestantibus armis, / hic pietate prior" [both were outstanding for courage and for their exceptional military skills, but Aeneas is superior in *pietas*], 11.291–92. This passage not only praises Aeneas for highly masculine qualities but subtly suggests that *pietas* is the most masculine of all.

Finally, Aeneas himself links his prowess with that of Hector in a scene that dramatizes the contested gendering of *pietas*. After Turnus finally agrees to single combat, Aeneas is shown as both warlike and *pius*, rejoicing that the battle will be fought on an orderly and rational basis ("oblato ... foedere" [according to the solemn compact that he had offered], 12.109). After the treaty is treacherously broken through the interference of Juturna, however, only Aeneas's *pietas* is emphasized: "at pius Aeneas dextram tendebat inermem / nudato capite atque suos clamore uocabat" [but dutiful Aeneas stretched out his unarmed hand and with uncovered head called his men with a shout], 12.311–12. The juxtaposition of *inermem / nudato* emphasizes weakness and vulnerability (the words mean "defenseless / naked"); here, *pietas* appears almost feminized, and the "naked" Aeneas is immediately penetrated by an arrow, although the text suppresses the phallic implications by stressing the arrow's unknown origin rather than its impact.

Aeneas's impatience to return to the fighting even if the arrowhead has to be cut out somewhat recuperates the masculine imagery, and Venus's healing of the wound invests him with ideological power from the figurative register: "maior agit deus atque opera ad maiora remittit" [a greater god intervenes and sends you back to greater deeds], 12.429. Even Hector removed his helmet before lifting up his son, but now Aeneas embraces Ascanius in full armor and kisses him through his helmet (12.433–34), telling his son to learn manly valor ("uirtutem") and true effort (or suffering? "laborem") rather than good fortune from him (12.435–46). This is when he links himself to Hector: "te animo repetentem exempla tuorum / et pater Aeneas et auunculus excitet Hector" [may your father Aeneas and your uncle Hector inspire you with courage, as you follow the models of your people], 12.439–40. Finally, Aeneas erupts into battle like a storm (12.450–55). When his efforts to track down Turnus are thwarted by Juturna, he first calls to witness the commands of Jupiter and the violated treaty and then unleashes indiscriminate slaughter ("nullo discrimine caedem" 12.494–99). The scene has come full circle, returning to the combination of military valor and *pietas* with which it began; the heavier stress on masculine violence at the end of the scene can be seen as an effort to counterbalance the feminized vulnerability earlier associated with *pietas*.

A closely related narrative strategy involves Aeneas in highly masculine activities that go beyond the dictates of his fated role; this strategy is riskier than the former because it reveals some of the cracks in the dominant ideology and calls attention to the tensions between the level of action and the figurative argument. In book 10, Aeneas goes berserk with rage and grief after the death of Pallas, rampaging through battle like Achilles, even to the point of taking prisoners to sacrifice at Pallas's funeral. The blood-lust of war leads him to scornfully dismiss *pietas* itself, as he taunts young Lausus with weakness: "quo moriture ruis maioraque uiribus audes? / fallit te incautum pietas tua" [Why are you rushing to your death, and why do you venture beyond your strength? Your *pietas* deludes and blinds you], 10.811–12. Although the image of his own *pietas* reflected back at him from the face of the dead youth later brings Aeneas back to his senses (10.821–24), the implication that *pietas* can be a deceptive and weakening force resonates uneasily with Aeneas's occasionally bitter defiance of the role he has been compelled to play.

This defiance surfaces most strikingly at the very end of the epic, when the humbled Turnus publicly admits defeat ("uicisti" [you have won], 12.936) and asks that his father be spared further grief. This appeal to *pietas* makes Aeneas hesitate, and Turnus's mention of Anchises recalls the latter's command to spare those who have submitted and make war on the arrogant ("parcere subiectis et debellare superbos" 6.853). But the sight of the sword belt plundered from the body of Pallas kindles a terrible fury in Aeneas, and he plunges his sword into the breast of the kneeling Turnus. The epic ends with the protesting cry of Turnus's ebbing life, and the reader is left with a profoundly ambiguous—and conspicuously masculine—image.[23]

Thus, the narrative strategies that emphasize Aeneas's masculinity reveal the difficulty of transgendering feminized space. The last strategy I will discuss involves an alternative move that seeks to dignify feminine imagery, either by associating it with young males who die tragically or by transgendering female characters. The lilies and purple flowers that Anchises proleptically offers to Marcellus (Augustus's nephew and destined heir who died just as he was reaching adulthood) in the underworld find an echo in the later descriptions of the dead Euryalus and Pallas. Blood covers the "beautiful limbs" of Euryalus ("pulchrosque per artus" 9.433), and his head droops like that of a purple flower that is dying after it has been cut by a plough (9.435–36); the body of Pallas resembles a flower picked by a young maiden, either a violet or a drooping hyacinth, which has not yet lost its bloom though cut off from the earth that nourished it (9.68–71). The feminine imagery characterizing these young men is quite striking; it is also safe, because it is invoked after they have died on military missions. Thus, these tragic males dignify the feminine imagery associated with them instead of being themselves contaminated by it, as Turnus was infected by the fiery feminine imagery carried by Allecto. Even the hint of sexuality suggested by the reminiscence of Catullus (62.39–44 and 11.21–24, both drawing on the sexual imagery of flower and plough) takes on an affirmative note.

Similarly, the transgendered moments of Dido and Camilla serve to elevate the feminine, and it is not coincidental that Camilla's death is imagistically linked with that of Euryalus and Pallas through the mention of purple (11.819) and the reference to her drooping neck (11.829). If the transgendering of Aeneas's role is to succeed, the epic needs to present the feminine in some positive contexts that will interrogate the relentlessly negative scapegoating of the feminine on the figurative level. When Dido is portrayed as a woman who can effectively, even brilliantly, carry out a traditionally masculine role while still retaining her feminine gender, Vergil can parallel her experience with that of Aeneas, who must retain his masculinity while performing a new, partially feminized role. Transgendering masculine space for the female aids the more complex process of transgendering feminine space for the male.

FEMINIST APPROACHES TO CLASSICAL LITERATURE

Revisiting the *Aeneid* has helped me to appreciate how much my own process of reading and interpreting classical literary works has been changed by feminist theory. My current reading does not contradict the first but deepens and enriches it; feminist theory has given me "eyes to see" in much the same way that Venus lifted the mist that dulled the mortal vision of Aeneas during the last night at Troy, enabling him to see the mighty forces ("numina magna deum" 2.623) at work beneath surface appearances. Neither I nor anyone else could have produced this reading of the *Aeneid* in 1976; 20 years of feminist scholarship have made it possible to understand not only the misogyny in the epic but also the way the narrative action problematizes gender and contests the ideological scapegoating of the female.

This interpretation of the *Aeneid* is not intended to be comprehensive or to supersede the many other possible approaches to the epic. A full exploration of transgendering in the epic would require a much longer and more complex study. However, it does illustrate one way that a feminist reading can contribute to "mainstream" studies of the *Aeneid*. Although most of the work on this epic that has been influenced by feminist theory has concentrated on the women and/or goddesses, this need not be the case. Using gender as a category of analysis can make a significant difference in how we interpret many of the "big" questions that have preoccupied Vergilian scholars: the characterization and development of Aeneas, the relation of the hero to Augustus and to Roman imperial ideology, and the significance of the epic's ending. Scholars could also use the concept of transgendering as a springboard for fuller studies of the struggles over gender surrounding historical individuals contemporary with the epic (e.g., Augustus, Antony, Cleopatra, Livia, etc.).

Let me give just two brief examples of recent work on the *Aeneid* that I believe would have been deepened and enriched by a feminist analysis of gender. Francis Cairns (1989) analyzes the *Aeneid* from the perspective of ancient kingship theory, presenting Aeneas's story as that of the development of a "good king," particularly of "a toiling and suffering ideal monarch" (32). In contrast, Dido is analyzed as a "good king" who degenerates into a bad one under the influence of passion, while Turnus is depicted as a "bad king" from the beginning, one "who cannot be exempted from punishment" (82). However, Cairns never analyzes the role that gender plays in this topic, even when he repeatedly applies the term *king* to Dido. The concept of transgendering not only would have brought more depth to his discussion of Dido's kingship but also would have helped him explore the conflicted aspects of Aeneas's kingship.

David Quint's (1993) insightful discussion of the *Aeneid* does pay attention to gender, but primarily as a symbolic category in a polarized scheme of opposites relating to the narrative forms of epic and romance and their concomitant political meanings. Using the Battle of Actium depicted on Aeneas's shield as emblematic of this scheme, Quint argues that Cleopatra, along with Juno elsewhere in the epic, "gives the name of woman to the anarchic forces inherent in the East, in the cosmos, and in the human psyche. Woman, like the boat of Cleopatra, is a passive, open vessel, unable to direct her destiny, subject to the everchanging winds of circumstance" (28–29). He demonstrates "the affinity of Cleopatra's fleeing ship to the patterns of romance" (34) by discussing scenes of characters from many later romance narratives who are carried off by mysterious boats or unbridled horses. In contrast, Augustus, who "stands firmly in control at the stern" of his ship (29), represents the epic genre, the masculine, end-directed, empire-building narrative of history's winners.

However, in discussing this ideological scheme, Quint fails to distinguish gender from sex (as can be seen in his use of the word *woman* in the above quotation), and he does not acknowledge the problematic role played by gender expectations in the *Aeneid*'s redefinition of the epic hero as a man who must sacrifice "his own individuality, even . . . his heroic agency" (84). The concept of transgendering would have been particularly useful in helping Quint avoid a crux in his argument: although Quint acknowledges that Aeneas often perceives himself as carried away by forces beyond his control and at one point literally rides in a ship without a rudder or helmsman (after the death of Palinurus), he rather unconvincingly declares that Aeneas's situation is *not* the same as that of Cleopatra ("at the mercy of the winds of chance") because his ship is directed by Fate (92–93). Instead, a recognition of the affinities between these two situations—the feminized aspects of the role Aeneas is forced to play, the masculinized aspects of Cleopatra/Dido's role, and the transgendering of both—would have led to a more complex and persuasive interpretation.

The reading of the *Aeneid* that I have presented in this chapter exemplifies some of the distinguishing features of feminist approaches to classical literary texts. For example, feminist classicists seek to view a literary text as part of the cultural discourse of its specific time and place, especially the sex/gender system. This broader discourse has shaped the literary work, as it also shaped the author and audience, and the text in turn contributed to the further construction of the discourse. Twenty plus years of feminist scholarship in classics have brought us to some understanding of ancient discourses of sex and gender, and feminist literary study involves both "reading in" and "reading out": we bring our knowledge of these cultural discourses to bear on our interpretation of the text, and we study the text to help us understand the culture. My earlier, New Critic self would have dismissed such a process as "extrinsic," but I now realize that so-called "intrinsic" approaches to literature merely "read in" and "read out" the critic's own cultural discourse without awareness or acknowledgment. Therefore, my current reading of the *Aeneid* draws on studies that piece together elite Roman conceptualizations of gender and sex roles using evidence spanning every aspect of the society, though the brevity of this chapter prevents any demonstration of how these sources have influenced my interpretation. A much fuller illustration of this approach can be seen, for example, in Helene Foley's presentation of the Homeric *Hymn to Demeter* (1994).

Like many other feminist studies of classical literature, my approach to the *Aeneid* explores the ancient text with the help of a theoretical concept articulated by modern scholars from another field, in this case the concept of the transgendered as defined by two political scientists. Barbara Gold (1993b) provides an excellent example of another such application of theory, as she reads the elegiac poetry of Propertius through the lens of Alice Jardine's theory of "gynesis" (Jardine 1985). This theoretical perspective enables her to demonstrate that Propertius "does at least temporarily destabilize the feminine in such a way that his readers can see in his text new possibilities for gender reversals and gender confusion" (Gold 1993b, 89). Although Gold contrasts this gender bending with Vergil's treatment of Dido, who she says remains imprisoned by traditional gender expectations, I believe my reading has shown that Vergil subtly contests the concept of polarized sex roles and fixed expectations of gender performance through his portrayal of transgendered moments (I would not, however, go so far as to say that Vergil destabilizes gender; indeed, the very concept of transgendering would seem to preclude gender reversals).

Another characteristic that distinguishes many feminist studies of classical literature is an awareness of the work's readers and audience, both ancient and modern. Feminist critics seek to ascertain what subject positions the text offers to its readers, how these differ for males and females, whether (and how) the text works to reinscribe and reinforce or to disrupt and subvert dominant gender ideologies, and what effect the text may have on modern readers. For example, both Nancy Rabinowitz (1993a) and Froma Zeitlin (1996) ask these questions of Athenian tragedy, and though their perspectives and methods vary, both conclude that Greek tragedies were "designed primarily for exploring the male project of selfhood in the larger world" (Zeitlin 1996, 347) and "impose a gender hierarchy consistent with and supportive of the sex/gender system of the time" (Rabinowitz 1993a, 14). Rabinowitz warns the contemporary feminist reader that female subject positions that appear to promote independent agency may be undermined by the text in ways that actually support androcentric hierarchies.

The *Aeneid* offers no such potentially affirmative and autonomous female subject positions as Penelope, Antigone, or Medea; the figurative register demonizes and ultimately subjugates the female deities, and female characters on the level of action, like Dido and Amata, are compromised and destroyed. Even the transgendered moments proffer only a male subject position, that of Aeneas, for Camilla never focalizes[24] the narrative, and we enter the mind of Dido only as it is being penetrated by Cupid. Although Dido provides the center of consciousness for most of book 4, the reader shares her subjectivity only in its process of dissolution; her transgendered moment is perceived through the eyes of others. However, even though the figurative level clearly reins in the subversive potential of the transgendered Dido within the epic, outside the parameters of the text, the figure of Dido has been the locus of a number of readings that contest androcentric norms, as ably demonstrated by Marilynn Desmond (1994). It is possible to imagine that some ancient Roman women found affirmative possibilities in reading Dido against the grain of the text, and Juvenal, though his intention is clearly to mock, gives some credence to such imaginings (see above, n. 5).

Lillian Doherty has recently pointed out two complementary feminist strategies for rereading canonical texts: "the closed oppositional reading, which identifies patterns of textual determinacy as forms of constraint on the (female) reader; and the open affirmative or celebratory reading, which identifies textual openings as opportunities for subverting androcentric norms or imagining alternatives to them" (Doherty 1995, 40).[25] The approach to the *Aeneid* that I have sketched out here demonstrates the importance of both strategies. On the one hand, the figurative level of the epic, which presents and continually reinforces Roman imperial ideology, clearly requires a feminist reading that reveals and resists the symbolic elements working to idealize the masculine and to demonize and subordinate the feminine. On the other hand, the concept of the transgendered helps the feminist reader to find the gaps and openings on the narrative level that problematize such rigid polarizations. What this approach offers, I think, is a way of reading that requires neither "immasculation" nor rejection; we can savor the richness of the text without swallowing *or* spitting out the dominant ideology.

5

COMMUNICATING
CLASSICS AND FEMINISM

Up to this point, I have been largely speaking for others, of necessity impos-
ing my own perspective and angle of vision on what I am describing. But
this chapter will include many other voices, speaking for themselves through
the medium of a survey that I distributed through a number of channels (primarily electronic) in the summer and fall of 1995 (see table 6, page 147, for
details on survey distribution and results).

The survey is not—and was not intended to be—a scientific sampling.
Respondents were totally self-selected and primarily drawn from venues that
presupposed some interest in ancient gender studies. However, there were
enough responses (202) to give the survey some weight, particularly considering the overall size of the classics profession (compare, for example, the
approximately 2,740 individual members listed in the 1995 *American Philological Association Directory of Members*). Predictably, the responses
included high percentages of women (64%) and college/university faculty
(66%), but the distribution was not wildly skewed, and there was a nice balance with regard to differing lengths of time in the profession. Since only

119

55% of the respondents are members of the Women's Classical Caucus, it is reasonable to assume that not all are committed feminists (as indeed some responses demonstrate). While the first seven questions were multiple choice, the remaining seven asked for open-ended comments about responses to feminist influence in specific areas, and the number of people who took the time to send extensive and thoughtful comments is quite remarkable. It seems that many classicists have a great deal to say about feminism and have been looking for an opportunity to say it.

SURVEY OF INDIVIDUAL CLASSICISTS: SUMMARY

Table 6 presents the quantifiable results of the survey, including total responses, breakdown according to sex, and a comparison of the responses of those with the greatest and the least longevity in the profession. The most immediately obvious result is the degree of change perceived by respondents; if we combine the "a great deal" and "moderately" categories, approximately three-quarters of the respondents see significant feminist influence on their perception of the discipline (87%), their scholarly work (74%), and their teaching (79%), and very few see no influence at all.

It is interesting to note that the strongest influence involves the way classicists think about their discipline, particularly among those who have been around the longest (93%, with no one claiming a complete lack of influence). These individuals remember what classics was like before the challenges and questions posed by modern feminism, and even the 13 (22%) who say that their own scholarship has changed little now think about the discipline differently. The contrast with the responses of the newest members of the profession, 27% of whom see little or no change in their perception of the profession, may be partly explained by the emphasis on *change* (as a number pointed out in their comments, they grew up with feminism). However, it may also be partly attributable to the conservative nature of classics graduate programs. Of the five people who saw no feminist influence in any area (as one male stated succinctly, "Feminism has made no impact whatever on me"), three were in the profession 5 to 10 years, and two less than 5 years; four were males; one was Canadian and one Italian. The three classicists from the United States in this category were all males—one an independent scholar and two students in major research universities (one a graduate student and one an undergraduate).

When we compare the responses of women and men, the women are consistently higher than the total responses, and the men slightly lower. The greatest contrast, however, occurs in the area of scholarship, where 81% of the women but only 63% of the men see a great or moderate feminist influence (even here, however, well over half the men report such influence). This is not surprising, since all my studies of scholarship directly concerned with gender issues have turned up more female than male authors. It does, however, suggest that even among classicists interested in gender and feminism (as the vast majority of the respondents clearly are), men are less inclined than women to alter their scholarly focus and approach. In the words of one male graduate student who indicated that feminism had influenced his concept of the discipline and his teaching but not his scholarship, "My work tends to be gender neutral."

The last section of table 6 indicates how many respondents included comments describing specific areas of feminist influence. These comments, often quite detailed, provide strong confirming evidence for the respondents' claims that feminism has made a significant impact on their course offerings, pedagogy, and scholarship. Over half of the respondents described changes that they had made in traditional courses like language courses and mythology; moreover, 36% said that they had created completely new courses, for a total of 115 new courses. Among the most frequently mentioned new courses, unsurprisingly, were courses on women in classical antiquity, but table 7 (page 149) lists 65 courses with different titles, grouped according to the rubrics suggested to me by their titles. This information can be put in context by looking at table 8 (page 151), which presents national statistics gathered by the APA's Committee on the Status of Women and Minority Groups. Nearly half of the programs responding to the CSWMG's 1995 survey stated that they offer courses on ancient Greek and Roman women, a really remarkable number when we consider that the first women in antiquity course in the United States was taught in 1971. The variety of topics and approaches indicated on table 7 is also beginning to be reflected in the CSWMG survey. The fact that a higher percentage of classics departments with graduate programs offer gender-related courses is most probably due to the size of their undergraduate as well as graduate programs, since there is no way to tell from the survey whether the specified courses are undergraduate or graduate offerings (in fact, I surmise that most are undergraduate offerings). It is harder to account for the fact that courses on ancient sexuality seem to be taught mainly in departments with Ph.D. programs; perhaps this is also a matter of size coupled with their faculty's freedom to choose what courses they will offer.

Besides these detailed curricular changes, 78% of the respondents to my survey indicated that feminism had exerted a great or moderate influence on their teaching, and half described the nature of these changes. This answers a challenge recently posed by John Heath in a special issue of the journal *Classical World*, when he calls upon feminists to provide "supporting evidence" for their claim to be particularly committed to undergraduate teaching (Heath 1995a, 57).[1] While this survey does not compare respondents with others in the profession, it does provide evidence that a significant number of classicists interested in gender issues are dedicated teachers who credit feminism with enhancing that dedication and helping them evolve a more student-centered pedagogy.

SURVEY OF INDIVIDUAL CLASSICISTS: COMMENTS

Reading the survey comments has been a very enriching experience for me and an exciting introduction to the profession for the undergraduate student who helped me tabulate them. The excerpts that follow are representative of the whole, presented without names but as much as possible in the voices of those who made them. The divisions are somewhat arbitrary but are included to give some sense of organization to the discussion. Except for providing this organization, I have tried to allow the comments to speak for themselves.

One survey respondent pointed out the need to counteract nonclassicists' often inaccurate and reactionary concept of the discipline: "We need to communicate better with other disciplines and with the general public—advertising not only the new approaches, but the more subtle changes in the 'traditional' methods as well." This section of the book is an attempt to address that need; anyone who really listens to the voices of these classicists cannot fail to recognize that (as another respondent put it) "these are exciting times—so many ideas to revitalize our discipline."

Influences on Curriculum and Pedagogy

A major factor mentioned in some form by almost everyone was the integration of questions about women and gender into every type of course. A male French-Canadian professor says, "Since the 70s the questions regarding women (status, role, functions in society) are parts of my teaching"; another male professor says he always "brings in the women's viewpoint, or the fact that one must have existed"; a female professor notes that she places "considerably more emphasis on text as indicative of gender roles, and of engendered rhetoric in ancient politics than I had when I was a student in similar courses." A female professor from Sweden makes sure "the students *see* the women appearing in the texts. I also try to *see* female students and their needs." A male professor at a major research university states, "I would not feel comfortable teaching a women in antiquity course, but no course I give in Roman poetry or comparative literature is untouched by feminist perspectives—I make a concerted effort to look for these and use them." A female professor, however, stating that she is "too much of a traditionalist" adds, "I think it's unwise to overdo the feminist slant, but I do try to treat feminist issues when appropriate. There is . . . so much more to classical works to cover, and too much emphasis on purely feminist issues can undermine the power of it all."

A British female professor emphasizes the importance of broadly based gender integration: "I try to incorporate gender into all aspects of the classical world. I am particularly concerned that gender not be perceived as a 'girls' game,' which can be ghettoized into courses which only women teach and attend and can therefore be devalued as 'lightweight.'" Apparently agreeing, a male professor states, "Greek History, Roman History, both now incorporate substantial sections on the role of women, and I have tried to weave this material in at every stage, not just on 'topics' days." A female professor indicates that this procedure keeps her, as well as her students, intellectually vital: "I now have either specific lectures dedicated to women in my traditional courses or I include women or feminist material throughout the course to balance the traditional views. I find this invigorating intellectually to me as well as pedagogically."

Quite a few responses stressed the necessity to relate the classical materials (texts, art, artifacts, etc.) to their social context, to bring *people* back into the study of classics: "More emphasis on interconnections between literature and the social system, the consequences of 'choices' in the value system and construction of relations between self and other in society and literature" (female professor); "I try to bring in material that addresses to some extent what the women of the period would be doing at the time" (female art professor). A male professor indicates that his course in archaeological principles includes emphasis on "peopling the landscape, retrieving women, etc."

Another area of agreement involves the choice of texts to read, both ancient ones and modern textbooks. Many classicists emphasized how they had added to their courses works that focus on women and gender or pieces that were actually written by women, though one female high school teacher cautioned, "Teaching the results of research into how women lived in ancient times is valid, but I really will never include Sulpicia in a course on literature if Ovid or Catullus or Horace must be excluded because that would mean that I would have to admit that the poetry of Sulpicia is similar in quality to that of her male contemporaries." However, she indicated that she does in fact teach Sulpicia and finds her poetry very effective in the classroom.

One female professor from a major research university characterized the greatly increased interest that feminism had brought to noncanonical texts as a major contribution to the discipline: "It is particularly gratifying to me that the Classics profession has become more tolerant of these texts' contribution to our understanding of the world of the ancient Mediterranean. Feminist approaches have heightened my ability to bring more nuanced judgments to a wide range of socio-cultural inquiries." A male professor tries to select modern textbooks "that will reflect a wider range of attitudes toward gender," and another laments that "we desperately need elementary Latin and Greek texts that pay attention to women and integrate them fully into the content of the elementary language sequence." However, a female graduate student finds that the standard language textbooks provide "a very useful springboard for discussions of both gender in antiquity and the representation of these cultures by later societies," and a male high school teacher positively prefers the old misogynist textbooks:

> I find it useful to keep the books, which are otherwise quite good, and to encourage the student to look critically at the depictions of women. Are they true to antiquity, and if so, how then do the expectations of antiquity differ from those of today? Are they merely the shortcomings of the editors, and if so how can that be compared to similar examples in popular literature and media? I think my students get a more balanced view of the meaning of feminism this way than they would if we had a textbook that had done the balancing for us. In fact, I am not sure this is achievable; for how can one represent a decidedly patriarchal society without showing the warts? Having a fair view of the hardships of the past gives today's students a chance to appreciate fairly the mission and accomplishments of feminism.

Other respondents stressed incorporation of multiple perspectives from various marginalized groups. A female professor noted that "ethnic/multicultural studies and experiences ... provide me with analytical tools different from the predominantly patriarchal ones we're usually taught, and enable me to see aspects of the ancient world, in particular ancient Greece, that tend to remain camouflaged from the typical western forms of approach." A male high school teacher is "trying to introduce cross-cultural presentation devoid of traditional ethnocentric and sex biases," and a male professor from a major research university sees this as the major contribution of feminism for him:

> Not just women, but the role of all marginalized groups (the poor, slaves, etc.) plays a much larger role in determining what questions I ask, and in evaluating whether questions others ask are worth asking. . . . I think that the greatest value has been in the opening up of new perspectives and so new questions. Again, this is not just about women; for me, thinking about women's role in the ancient world has been a wedge which has forced open the door to much broader thinking about the other non-male-elite participants in the culture and society of that world.

A British female professor put it most simply: "I ask the obvious questions: Where are the women? Where are the slaves? Where is everyone else?"

With regard to methods of pedagogy, most respondents mentioned a less authoritative classroom manner ("less pontificating," as one female professor put it succinctly), a heightened attention to student needs, especially those of women and members of minority groups, much more collaborative work, and in general a more student-centered approach. A female professor comments, "My goal is for every student to speak and know that his/her voice is valued in the classroom," and another states, "I spend as much time as possible reaching out to people in other disciplines and reaching out to students who may need a safe place to test their abilities." A male professor says that he has now acquired "more realization that half the class is female and may perceive and be interested in materials somewhat differently from what I tended without thought to regard as the male 'norm.' " Another indicated that reading the book *Women's Ways of Knowing* (Belenky et al. 1986) made him more sensitive to diverse learning styles: "In my own experience, the alterations have been far more than reactions to pressure from marginalized groups, but rather enormously pleasant and powerful insights into teaching as a profession." Still another credits his students with providing the impetus for him to use feminist theory in the classroom: "In graduate school in the late seventies . . . feminist theory was not emphasized in my course work, and I put that section of my brain on hold while I learned the tools of classics. It was when I started teaching and trying to reach 20-year-olds that it became clear to me how seriously I needed to integrate feminist theory into my course design and intellectual work." Another male professor, however, seems very ambivalent about feminist pedagogy:

> I have read enough horror stories about gender bias in the classroom to be on
> my guard, and in general I try to allow for a great deal of difference in learn-
> ing styles among the students in my classes. I'm afraid the net result is that I
> am too easy on everybody. I am a bit envious of the glowing reports from
> the feminist classroom of the life-changing, meaningful discussions they
> claim to have; but the little actual experience I have had of such classrooms
> produces in me a profound distaste and suspicion.

Two other professors, both male, described the ways they thought gender-related discussion enhanced their classrooms: "When I taught *Lysistrata*
a few weeks ago, I broke the class up along gender lines and started discussion going before reuniting the groups. The final discussion was explosive,
but it also became a turning point for many students opening up and speaking more"; "What I find is that questions relating to gender arise more in my
classes, especially in those taught in English. . . . Even in teaching Plato's
Republic to a graduate seminar a few years ago, I spent a good deal of time
on feminist interpretations of those philosopher rulers. This adds new perspective to old courses and enlivens discussion (and wakes male students out
of their old, not-at-all-well-thought-out ways)." Finally, a female graduate
student claims, "I'd say that feminist theory has informed and expanded my
pedagogical toolbox. I like to focus on ancient views of women and the narratives created about women's roles to demonstrate the broader (pardon the
pun) function and mechanics of ideologies."

New Scholarly Topics and Questions

Many respondents referred to the explosion of studies on ancient women,
family, gender, and sexuality (described in chapter 3) as one of the most visible manifestations of feminist influence in classics. As one male graduate
student puts it, "As a latecomer to classical philology, I am busy enough
working on the basics and reading, so far. Maybe later I can work my way
into topics such as feminism. I suppose that I can feel the impact of feminist
theory on our discipline, though. All I need to do is flip through a catalogue
of classics publications to see the works being published. I suspect that there
is a 'trickle' effect—feminist scholarship has impacted the 'standard' works
to some degree and hence the whole field." Scholars praise the availability of
such work for making it possible now to explore different types of questions:
"My understanding of 'women/woman' in Greek art and society, a primary
focus of my research, has benefitted immeasurably from feminist theory,
data, and the actual existence of studies to draw on, something I could not
say when I set out to study this area in 1974. . . . Imagine our understanding

of Greek society before Pomeroy's *Goddesses, Whores, Wives, and Slaves* to see how far we've, and I've, come!" (male professor). Noting that so many interesting feminist studies have now been published, one male professor even admits, "I generally don't bother to read an article if it isn't at least tangentially related to the study of women. It just doesn't seem worth the bother."

Several respondents indicated that the scholarly topics on which they had chosen to focus (e.g., Roman satire, Latin elegiac poetry) led them to feminist theory as they sought to explain these works. However, most respondents described the reverse of this process; as they became acquainted with feminist theory, they were drawn to change the focus of their scholarship, sometimes quite radically: "I had intended to focus on the provincial army and now I am studying Hispano-Roman women" (female graduate student). "I've researched and published on women (elite Roman women), which was something never thought of (by my teachers, colleagues, or myself) during undergraduate or graduate school days" (female professor). Five professors (male as well as female) described scholarly projects that deal with classical influences on later women writers or intellectuals, and one male professor explained how a student's question about women rhetoricians led to his current investigation of this topic. One male professor describes how his interest in language has modulated into " 'gender-voice' questions as well as issues of gender-based use of semantics and grammar." And one female professor at a major research university, apparently concerned that feminism not be identified with the study of women, cautions, "I do not expect to stay with 'women' exclusively for the rest of my career."

Feminist Perspectives in Scholarship

As mentioned above, quite a few of the respondents, particularly younger scholars, objected to the emphasis on change in the questionnaire, stating that feminism had "shaped" or "formed" their work in classics rather than changed it: "My perspectives on gender and the way I approach these issues in the classroom haven't changed, but that's not because I've been unaffected by feminism—it's because I started out what I consider 'feminist' and haven't 'changed,' except to keep refining my ideas as I will do to the end of my life" (female professor). "Feminism and I matured academically together: How to tell the dancers from the dance?" (male professor). "I was a feminist before I was a professional classicist. Feminism changed me, and the work I do is certainly different than if I had not been inspired by feminism from an early age. I think I discovered the women's movement and Catullus at about the same time, and have been trying to make that combination work (to use shorthand) ever since" (female professor).

Even a male graduate student who checked all the "not at all" categories qualified his response a bit: "Let me suggest that feminism has to some extent entered into classics education to the extent that I probably take certain aspects of it as it applies to classics for granted without thinking that it is particularly feminist." His further comments certainly illustrate this point, for while continually denying any feminist influence, he describes how he modified a very traditional Latin textbook by writing his own Latin stories, "about women who actively participate in the world around them," in order to "overcome the limitations of a largely phallocentric text." About his scholarship, he says, "I am interested in the ancients, and women make up an important part of those people. Thus my choice to write about the topic of women in Aeschylus is not written because of an undercurrent of feminine [*sic*] scholarship but because it was a topic that interested me."

Another male graduate student also indicates interest in focusing his scholarship on ancient women while explicitly rejecting feminist perspectives, though he acknowledges the important role of feminist classicists in making this type of scholarly focus possible: "The existence of opportunities to write and publish about women in the ancient world has helped me to focus on the historical role of women in antiquity. I should add that all theoretical considerations of women in the ancient world in my professional world come not from feminism but from training in another historical outlook. I consider myself an advocate of the study of women in antiquity quite in opposition to the theoretical methods and political stance(s) of modern feminism, with which I hope to enter into a debate in the coming years."

A number of respondents who strongly supported feminist classical scholarship nevertheless expressed concern about the highly theoretical and sometimes conflictual stances it can assume: "Sometimes I don't get the point—anthropological readings are more concrete than many feminist classical writings" (female professor). "I've always been interested in women in the ancient world, but contemporary work by feminist scholars in classics and by feminist theorists has helped me to become more committed to this work. . . . I consider myself critically informed, but I still consider myself a philologist. I have found literary theory interesting to read and quite useful for framing the larger issues, but I am often discouraged by how politicized it can get" (female professor). A male professor complains that the survey "doesn't allow the effects of feminism to be distinguished from the effects of other kinds of sex and gender study," noting that "all these areas are mutually implicated despite the (sometimes bitter) ideological differences." Finally, a female professor states quite firmly, "The part of modern feminism that is divisive has no place in what I do or who I am. The feminism that is about understanding and enlightening is what interests and intrigues me as a woman, as a teacher, and as a scholar."

Two male professors whose responses were generally sympathetic to feminism nevertheless found fault with some feminist scholarship. The first terms it "disappointing": "To me it seems all too much scholarship related to feminist theories is either 1) not very different from non-feminist scholarship or 2) belaboring one good point tediously." The second, though welcoming "the fact that feminism has opened whole areas of research which were formerly ignored," advocates "gender studies" instead of "feminist or women's studies": "I feel that much of the work by feminists ignores male figuration or distorts it in order to make a rather narrow polemical argument."

A few respondents worried that feminist theory had not carved out a distinctive enough identity in classics: "After nearly 15 years in this field, I am struck by how little feminism has been able to establish itself as a methodology fundamentally different from other recent trends. It remains simply an available mode, to be added where useful to the existing repertoire of techniques" (male professor). A female professor at a major research university, who expresses a "continuing interest" in ancient women though it is "not the main focus" of her scholarship, feels that "feminism is hard to distinguish from other theoretical influences. Certainly it has given my view of the Greeks in general a more anthropological side." A male professor who describes how feminist perspectives have prompted him to integrate many previously separate subspecialties in classics into his courses and scholarship wonders how widely this integrative approach is being utilized in classics as a whole: "You could say that a discipline hasn't really been influenced at all by feminism if this influence is confined only to certain subgroups—which part of the ancient evidence is not affected by gender and class constructions? . . . If classics has not been redirected in a fundamental way by modern feminism, it would be more accurate to say that it, as a discipline, has so far resisted feminism successfully, rather than being influenced by it in part—such partial accommodation really blunts the ability of feminism to require study across disciplines."

However, the vast majority of respondents felt that feminism and feminist theory influenced their work in ways that were distinctive, pervasive, and profound. This position was expressed by both male and female respondents but was most heavily stressed in women's comments. A female professor of art history describes how her scholarly approach "has completely changed in the last 20 years—from traditional views of date, artist, and style of Classical Greek sculpture to structuralist and feminist theory as applied to the content and form of Greek art." A female professor of archaeology says, "I ask now not 'what does this tell me about general historical trends or the development of the culture?' but 'what can I find out about the lives of ancient people, how they interacted with their environment, and how gender, age, status affected their experiences?' The methods come out of the questions." Describing her approach to classical literature, a female professor states, "When I am dealing with questions centered on male-produced texts or areas where women are not a major issue, I try to find ways of opening up the texts or questions by focusing on gender, class, race, and issues that have traditionally not been touched." A female professor of history stresses the holistic nature of the feminist approach: "My interests (religion and social history) have become both more inclusive of the total population and at the same time more focused on women. In other words, my concern is that women be placed squarely in their historical setting. They should not be ignored (as they were for so long); but neither should they be studied in isolation."

Quite a few respondents mentioned the fact that feminist perspectives informed all their work, whether or not the topic was overtly connected with women or gender issues: "Even the work I do that is not explicitly about gender is influenced by my attention to feminist issues" (female professor). "All questions I ask now have a feminist component; my methodology always uses feminist theory even if a feminist question is not the primary one" (female professor). A female graduate student relates this influence to the nature of feminist discourse:

> I find the way I present my material has greatly changed. I have been very favourably impressed with what I perceive to be a more "honest" presentation of the feminist scholar's argument, that is to say, without attempting to hide the flaws and weaknesses beneath a thin veneer of "it seems likely that" or "it is probable." I also approve of including "I" in one's paper. I always thought referring to oneself in the third person in one's own paper was pompous, stupid-sounding and somehow cowardly. There is very much a spirit of engaged, committed scholarship within the feminist movement in Classics which is long overdue.

The following two comments by female professors should perhaps be read in counterpoint with the worries (quoted above) that feminism has exerted only a partial or insufficiently distinctive influence on scholarship in classics:

> The two biggest influences on my intellectual formation have been a) the old-fashioned historical/philological approach, which I learned in graduate school and treasure beyond belief; and b) radical feminist theory, historiography, and literary criticism, which I taught myself and treasure beyond belief. As Gerda Lerner says, once we put women in, everything changes.

> My scholarly approach has evolved so extensively since my positivistic graduate school training that I could say that every intellectual trend of the last 20 years has had some influence. But feminism, both French and American, has been a major factor. It has taught me to ask questions about ideology, about what counts as important, about rhetorical silences in our evidence, and it has forced me to shift my imaginative construct of antiquity. I am currently interested in how women spoke and acted in significant public situations (in religious ritual, in poetic performance) within the framework of Greek culture especially. That is not a question I would have been able to pose, let alone have some idea how to understand the evidence, without the paradigm shift and conceptual tools provided by feminism.

Professional and Personal Issues

A number of respondents praised feminism for effecting improvements in the professional climate within which classicists work. Several male professors commented on this. One muses, "I think one's attitude and behavior toward female colleagues and students has had to be re-examined, also the attitude of the professional establishment toward women and ethnic minorities." Another cites the influences on himself and his department (at a prominent research university): "Dynamics within the department and university (faculty/student, interfaculty, hiring, relations with staff, etc.) have benefitted, and I am more conscious of issues of bias, prejudice, harassment, etc." Still another describes himself as now "taking care to be positive and open about others' work, looking for the best in what people say." Several women note that feminism has made it easier for them to pursue an academic career in classics and indicate that they are now "less patient with 'business as usual' from the dominant male elite in the profession." A female professor sums up the changes that she perceives:

> Feminism has had a very positive influence on professional organizations (APA especially), and through them on the profession generally. The "old

boy" system is no longer unquestioned, hiring is more open, people are at least aware that anti-female sentiments are not accepted by many. Gender-neutral language has become the norm, and now the "generic masculine" sounds as odd as gender-neutral language did at first.

Another factor mentioned by many respondents was the way that feminist theory encourages attention to personal as well as professional issues and compels consideration of their intersection. As one female professor puts it, "The overall effect of feminist theory on my scholarship has been to make me much more self-conscious about what we as classicists do in our professional lives and how that, in turn, impacts on our personal lives." Several respondents found this very empowering: "The way I see the world and ask scholarly and daily-life questions has been profoundly influenced by my research on feminism. Feminist scholarly work has reinforced and validated a host of rather inchoate feelings about both personal relationships and about professional/academic goals which might otherwise have remained formless and dissatisfied" (female professor). However, a number of respondents worried that this integration of personal and professional issues would make it more difficult for the classics profession to accept feminism. One male scholar, a strong supporter of feminism, describes his scholarly approach as relying upon "the same sort of questions and approaches I use in thinking about my own life. In a way, truth be told, I think our discipline avoids these questions because a lot of people would rather not think in too much detail about their own lives." Another male professor rejects this aspect of feminism: "I am in sympathy with equity feminism, but not gender feminism, and I resist the morally repugnant aspects of the sexual revolution. Feminism on this campus and in our profession seems very tightly linked to a movement of homosexual advocacy that asks one to believe five impossible things before breakfast. I would rather teach people to read Latin and Greek, and to read well." A third sees the new feminist emphasis as transforming a much older ideal:

> Feminism has had more of an impact on me in my non-Classics identity. I do not think that this is because Classics is especially resistant to feminism, but has become resistant to meshing a non-scholarly life with the life of a professional Classics scholar. The ideal of a "gentleman and scholar," to say nothing of a truly heroic scholar, finds no support in the profession, I fear. The choice of "gentleman" may at first seem antithetical to support of gender studies within such an ideal, but I believe that this ideal embraces a certain humanity and respect for which feminism also strives. The withering of this ideal has, perhaps paradoxically on the surface, made it more difficult for the broad goals of feminism to make any inroads into Classics as a profession, as a vocation if you will. . . . In as much as I try to approach Classics

much more broadly, I try to incorporate the goals of feminist theory, scholarship, pedagogy, and appreciation for gender-based issues.

Establishment Resistance to Feminism

Some respondents described negative reactions to feminism that they had encountered in the profession. One female professor speculates about the effect on her professional advancement: "Perhaps being labeled 'a feminist' has hampered my career, but I would not give it up." A male professor observes that "many younger women entering the job market are careful not to identify themselves as feminists primarily and indeed resist to some degree attempts to persuade them to teach and research in areas obviously related to women's studies." Graduate students were particularly likely to describe either the absence of feminist perspectives or hostility to feminism among their professors. One female high school teacher who is also a graduate student says, "It is very clear to me that there are many professors who do not take a 'feminist approach'—by this I mean there are some professors I have worked with who don't ever really mention women's role in the ancient world, the problems we face in our approach to their role, etc." Another female graduate student characterizes both her undergraduate and graduate experience as "frustrating": "Whenever I have proposed research or papers which do approach classics from a feminist perspective, my ideas have consistently been rejected—not because they have no merit (at least nobody has said as much), but because they are 'too controversial.' It would appear that nobody wants to eat the hamburger that I make of their sacred cows. There is only one female—much less feminist—here, and I have not yet had the opportunity to work with her."

One woman points to her graduate school experience to emphasize the importance of continuing vigilance about the profession: "We must not heed those who say that classics is being (or has been) taken over by 'special interest' groups (code for feminists). From my perspective as a graduate student, this is far from the case. We must continue to press for oversight, affirmative action, and harassment guidelines in order to create a truly equal playing field." Another, who attributes her own positive experience to "very strong mentors," recommends, "One of the most important questions about feminism and classics should revolve around the question of mentoring—how we can encourage, inspire, and support students in taking up these often politically dangerous intellectual positions." A female graduate student who did attempt to foster a more feminist atmosphere in her department describes her experience:

My undergraduate professors were very supportive of my work in both feminist theory and the study of women in antiquity. In graduate school I have found that support largely from outside the classics department. I have tried to organize reading groups on issues of gender in antiquity in the classics department, but this effort has not gotten me farther than being deemed a sort of imposter/hoyden from comparative literature. Work on feminism is always "extra" and, in the world of classics department qualifying exams, secondary. It has been very frustrating. I find I have more to talk about with feminist scholars in other disciplines than I do with classicists.

Finally, another female graduate student, who found her undergraduate experience hostile to feminism, emphasizes the difference feminism has made in her own personal outlook:

I think that as an undergrad I swallowed so much hook, line and sinker. I actually believed professors who told me that issues of theory, women, and comparative studies were peripheral, unimportant, or, worse yet, unmarketable. I'm not sure if the atmosphere has become more friendly or if I finally realized the importance of job satisfaction. In any case, my work is becoming more self-consciously oriented toward questions of gender and social history, as opposed to Ciceronian periods and Homeric formulas. Perhaps more than anything, feminism has created for me an interest in ancient people, and not just the words they left behind.

GRADUATE PROGRAMS

As this survey has made very clear, efforts to communicate classics and feminism are many and varied in classrooms across this country. But the programs that *prepare* classicists to communicate their subject to others appear to be far less influenced by feminism than other areas of the profession. The reasons for this are surely manifold, but two mutually reinforcing explanations stand out: the low proportion of women faculty and the concern with "standards." The quotation from George Goold with which I opened chapter 2 amply demonstrates the way that standards forged according to a male norm tend to exclude women, whereupon the scarcity of women tends to continually validate the standards. A more recent quotation from Ernst Badian, a professor of ancient history at Harvard, further illustrates the connection. When asked in a survey whether he agreed with Allan Bloom, author of *The Closing of the American Mind*, that feminism posed a threat to the classics, Badian replied:

Only in the limited sense that "affirmative action" is a certain way of lowering standards in any field (and whoever its beneficiaries), since quality is no longer the only (or even chief) criterion. But the "threat" is less in classics than in many other fields, since women have on the whole been much better treated in classics than in (say) engineering or banking, so that there is less need for, and less application of, such anti-quality principles in the classical field. (quoted in Richlin 1988, 24)

The circular reasoning in this statement can only be understood in the light of certain (probably unconscious) assumptions: *feminism* equals *affirmative action* (and nothing else), *high quality* equals *male,* and *female* equals *lower quality.*

If these were idiosyncratic assumptions, there would be no need to belabor this point. However, I have already shown how deeply entrenched they are in the profession of classics. Since one major purpose of graduate programs is to certify the credentials of new members of the profession, these programs tend to view the "preservation of standards" as a primary function. This concern is particularly strong in classics; James Redfield describes the classicist as "uniquely threatened by any tendency to lower standards. In other fields, if standards are lowered the work goes on, although at a lower standard; since the *raison d'être* of classics is the maintenance of a certain standard, the lowering of standards here threatens the abolition of the field" (Redfield 1991, 15). While I think Redfield's formulation here a bit extreme, it is true that classics' self-definition is closely bound up with the idea of standards (as can be seen from the field's name), standards that were established a very long time ago and according to a very masculine norm. Feminists do not question the importance of quality or standards, but they do require that these concepts be interrogated: Who determines quality? According to what criteria? How and by whom were these criteria generated? Do these criteria disproportionately benefit or exclude any groups? Unless such questions are confronted and answered honestly, no standards can claim to represent quality pure and simple.

However, information is needed to answer questions such as these, and that information is hard to find, particularly since most assessors of quality do not even look for it. For example, the idea that "quality" can be assessed with no attention to gender, that the sex of the rater and the rated are totally irrelevant, is structured into the design and implementation of the National Research Council's latest study of *Research-Doctorate Programs in the United States* (Goldberger et al. 1995). Although this study collected information about the number and percentage of women students enrolled in graduate programs, it totally ignored the sex of faculty. The "objective measures" for faculty quality in the humanities included total number of faculty, percentage of full professors, percentage with research support, number of honors and awards, and percentage of faculty receiving honors and awards; this was supplemented by "reputational ratings" of quality by faculty at other research universities, whose sex was also not ascertained.

Since I do believe that gender is relevant to questions of quality, I used the 1995 *APA Guide to Graduate Programs in the Classics in the United States and Canada* to try to find some information about the sex ratios of faculty in various graduate programs. Tables 9 and 10 (see pages 152–154) show what information can be gleaned from the directory with regard to doctoral-level and masters programs in classics. Although this information is neither totally complete nor completely accurate (see notes at the bottom of table 10), it does give a sense of the low proportion of women in classics programs that offer graduate degrees (according to this tally, 24% in doctoral programs and 27% in masters programs). Since the directory gives no information about rank, it is impossible to ascertain how many of the women in these programs actually teach graduate courses. However, if we couple this information with the data regarding dissertations (see fig. 2), we can conclude that there are not many women in positions of seniority in classical graduate programs.

Of course, not all women are feminists, and not all feminists are women, but the simple *dearth* of women is significant in and of itself. Out of all the classical dissertations reported to the APA as completed between 1987 and 1995, only 44 female graduates had women professors directing their dissertations (18% of female doctoral recipients). As has been pointed out frequently, this means a lack of role models for female graduate students. But to my knowledge, no one has lamented a fact that is just as meaningful—in the same period, only 40 male graduate students had women dissertation directors (13% of male doctoral recipients). This means that few men being trained in classics work closely with women who are in positions of authority. It is hard to see how this would not affect their perception of the role of women in the profession, their ideas about "standards" and "quality," and even their later attitudes toward female colleagues. Feminism is an important support and corrective for female graduate students, but it has an equally important role to play for male graduate students.

The 1995 directory lists very few graduate faculty with a specialization in women in classical antiquity: only 8 out of 629 faculty in doctoral programs (1.3%) and only 3 out of 181 in masters programs (1.6%).[2] Indeed, a glance at tables 9 and 10 shows that very few specialities even minimally related to gender studies are mentioned; the most frequently named is social history. Furthermore, when programs cite their particular curricular strengths, only 2 out of 50 doctoral programs (4%) and 1 out of 26 masters programs (3.8%) name women in antiquity or women's studies. Since the information for the directory is generally submitted to the APA by the department chair or the director of graduate studies, individual faculty may have little control over the specialities that are listed, and some feminists who have made substantial contributions to the study of women in classical antiquity are not listed with this speciality. However, the reluctance of programs to include this kind of information is itself indicative that such work is still considered peripheral by many classicists in positions of authority.

In such a climate, then, it is not surprising that gender studies do not count on qualifying exams, that feminist work is considered "extra" or "secondary" to the serious business of classics. Critics of feminism draw on this attitude when they praise only "scholars who work in a number of areas and happen, for one reason or another, to take an interest in women's studies," scholars " who established their credentials in other areas" (Fleming 1986a, 74). The powerful effects of the disciplinary socialization provided by graduate programs (Ruscio 1987) also help to explain why so few classics dissertation topics deal with gender studies, feminist theory, or even other forms of contemporary theory; why some scholars may be worried about being seen as feminists or identified with work on ancient women; and why the strongest feminist influence was found among the classicists in my survey who were furthest from their own graduate school experience.

It seems that classicists have not yet succeeded in communicating the message of feminism very effectively to and within graduate programs, but there is a promising initiative underway (begun in 1993 by classicists at the University of Pennsylvania) to bring together representatives from various departments to examine the nature of graduate study in classics. Several prominent classical feminist scholars (e.g., Susan Guettel Cole, Judith Hallett, and Sheila Murnaghan) are actively involved in this effort.

COMMUNICATING OUTSIDE THE FIELD

In the heady 1970s, feminists in classics were visible partners in the feminist dialogues about recovering women's history and transforming the disciplines; along with colleagues from other disciplines, they delivered papers at the Berkshire conferences, published articles in *Signs* (Arthur 1976) and in early collections such as *Liberating Women's History* (Pomeroy 1976) and

Becoming Visible (Arthur 1977), and accounted for an entire special issue of the journal *Women's Studies* 8.1–2 (1981). This level of communication was hard to sustain, however, particularly as feminist classical scholars concentrated their efforts on communicating to their fellow classicists through panels, conferences, publications in classical journals, or books on classical topics. Most recent collections on feminism in the disciplines have not included classics, with the notable exceptions of *(En)gendering Knowledge* (Gutzwiller and Michelini 1991) and *Feminisms in the Academy* (Kampen 1995; Pomeroy 1995). Despite the continuing efforts of some feminist classicists to speak out in venues not connected with classics (as, for example, Richlin [1992c], a discussion of the Anita Hill hearings from the perspective of Cicero's *Pro Caelio,* published in a law journal), many feminists outside the discipline do not read classicists' work.[3]

Since, as I have shown, there are now so many more voices swelling the feminist chorus within classics, it is perhaps time to make a concerted effort to share our song with others. This book is one step in that effort, and the conference on "Feminism and Classics: Framing the Research Agenda," scheduled for November 1996 at Princeton, is another, since the conference has an interdisciplinary organization, including speakers and participants from outside of classics and attention to methods of fostering dialogue with feminists from other disciplines. Electronic communication may also encourage such dialogue, particularly the visually and intellectually exciting World Wide Web site called *Diotima: Materials for the Study of Women and Gender in the Ancient World*, begun in 1995.[4]

Feminist classicists have also been communicating, at times perhaps unwittingly, with those outside academia altogether. When Sarah Pomeroy's *Goddesses, Whores, Wives, and Slaves* was first published, it received a good deal of media attention, and its subsequent influence has been widespread and sometimes unexpected. While attending a recent gallery show in Greenwich Village, for example, Pomeroy was startled to see that a number of paintings by the avant-garde artist Nancy Spero were graphic designs featuring images and words from her book. In the spring of 1995, the National Museum in Athens mounted an exhibition dedicated primarily to representations of mythical women, *From Medea to Sappho: Radical Women in Ancient Greece*, and fall 1995 saw a major exhibition at Baltimore's Walters Art Gallery, *Pandora's Box: Women in Classical Greece*, containing 138 works of art from fifth-century Greece (Reeder 1995). A two-day symposium on "Gender, Sex, and Mythology in Ancient Greece" was presented in conjunction with the exhibition. Events such as these reach far beyond the discipline and may in fact help to revitalize classics' image among the general public. One respondent to my survey, an independent scholar who has been teaching private courses on ancient women to adolescents and adults, commented about the role of feminism in such a revitalization: "Male scholars often forget that there is a world apart from academia. In that larger world, feminism and the reinterpretation of the classics have had a large impact. His [*sic*] work has had none."

CODA

Feminists often speak of "revolutionizing" disciplines, but I doubt whether feminists in classics can reasonably expect to achieve such a profound change. Classics does not offer feminists enough ammunition for a true revolution: the subject matter is too patriarchal, the evidence too scarce, the history too long, the traditions too deeply ingrained.[5] I have instead used the concept of crossing a "rational frontier" that leads to a redirection of the discipline and a redefining of professional boundaries, and I have demonstrated that both of these processes are well under way in classics.[6] When I began the work for this book, I expected a much more negative outcome, but I am now convinced that we have already crossed the most dangerous part of that frontier; we have made our case too strongly for classics ever to go back. Military metaphors may have been appropriate when we were crossing the minefields, but my musical analogy now seems a more apt and attainable goal: creating a richly textured contrapuntal composition that promotes cooperation while preserving diversity.

TABLE 1 *Women Presidents of the American Philological Association, 1869–1995*

Name	Year	Degrees	Primary faculty positions	Married?
Abby Leach	1899–1900	Harvard Annex; Vassar	Vassar	no
Elizabeth Hazelton Haight	1933–34	Vassar; Cornell University	Vassar	no
Lily Ross Taylor	1941–42	University of Wisconsin; Bryn Mawr	Vassar; Bryn Mawr	no
Cornelia Catlin Coulter	1947–48	Washington University; Bryn Mawr	Vassar; Mt. Holyoke	no
Gertrude E. Smith	1957–58	University of Chicago	University of Chicago	yes
Inez Scott Ryberg	1961–62	University of Minnesota; University of Wisconsin	Vassar	yes
Dorothy Mae Robathan	1964–65	Wellesley; University of Chicago	Wellesley	no
Agnes Kirsopp Lake Michels	1971–72	Bryn Mawr	Bryn Mawr	yes
Helen F. North	1975–76	Cornell University	Swarthmore	no
Helen H. Bacon	1984–85	Bryn Mawr	Smith; Barnard	no
Emily Townsend Vermeule	1994–95	Radcliffe; Bryn Mawr	Boston University; Wellesley; Harvard University	yes

Note: In 1995, Susan M. Treggiari was elected to the APA presidency, to serve as president in 1997. The first feminist activist ever elected to this office, Helene Foley, will assume the APA presidency in 1998.

TABLE 2   *Library of Congress On-Line Search*

Publications: Books	All	English	English Greece	English Rome	English Both
total number	293	160	85	40	35
total known gender	284	159	84	40	35
number unknown gender	9	1	1	0	0
number by women	146	92	47	22.5	22.5
number by men	138	67	37	17.5	12.5
number on Greece	156	85	85	NA	NA
number on Rome	83	40	NA	40	NA
number on both cultures	54	35	NA	NA	35
number historical/social focus	180	97	39	30	28
number literary focus	84	51	37	9	5
number art/archaeology focus	11	1	1	0	0
number other (mostly translations)	18	11	8	1	2
number 1990–present	112	78	43	18	17
number 1985–89	59	23	10	7	6
number 1980–84	50	22	10	7	5
number 1975–79	40	15	8	2	5
number 1970–74	13	7	4	1	2
number before 1970	19	15	10	5	0
% by women	51%	58%	56%	56%	64%
% by men	49%	42%	44%	44%	36%
% on Greece	53%	53%	100%	NA	NA
% on Rome	28%	25%	NA	100%	NA
% on both	18%	22%	NA	NA	100%
% social/historical	61%	61%	46%	75%	80%
% literary	29%	32%	44%	23%	14%
% art/archaeological	4%	1%	1%	0%	0%
% 1990–95 (fall)	38%	49%	51%	45%	49%
% 1985–89	20%	14%	12%	17.5%	17%
% 1980–84	17%	14%	12%	17.5%	14%
% 1975–79	14%	9%	9%	5%	14%
% 1970–74	4%	4%	5%	2.5%	6%
% before 1970	6%	9%	12%	12.5%	0%
% in English (N=160)	55%				
% in German (N=50)	17%				
% in Italian (N=36)	12%				
% in French (N=24)	8%				
% in other languages (N=23)	8%				

Using the database of books acquired since 1968, I searched the Subject category for variants of *Greece* or *Rome* plus variants of *women, family, marriage, sexuality*. I manually eliminated all irrelevant items and used the full records to classify books under the broad headings listed above. Search conducted in August 1995. Percentages do not always add up to 100 because of rounding.

TABLE 3   Database of Classical Bibliography *Study*

Year	Books or monographs	Collections	Articles in collections	Articles in journals	Dissertations	Total number
1976	2	1	1	28	5	37
1977	4	0	1	23	2	30
1978	3	2	0	39	3	47
1979	4	1	4	30	4	43
1980	1	0	0	36	5	42
1981	7	1	16	32	4	60
1982	10	0	2	45	3	59
1983	6	1	12	48	4	71
1984	8	1	17	51	2	79
1985	4	1	4	37	2	48
1986	4	2	22	29	0	57
1987	2	1	1	36	0	40
Totals	55	11	80	434	34	614
	9%	1.8%	13%	70.7%	5.5%	

TABLE 4   *Journals Study*

1971	*AJA*	*AJP*	*ARETH*	*CSCA*	*CJ*	*CP*
articles by women	12	5.5	5	1	5	6
articles by men	27	42.5	11	15	16	36
% articles by women	31%	11%	31%	6%	24%	14%
% articles by men	69%	89%	69%	94%	76%	86%
gender-related articles	1	1			3	
% gender-related articles	3%	2%			14%	
category 1 articles					1	
category 2 articles	1	1			2	
category 3 articles						
category 4 articles						

1981	*AJA*	*AJP*	*ARETH*	*CSCA*	*CJ*	*CP*
articles by women	14	4	3	5	10	4.5
articles by men	26	42	13	13	21	24.5
articles of unknown sex					1	
% articles by women	35%	9%	19%	28%	32%	16%
% articles by men	65%	91%	81%	72%	68%	84%
gender-related articles	7	2	1	1	2	2
% gender-related articles	18%	4%	6%	6%	6%	7%
category 1 articles						
category 2 articles	7	1	1	1	1	2
category 3 articles		1			1	
category 4 articles						

1991	*AJA*	*AJP*	*ARETH*	*CA*	*CJ*	*CP*
articles by women	5.5	7	7	5	5	2.5
articles by men	8.5	30	4	10	20	20.5
articles of unknown sex						
% articles by women	39%	19%	64%	33%	20%	11%
% articles by men	61%	81%	36%	67%	80%	89%
gender-related articles	4	5	7	4	11	3
% gender-related articles	29%	14%	64%	27%	44%	13%
category 1 articles					1	
category 2 articles	2	3	5	2	9	2
category 3 articles	2	2	1	1	1	
category 4 articles			1	1		1

Study encompassed all articles except brief notes and individual book reviews, though review articles were included. **Journals:** *American Journal of Archaeology* (AJA), *American Journal of Philology* (AJP), *Arethusa* (ARETH), *Classical Antiquity* (CA; formerly *California Studies in Classical Antiquity*), *Classical Journal* (CJ), *Classical Philology* (CP), *Classical World* (CW), *Échos du monde classique/Classical Views* (EMC), *Helios* (HEL), *Hesperia* (HESP), *Harvard Studies in Classical Philology* (HSCP; used 1992 because no volume was published in 1991), *Illinois Classical Studies* (ICS),

CW	EMC	HEL	HESP	HSCP	ICS	PHOEN	TAPA	VERG	TOTAL
8	3	NA	3.5	3	NA	0	2	0	54
16	10	NA	18.5	12	NA	24	24	6	258
33%	23%	NA	16%	20%	NA	0%	8%	0%	17%
67%	77%	NA	84%	80%	NA	100%	92%	100%	83%
1	2	NA		2	NA	3	1	1	15
4%	15%	NA		13%	NA	13%	4%	17%	5%
	2	NA			NA			1	4
1		NA		2	NA	3	1		11
		NA			NA				0
		NA			NA				0

CW	EMC	HEL	HESP	HSCP	ICS	PHOEN	TAPA	VERG	TOTAL
4	2.83	3	5.5	0.5	2.5	2	2.5	4	67.33
14	10.17	9	18.5	15.5	26.5	14	18.5	5	270.67
									1
22%	22%	25%	23%	3%	9%	13%	12%	44%	20%
78%	78%	75%	77%	97%	91%	88%	88%	56%	80%
2	4	5				3		1	30
11%	31%	42%				19%		11%	9%
1	1								2
1	3	5				3		1	26
									2
									0

CW	EMC	HEL	HESP	HSCP	ICS	PHOEN	TAPA	VERG	TOTAL
7.5	3.33	6	12.67	2	4	5	5	2	79.5
10.5	11.67	8	10.33	20	21	13	14	6	207.5
						1			1
42%	22%	43%	55%	9%	16%	28%	26%	25%	28%
58%	78%	57%	45%	91%	84%	72%	74%	75%	72%
6	3	8	2	4	2	2	5	1	67
33%	20%	57%	9%	18%	8%	11%	26%	13%	23%
		1		3					5
5	1	1	2	1	2	2	4	1	42
	2	4					1		14
1		2							6

Phoenix (PHOEN), *Transactions of the American Philological Association* (TAPA), *Vergilius* (VERG). **Categories:** 1—articles that treat feminism, women, or gender studies with flippancy and/or hostility; 2—articles on topics relevant to gender studies that do not employ a feminist approach; 3—articles on topics relevant to gender studies that employ a feminist approach; 4—articles not obviously relevant to gender studies that show significant feminist influence.

TABLE 5 Classical Dissertations in the United States and Canada

	87–88	88–89	89–90	90–91	91–92	92–93	93–94	94–95	Totals and means
dissertations by women	25	23	29	36	22	26	43	32	236
dissertations by men	42	38	23	37	41	45	50	30	306
female directors	9.5	6.5	7	9.5	12	6	25	8.5	84
male directors	57.5	54.5	45	63.5	51	65	68	53.5	458
% dissertations by women	37%	38%	56%	49%	35%	37%	46%	52%	44%
% directed by women	14%	11%	13%	13%	19%	8%	27%	14%	15%
number of women directed by women	3	3.5	2.5	3	7	4	15.5	5.5	44
number of men directed by women	6.5	3	4.5	6.5	5	2	9.5	3	40
% women directed by women	12%	15%	9%	8%	32%	15%	36%	17%	19%
% men directed by women	15%	8%	20%	18%	12%	5%	19%	10%	13%
topics related to classical gender studies	5	1	3	2	7	7	13	10	48
% related to classical gender studies	7%	2%	6%	3%	11%	10%	14%	16%	9%

Based on information supplied by graduate programs in the United States and Canada and published in the American Philological Association Newsletter.

TABLE 6   *Survey of Individual Classicists*

	Total responses	Women	Men	More than 20 years	Less than 5 years
total responses	202				
respondents who are WCC members	112	55%	65%	39%		
respondents from foreign institutions	25	12%	12%	13%		
Sex of respondents					
unknown sex	3	1%			
female sex	130	64%			
male sex	69	34%			
Status of respondents					
college/university faculty	134	66%	65%	68%	90%	18%
high school faculty	10	5%	4%	7%	3%	8%
graduate students	36	18%	17%	20%	0%	44%
undergraduate students	7	3%	3%	3%	0%	13%
other	15	7%	11%	1%	7%	18%
Respondents' length in classics profession					
less than 5 years in profession	39	19%	21%	16%		
5–10 years in profession	48	24%	22%	28%		
11–20 years in profession	53	26%	27%	25%		
more than 20 years in profession	60	30%	29%	30%		
unknown length	2	1%	1%	1%		
Modern feminism has changed the way I think about the discipline of classics					
a great deal	109	54%	58%	48%	63%	36%
moderately	66	33%	32%	33%	30%	38%
to a small degree	20	10%	9%	12%	7%	21%
not at all	7	3%	2%	7%	0%	5%
Modern feminism has influenced my scholarly work in classics					
a great deal	79	39%	47%	25%	37%	33%
moderately	71	35%	34%	38%	42%	44%
to a small degree	35	17%	12%	28%	20%	15%
not at all	15	7%	5%	10%	2%	5%
not applicable	2	1%	2%	0%	0%	3%

continues

TABLE 6 *Continued*

	Total responses	Women	Men	More than 20 years	Less than 5 years
Modern feminism has changed what and how I teach in classics					
a great deal	87	43%	45%	39%	50%	33%
moderately	70	35%	38%	36%	38%	21%
to a small degree	19	9%	7%	14%	10%	8%
not at all	10	5%	4%	7%	0%	10%
not applicable	16	8%	5%	3%	2%	28%
Included comments explaining specific areas of feminist influence					
offered new courses (115 courses listed)	72	36%	38%	32%	48%	5%
changed traditional courses	118	58%	58%	61%	75%	23%
changed pedagogy	100	50%	52%	46%	57%	28%
changed content of my scholarship	101	50%	55%	43%	55%	28%
changed approach of my scholarship	94	47%	50%	42%	47%	15%

This survey is not intended as a scientific sampling. The respondents were self-selected, and the methods of distribution for the survey tended to favor those with some interest in ancient gender: the *Women's Classical Caucus Newsletter* and E-mail list; the web site *Diotima: Materials for the Study of Women and Gender in the Ancient World* and its related electronic discussion list ANAHITA. But the questionnaire was also posted twice on the large CLASSICS and CLASSICS-M electronic discussion lists, which are not gender-related. Percentages do not always add up to 100 because of rounding.

TABLE 7   *New Courses Listed in Survey of Individual Classicists*

Type	Course title
archaeology	Archaeological Method and Theory (special section on gender)
archaeology	Domestic Roman Archaeology
archaeology	Greek Sanctuaries
archaeology	Pompeii
art	New Ways of Seeing Art in Greece & Rome: Body Image, Gender Symbolism, Feminist Theory
art	Women in Ancient Art and Society
art	Women in Classical Art
civilization	Gender and the Gift: Ancient Texts and Modern Ethnographies
civilization	Gender in Ancient Society
civilization	Graduate Reading Seminar on Ancient Women
civilization	Hellenistic Civilization
civilization	Senior Thesis Seminar on Women in Antiquity
civilization	The Family in Greece
civilization	The Women in Greek and Roman Egypt
civilization	Women and Family in Greece and Rome
civilization	Women and Gender in Antiquity
civilization	Women and Gender in the Classical World
civilization	Women in Ancient Greece
civilization	Women in Ancient Greece and Rome
civilization	Women in Ancient Rome
civilization	Women in Classical Athens
civilization	Women in the Greco-Roman World
civilization	Women in the Roman Provinces
history	Athenian Democracy
history	Freshman Seminar on Cleopatra
history	Images of the Twelve Caesars
history	Women in Ancient History
language	Latin Readings on Roman Women
language	Seminar in Koine Language and Literature: Thekla, Aseneth, Perpetua
literature	Aristophanes, Lysistrata, and Thesmophoriazusae
literature	Greek Drama in Modern Performance
literature	Greek Tragedy in Critical Perspective
literature	Heroines

continues

TABLE 7 *Continued*

Type	Course title
literature	Sappho and the Lyric Tradition
literature	Sex, Gender, and Representation in Greek and Roman Literature
literature	The Ancient Novel
literature	Women Writers in World Literature
literature	Women in Ancient Comedy
literature	Women in Greek Literature
literature	Women in Traditional Folktales
literature	Women's Texts and Women's Experience in Classical Antiquity and the Middle Ages
literature	Written Roman Women
mythology	Feminine Archetype in Myth and Art
mythology	Goddesses and Women in the Literature and Myth of the Ancient Near East
mythology	Myth and Gender
philosophy	Ancient Views of Justice
philosophy	Hellenistic Philosophy
philosophy	Women and Utopia in Classical Greek Thought
postclassical	Classics and Post-War German Literature
postclassical	Women and the Classical Tradition
religion	Women Thinking God
religion	Women in the Early Church
sexuality	Gender and Sexuality
sexuality	Gender and Sexuality in Ancient Rome
sexuality	Gender and Sexuality in the Classical World
sexuality	Issues of Gender and Sexuality in Ancient Greece
sexuality	Perspectives on Gay, Lesbian, and Bisexual Studies
sexuality	Sex and Gender in Greece and Rome
sexuality	Sex and Gender in the Ancient World
sexuality	Sex and Power in Ancient Greece
sexuality	Sex and Society in Ancient Greece
sexuality	Sex and Society in Antiquity
sexuality	Sex in the Ancient World
sexuality	Sexuality and Gender in Classical Antiquity
theory	Feminist Theory (cross-listed in classics)

A total of 115 new courses were listed; 65 titles are included here, and the remaining courses were all titled Women in Antiquity. For ease of grouping, I have used broad rubrics to classify the courses based on their titles. Of these 65 courses, 57% include both Greece and Rome, 25% focus on Greece, 14% focus on Rome, and the rest were unclassifiable.

TABLE 8   *CSWMG Data on Course Offerings, 1991–94 Mean Percentages*

	All programs responding	*Baccalaureate programs*	*MA/MAT programs*	*Ph.D. programs*
number of programs	190	124	26	36
offer courses on women	45%	34%	67%	61%
offer courses on minority groups	4%	5%	0%	4%
offer courses on sexuality	6%	2%	4%	21%
offer courses combining categories	15%	14%	8%	27%

Table is based on data from the 1995 survey of classics departments in the United States and Canada conducted by the American Philological Association's Committee on the Status of Women and Minority Groups. Programs are classified according to highest terminal degree offered in classics; four programs listed in the total responses are not included in the program breakdowns (two were from community colleges, and two did not indicate terminal degree).

TABLE 9 *Faculty in Doctoral Programs in the United States and Canada*

Institution	Women	Men	% Women	Sex unknown	Women in antiquity	Related specialties
Alberta, University of	3	6	33%		1	
Arkansas, University of	1	4	20%			
Berkeley, University of California (Classics)	2	15	12%			ancient society
Berkeley, University of California (History & Archaeology)	4	25	14%			
Boston University	4	9	31%			
British Columbia, University of	2	9	18%			
Brown University	3	10	23%			
Buffalo, SUNY	2	9	18%		1	social history
Catholic University of America	1	8	11%	1		
Chicago, University of	3	9	25%			social history; anthropology
Cincinnati, University of	3	8	27%			
*City University of New York	6	10	38%		1	
Colorado, University of	2	6	25%	4		
*Columbia University	5	9	36%		1	
Cornell University	3	12	20%	1		
Dalhousie University	0	10	0%			
Duke University	2	11	15%			
Fordham University	1	4	20%			
Georgia, University of	3	10	23%			
Harvard University	5	10	33%			
Illinois, University of (Urbana-Champaign)	1	9	10%			
Indiana University	4	9	31%		1	
Iowa, University of	3	5	38%	1		
Irvine, University of California	3	5	38%	1		
Los Angeles, University of California	4	9	31%			
Loyola University, Chicago	1	9	10%			
McMaster University	2	7	22%	1		social history
Michigan, University of (Classics)	9	17	35%			social history; anthropology
Michigan, University of (Classical Art & Archaeology)	5	7	42%			
Minnesota, University of	4	10	29%			
Missouri at Columbia, University of	2	11	15%			

Institution	Women	Men	% Women	Sex unknown	Women in antiquity	Related specialties
New York University	3	8	27%			ancient dress and culture
North Carolina, University of (Chapel Hill)	2	13	13%			
Northwestern University	0	6	0%			
Ohio State University	5	11	31%			social history
Ottawa, University of	1	9	10%			
Pennsylvania, University of	2	11	15%	1	1	social history; cultural studies
Pittsburgh, University of	3	6	33%			
Princeton University	4	7	36%			
Rutgers University	1	4	20%			social history
Santa Barbara, University of California	2	5	29%			Roman society
Southern California, University of	4	9	31%		1	cultural studies
Stanford University	6	15	29%			
Texas, University of	6	18	25%		1	ancient medicine
Toronto, University of	3	15	17%	1		
Vanderbilt University	3	6	33%			social history
Virginia, University of	1	6	14%			
Washington, University of	3	7	30%	1		ancient medicine
Wisconsin, University of	3	10	23%			ancient medicine
Yale University	6	8	43%			
Totals	151	466	24%	12	8	

Table 9 is based on information published in the 1995 edition of the *American Philological Association Guide to Graduate Programs in the Classics in the United States and Canada.* Some statistics are not entirely current, since not all departments update their entries regularly. Moreover, some departments are not included in the directory because they have failed to submit the required information to the APA. Programs marked with an asterisk have listed the study of ancient women as among their curricular strengths. The "Women in antiquity" column contains the number of faculty in the program who have this subject listed among their research specialties. The "Related specialties" column contains the names of specialties related to the study of gender that are listed among the research specialties of faculty in the department.

TABLE 10   *Faculty in Masters Programs in the United States and Canada*

Institution	Women	Men	% Women	Sex unknown	Women in antiquity	Related specialty
Albany, University at	2	6	25%			
Arizona, University of	3	7	30%		1	
Boston College	1	3	25%			
Calgary, University of	1	9	10%			
Florida State University	1	8	11%			
Florida, University of	3	5	38%			
Hunter College, City University of New York	4	3	57%			social history
Kansas, University of	2	5	29%			
Kent State University	1	3	25%		1	
Kentucky, University of	1	6	14%			
*Maryland, University of	3	4	43%		1	
Massachusetts, University of (Amherst)	1	7	13%			
Montana, University of	0	4	0%			
Nebraska–Lincoln, University of	0	5	0%			
New Brunswick, University of	0	5	0%			
Oregon, University of	3	7	30%			
Queen's University (Kingston)	1	5	17%			social history
San Francisco State University	5	3	63%			
Texas Tech University	1	8	11%			
Trent University	1	1	50%			
Tufts University	5	4	56%			
Tulane University	3	2	60%			social history
Vermont, University of	1	4	20%	1		
Victoria, University of	2	6	25%			social history
Washington University (St. Louis)	1	5	17%	1		
Wayne State University	3	5	38%			
Totals	49	130	27%	2	3	

Table 10 is based on information published in the 1995 edition of the *American Philological Association Guide to Graduate Programs in the Classics in the United States and Canada.* Some statistics are not entirely current, since not all departments update their entries regularly. Moreover, some departments are not included in the directory because they have failed to submit the required information to the APA. Programs marked with an asterisk have listed the study of ancient women as among their curricular strengths. The "Women in antiquity" column contains the number of faculty in the program who have this subject listed among their research specialties. The "Related specialties" column contains the names of specialties related to the study of gender that are listed among the research specialties of faculty in the department.

FIGURE 1   *Women's Slice of the Pie—Classics Faculty*

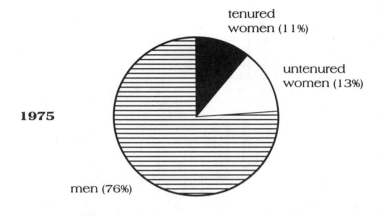

tenured
women (11%)

untenured
women (13%)

1975

men (76%)

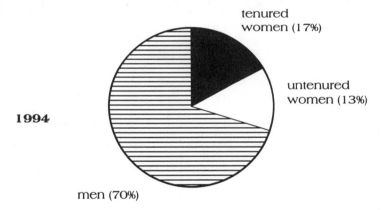

tenured
women (17%)

untenured
women (13%)

1994

men (70%)

FIGURE 2   *Classical Dissertations (United States and Canada)*

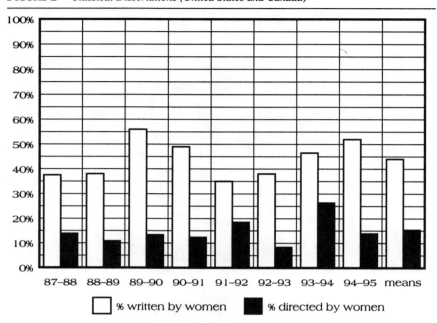

FIGURE 3   *Increasing Gap*

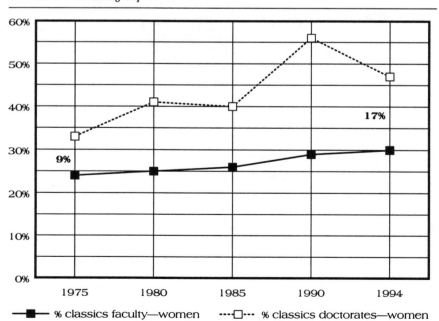

FIGURE 4 *Placement Service Statistics*

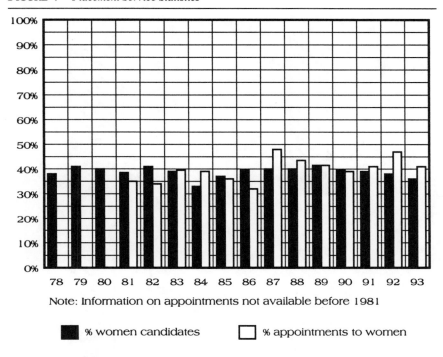

Note: Information on appointments not available before 1981

■ % women candidates   □ % appointments to women

FIGURE 5 *Classics Appointments (1989–94 Means)*

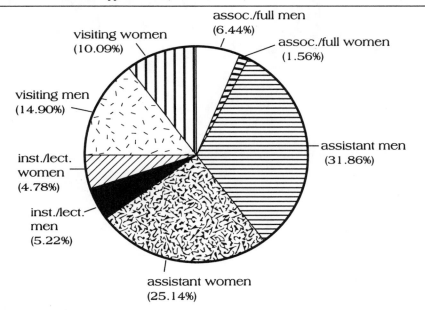

assoc./full men (6.44%)

assoc./full women (1.56%)

visiting women (10.09%)

visiting men (14.90%)

inst./lect. women (4.78%)

inst./lect. men (5.22%)

assistant men (31.86%)

assistant women (25.14%)

FIGURE 6   *Classics Faculty (1986–94 Means)*

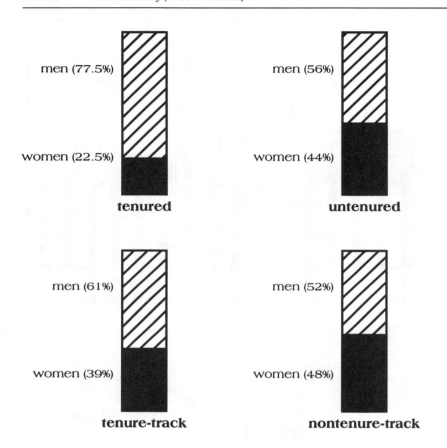

FIGURE 7 *Women in Classics Faculties—A Longitudinal Comparison*

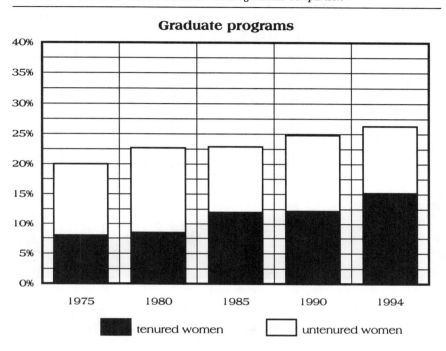

Graduate programs

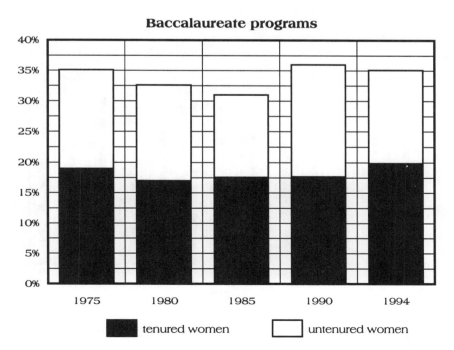

Baccalaureate programs

FIGURE 8   *Breakdown of APh Rubrics and Categories in DCB Study*

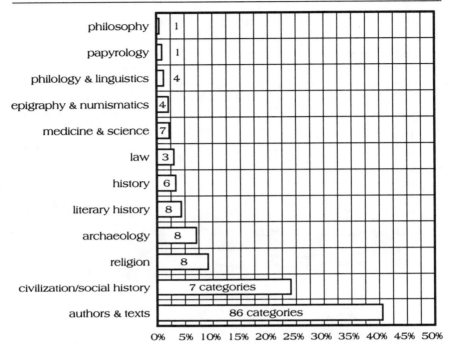

FIGURE 9   *CSWMG Journal Surveys (14 Classical Journals)*

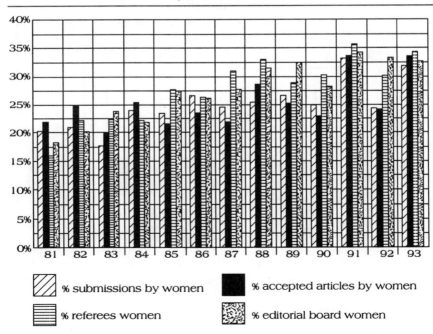

FIGURE 10 *Breakdown of Rubrics in Journals Study*

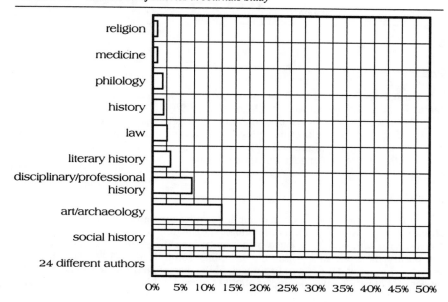

NOTES

Preface

1. Further discussion of the feminist debate over "decentering the text" in classics can be found in the special issue of *Helios* 17.2 (1990).

2. The URL is http://www.uky.edu/ArtsSciences/Classics/biblio.html; see also chapter 5, note 4. These useful bibliographies are searchable, frequently updated, arranged according to culture and topic, and include many literary studies as well as works with a theoretical or social/historical focus.

Chapter 1

1. In Anglophone countries, the discipline is now generally called "classics," "the classics," or occasionally "classical philology." The term adopted in Germany, *Altertumswissenschaft,* or "the science of antiquity," highlights both the universalizing and positivistic tendencies within the discipline. Judith Hallett (1993, 66) discusses the term *classics* and the general approach of the discipline from the perspective of a modern feminist: "I have the impression that many feminist scholars in other disciplines cannot fathom my love of what must seem to them a reactionary, elitist, and unlovable field, and that they regard the term 'feminist classicist' as the ultimate oxymoron."

2. Classics still fosters this sense of privilege in many practitioners despite its increasingly marginalized position in the modern academy. A good example of the strength of this tendency can be found in Michael Gagarin's 1990 presidential address to the Classical Association of the Middle West and South. Although Gagarin argues for innovation and openness to diverse perspectives within the discipline, his rhetoric betrays the assumption of "classic" status as he speaks of "defend[ing] the privileged position of the subject" and "justify[ing] its privileged status" (Gagarin 1992, 368, 369).

3. Segal is one of the more progressive of the prominent male scholars in classics. My comments here apply strictly to this article and should not be taken as criticisms of his current work, much of which does treat issues of gender (see, for example, his recent analysis of mythopoeic imagery of the female voice in a Pindaric ode [Segal 1994]); this in itself is testimony to the influence of feminism on classical scholarship. In fact, I remember reading the 1971 article with approbation when it was first published; at that time, I myself was completely unaware of the assumptions and omissions I now find so problematic.

4. Stephen Toulmin's distinction between discipline and profession provides the conceptual framework for the following discussion, although he draws most of his examples from the natural sciences and never mentions classics. Women and gender issues are also completely invisible in his book, which opens with the following statement: "The problem of human understanding is a twofold one. *Man knows, and he is also conscious that he knows* [italics original]" (Toulmin 1972, 1). From reading this book, one would surmise that no woman had ever played any role in intellectual history.

5. Calling classics "probably the most naive and least self-reflexive of the literary disciplines," Steve Nimis points out this contradiction: "With the possible exception of certain more technical areas of the field, classics lacks an essential prerequisite for the conduct of 'normal science': an explicit theoretical paradigm which has won the acceptance of most competent practitioners" (Nimis 1984, 113, 119).

6. Martin Bernal compares the disciplinary function of Latin and Greek to that of mathematics in the natural sciences: "they are seen both as essential to all work in the fields and as providing the rigor that elevates or 'hardens' classics and the natural sciences above other 'softer' disciplines" (Bernal 1989, 68). Some of these areas have recently begun to challenge their status as "subdisciplines" and to question the focus on the ancient languages as what one scholar has termed "the hard-to-scale propylaeum to the whole of antiquity" (Selden 1990, 163). This is particularly true of classical archaeology (see, for example, Dyson 1989 and Morris 1994).

7. The degree to which this positivist strain in classics results in a negative emphasis on limits, constraints, and error is indeed striking; note, for example, the following two statements by classicists: "as a scholar, I have been taught never to go beyond the evidence" (Lefkowitz 1985, 17) and "a competent classicist is one who does not make errors and notices other people's" (Redfield 1991, 6).

8. The historical connection of classics with institutionalized Christian religions and with institutionalized political power structures ensured that this identification of classics with the humanities would be deeply imbued with concepts of "morality" and "ethics" and that a classical education would be seen as inculcating these qualities. See Connor (1989) for an analysis of how this "ethical" concept of classical humanities was implicated in ideas about liberal education in the United States in the 1950s. It is this aspect of the humanistic strain in classics that makes classics so attractive to current proponents of a neoconservative agenda in education.

9. Sarah Pomeroy (1973) describes 121 books and articles relating to women in classical antiquity (excluding Christianity, which is covered in a supplement) dating from 1861 to 1973, most of which were written by classicists. Leanna Goodwater (1975), a librarian, compiled a less-scholarly and less-discriminating bibliography containing 386 books and articles published in English, German, French, Italian, and Latin between 1872 and 1974 with some connection to ancient women.

10. Robert Hamerling was a pseudonym of the Austrian classicist Rupert Hammerling, who published a highly romanticized and very popular novel about Aspasia in 1876. See Henry (1995) for more information about this novel and about Wilamowitz's treatment of Aspasia; see Nimis (1984) for Wilamowitz's status as the quintessential classical scholar.

11. Josine Blok (1987) examines this literature in the context of the tension between positivist and idealist historiography in nineteenth-century Germany, focusing particularly on the relation of the status debate to general and professional values; in a very perceptive article, Marilyn Katz (1992) analyzes this writing as part of the European ideological debate about the role of women in civil society, paying particular attention to its interaction with discourse about cultural racism and female sexuality.

12. Martin Bernal (1987) has analyzed the racial implications of this sense of affinity between "the Greeks and us," while Marilyn Katz (1990, 1992) and Joan DeJean (1989) have explored the interconnections between race, gender, nationality, and sexuality underlying this concept.

13. The two published reviews of this book clearly reveal the ambivalence that such a sexual topic engendered. One reviewer calls this chapter "distinctly unpleasant

reading" but necessary to show the "seamy and even revolting side" of Hellenic culture (Fairclough 1908, 22), while another refers to the chapter as "one of the not least interesting in the book" (Horton 1909, 285: note particularly the convoluted phraseology).

14. Mary Beard has recently called this book "the classic, groundbreaking account, . . . the first general treatment of women in the ancient world to reflect the critical insights of modern feminism" (Beard 1992, 12).

15. Although Badian finds "traces of feminist clichés" in the book, he concludes that "the actual evidence is fairly presented." He deduces from Pomeroy's avowed gratitude for the support of her husband and children that she "clearly has no patience with those women who feel guilty about not being in the kitchen when they are writing poetry or history. Such security in her own role was no doubt the necessary basis for the objectivity of her judgment" (Badian 1975, 28). It is hard to imagine any reviewer similarly basing a judgment about a male historian's objectivity on his security about his own masculinity!

16. One reviewer did complain about Pomeroy's "strident tones which on the sensitive—or should one say 'sexist'?—male ear sometimes jar" (Balsdon 1977, 207), but this review is clearly idiosyncratic; its dismissive tone is perhaps attributable to the fact that Pomeroy's book might be perceived as a competitor to Balsdon's own *Roman Women* (1962), which has been termed by a recent critic "misogynistically antiquarian" (Beard 1992, 12). Although Balsdon praised Pomeroy's scholarship, his concluding sentence reveals his generally flippant attitude: "Perhaps one day, after whatever series of cataclysms, man will regain his one-time equality and somebody will write a book about Man in the Ancient World—not, it is to be hoped, with the title, *Gods, Pimps, Rapists, Husbands and Slaves*" (208).

17. Marylin Arthur [Katz] criticized the lack of "a theoretical framework" in the book (Arthur 1976, 394); indeed, Katz's sensitivity to theory and ideology has proven very productive in her own work. However, given the scholarly climate in classics at the time (including the lack of self-reflection and hostility to theory discussed earlier in this chapter), it is very doubtful whether Pomeroy's book would have exerted the same influence on the discipline if it had been more explicitly theoretical. Marilyn Skinner (1992) has also recently endorsed this view, noting that employment of "the traditional voice" of classical scholarship was "exactly the right rhetorical strategy to embrace" at the time.

18. Although Pomeroy's book is individually authored, her acknowledgment of debt to her students (xiii) was unusual enough to elicit this patronizing comment from a reviewer: "the book originated in a course of undergraduate lectures, and this, I suspect, accounts for . . . a desire to stress contemporary relevance and current psychology" (Walcot 1976, 98).

Chapter 2

1. Goold is not unique in alleging such a standard for the doctorate. In the late nineteenth century, the United States imported from Germany the concepts of the research university and the specialized Ph.D. degree; Laurence Veysey describes how American academics, because of increasing claims about the democratic nature of American society, used the rhetoric of intellectual meritocracy to mystify the fact that this new degree actually intensified the elitism of the cultivated professions, which still demanded social suitability: "By emphasizing intellectual merit as a necessary further ingredient for success, a section of the elite redefined itself in a way

that made its role appear more widely justifiable. However much one might resent the exclusivist claims of Ph.D. holders, the requirements for the degree had been established on a disarmingly rational basis. The new form of advanced academic training thus threw up a facade of democratic opportunity" (Veysey 1979, 66).

2. Carl J. Richard argues that the standardization of classical education in the Western world was appealing to the American founders because of the "stable basis for awarding status" that it provided: "Classical knowledge, including a facility with classical symbols, was a badge denoting class, taste, wisdom, and virtue. Ironically, as American wealth and social mobility increased, the aristocratic classics became a means by which the rising middle class could acquire social status" (Richard 1994, 10). Richard's discussion, however, completely ignores the gendered nature of this badge of status and the role it played in excluding women.

3. The following statement from Benjamin Rush's "Thoughts upon Female Education" epitomizes the way early proponents of women's education in America used republican ideals about an educated male citizenry to justify educating women not for their own sake but for the sake of their sons: "The equal share that every citizen has in the liberty, and the possible share he may have in the government of our country, make it necessary that our ladies should be qualified to a certain degree by a peculiar and suitable education, to concur in instructing their sons in the principles of liberty and government" (Rush [1798] 1988, 45). Many modern studies of the early education of American women have drawn attention to this concept of "Republican Motherhood" (see Schwager 1988 for an overview of these studies), but as far as I have been able to determine, none has noticed a possible classical source for the idea in the Roman rhetoric about the beneficial influence of an educated mother. Two relevant Latin passages that were likely to be well known by Rush and others are Quintilian, *Institutio Oratoria* 1.1.6 and Cicero, *Brutus* 211, which praises Cornelia, mother of the republican reformers Tiberius and Gaius Gracchus: "her sons were nursed not so much by their mother's breast as by her speech."

4. The first edition of the journal of this association, the *Classical Weekly* (which was later renamed the *Classical World*), contained a pedagogical article by a female Latin teacher, Ella Catherine Greene, which she had delivered as a paper at the first meeting of CAAS on 27 April 1907 (Greene 1907). In a slightly later issue of the journal, a review of a Latin textbook by a male professor at Bryn Mawr College spoke disparagingly about the preparation of Latin teachers in America: "no American text-book in Latin of the last twenty-five years has had a more salutary influence than this one in giving half-trained teachers some much-needed data about the fundamentals of the Latin language" (Frank 1908, 100).

5. Ward Briggs (forthcoming) describes how Leach's "fierce determination coupled with unusual tact," plus her excellent Greek and Latin skills, overcame the initial reluctance of the classics professors to offer her instruction. James Greenough and William Goodwin supported the Annex largely because of Leach. Briggs quotes the tribute paid to Leach at Radcliffe's 25th commencement by president Le Baron Russell Briggs: "No one can speak more fitly at a Radcliffe Commencement than she who was the Commencement of Radcliffe."

6. Although Graham does not discuss this aspect of classics, she pointedly uses the discipline to illustrate the nature of increasing scholarly specialization: "A mid-nineteenth-century professor might have thought of himself as a professor of the classics; his successor was a classicist; his successor concerned himself only with ancient Greek; his successor became a specialist in the early plays of Aeschylus. His successor, expert in Aeschylus's use of the metaphor, is unemployed" (Graham 1978, 762).

7. Otto Skutsch's autobiographical lecture "Recollections of Scholars I Have Known" gives a good picture of the masculine atmosphere and attitudes of classicists in this period, particularly in Germany. He describes what is very much a man's world; anomalous women are referred to as "girl students," and the only female classical scholar mentioned among the 50 scholars discussed appears in an aside as the wife of another classicist. The following story about Otto Gradenwitz, professor of Roman law at Heidelberg, which Skutsch presents as an amusing anecdote, is emblematic of the attitude toward women in this closed community: "One day a girl student came to him and said she wanted to write a doctoral thesis on Bismarck. He talked to her for a short while, then said: 'Will you excuse me a minute,' and left the room. The girl sat there waiting, and suddenly from the floor beside her there was a loud 'Bow-wow, bow-wow.' She jumped up in terror, and there beside her chair on all fours was the Professor. He stood up, smiled at her and said: 'Young lady, if you are afraid when an old man says bow-wow, you can't write on Bismarck' " (Skutsch 1992, 402).

8. Judith Hallett quotes a 1919 letter to Harry Caplan from four of his non-Jewish colleagues at Cornell urging him to give up the idea of a university career and turn to teaching in the schools. Although the letter writers state that they do not share the "very real prejudice against the Jew," they believe that it is "wrong to encourage anyone to devote himself to the higher walks of learning to whom the path is barred by an undeniable racial prejudice" (Hallett 1992a, 56 n. 21; see also Calder 1992 and Metzger 1987, who discuss statistics for the American professoriate as a whole). In 1905, Jessie Fauset, a talented Black undergraduate who was elected to Phi Beta Kappa, had faced similar discouragement from her classics professor at Cornell, who bluntly told her that she should not go to graduate school because she would never be able to become a professional classicist (Solomon 1985, 136–37).

9. Haley discusses the issues confronting Black women classicists in America in her introduction to the reprint of Fanny Jackson Coppin's *Reminiscences of School Life*, originally published in 1913 (Haley 1995b); she is writing a much fuller treatment of this topic in her book-length study *To Teach My People: The Role of Classics in the Life of Fanny Jackson Coppin, Anna Julia Cooper, and Mary Church Terrell*.

10. Factual information and brief biographical studies of most of these women can be found in Briggs (1994); the issue of *Classical World* devoted to the lives of six North American women classicists contains more detailed studies of Leach (Briggs forthcoming), Haight (Lateiner forthcoming), and Smith (Gagarin forthcoming).

11. Gagarin (forthcoming) points out that 22.5% of the faculty at the University of Chicago were women in 1910; by 1940, this figure was 10.3%.

12. Leach served as president of the American Association of Collegiate Alumnae (which was later renamed the American Association of University Women) from 1899 to 1901; Briggs (forthcoming) suggests that her Harvard connections may have helped secure the APA presidency for her.

13. See Veysey (1979) for a discussion of the APA in the context of other professional associations of humanists in America.

14. Neither Shero nor Benario mentions the fact that no woman has ever held the office of APA secretary-treasurer, the person most responsible for the actual operations of the association.

15. Another way of expressing this situation is to say that the profession of classics had become "transgendered" earlier and to a greater degree in the United States than in other countries; see Georgia Duerst-Lahti and Rita Mae Kelly (1995a, 1995b) for an explanation of this term. I discuss the concept of "transgendered moments" more fully in chapter 4.

16. I am grateful to William M. Calder III for this reference; he discusses Meyer's ideas more fully in his introduction to the 1992 Classical Association of the Middle West and South panel on "Six North American Women Classicists," which is reprinted in the forthcoming special *Classical World* issue. Calder notes that this attitude was still present during his own graduate school days at Harvard: "There was certainly the conviction that the presence of women distracted the men and trivialized a noble subject. I recall Arthur Darby Nock at Harvard during the years 1954–56, driving an unwelcome woman from his graduate seminar by repeatedly asking her difficult questions until one day she fled in tears" (Hallett forthcoming/b).

17. It is instructive to note that Goold was born and educated in Great Britain.

18. I am grateful to Marilyn Skinner for helping me to clarify my thinking on this issue.

19. Judith Hallett quotes private correspondence among APA dignitaries indicating that there was some question about whether Taylor should be appointed APA delegate to the American Council of Learned Societies because the ACLS sometimes met in men's clubs, but they concluded that it would be "unreasonable" to exclude her on those grounds (Hallett 1992a, 58). Hallett's discussion of the political maneuvering surrounding Werner Jaeger's candidacy for high office in the APA incidentally reveals the degree to which Taylor, then serving as APA president, was "out of the loop" in APA politics.

20. This observation is quoted without comment in Walter Donlan's history of the journal (Donlan 1981, 12).

21. In his reminiscences, Otto Skutsch relates the following anecdote about the revered German classicist Wilamowitz, which he claims "characterizes the man": "One day his colleague Hermann Diels ... returned to his office and, greatly shocked, rushed out again. In the corridor he met Wilamowitz: 'Herr Kollege, Herr Kollege, what I have just seen in my office: my assistant, sitting on the sopha [*sic*], with a girl student!' Wilamowitz: 'Was she naked?' The aristocrat and man of the world, poking fun at his bourgeois colleague" (Skutsch 1992, 397).

22. For more information on the WCC, see also Hallett (1989b).

23. For the full text, see *Transactions and Proceedings of the American Philological Association* 102 (1971): v–lxix and 103 (1972): iii–lxxvii.

24. Mary Lefkowitz, I am told, deliberately chose to wear a red pantsuit to mark the occasion. No more invisibility for women classicists!

25. The founding members of the WCC were Marylin Arthur (now Marilyn Katz), Leona Ascher, Judith Hallett, Sarah Pomeroy, John Sullivan, and Dorothea Wender. In 1992, 20 years after its founding, the WCC was incorporated as a nonprofit membership corporation.

26. Although the official record gives no reason for this change of heart, then-president Harry Levy told Sarah Pomeroy it was due to the caucus's goal of transforming the profession: "Why should we give money to a group that is committed to opposition?" (*Women's Classical Caucus Newsletter* 8.2 [1984]: 4).

27. In 1991, the WCC also established annual awards for scholarship in these areas, including one for an oral paper presented at the annual meeting and one for a published article.

28. Gamel also quietly notes the personal costs of this kind of struggle, no matter how victorious in the end: "[T]he brandishing of rhetorical weapons didn't allow much room for the hurt and self-doubt that accompanied the exhilaration of battle" (Gamel 1990, 174).

29. By 1986, affiliated groups were granted control over their own panels on an experimental basis, later made permanent through a system of "charters"; by 1993,

members of the Program Committee were elected rather than appointed. By 1994, the program had been largely decentralized, with the Program Committee judging abstracts for only two out of the five types of program units. Significantly, all of these innovations were first suggested by the WCC, which worked with many different APA members and committees to bring them to fruition.

30. For much of the history of the APA, the Nominating Committee, itself composed of former APA presidents, proposed a single name for each of the major offices; hence, nomination by petition was the only way to hold contested elections. Even so, the device was rarely used. Judith Hallett (1992a) provides a fascinating picture of the behind-the-scenes maneuvering on one memorable occasion when it was used, the 1942 elections that denied the APA presidency to the noted German refugee scholar Werner Jaeger. The evidence Hallett discusses reveals how clearly the "politics" of the APA were dominated by men and male networks (note particularly the references to "our best men"); although Lily Ross Taylor was serving as APA president in 1941–42, she was apparently not consulted at all during this electoral scheming.

31. Before the official slate of candidates was announced, the newly formed Lesbian and Gay Caucus had added David M. Halperin by petition to the candidates for director.

32. Reprints of the entire series of articles and letters can be found in the 1992 issues of the *Women's Classical Caucus Newsletter* (19.1, 9–17 and 19.2, 5–8).

33. Thomas himself was not so naive, though he gave varied and somewhat contradictory explanations for his intervention in the election. He implied that there had been favoritism on the part of the Nominating Committee because both women had served on this committee the year before they were nominated. He also used the "breadth of choice" argument, maintaining that both women did "similar kinds of work" and both taught at "elitist East Coast colleges" (i.e., Barnard and Wesleyan); however, he then stated that they were "less senior and distinguished than Ludwig Koenen." He pointed to the election results—this was before the vote tallies were published—as vindication of his actions, saying that "a democratic process has exposed the maneuvering of a group as out of step with the rank and file." Finally, he described his position as "unwilling to hand one's field over to special interest groups" (Thomas 1992, 54).

34. The chair of the ad hoc committee on professional ethics and prime mover in the adoption of the code, Susan Guettel Cole, had formerly served as an officer of both the WCC and the CSWMG.

35. Ian Morris discusses the protest against the journal's editorial statement as though it were a spontaneous, grassroots movement: "A furious debate arose which crystallized as the book *Classics: A Profession and Discipline in Crisis?*" (Morris 1994, 44). He completely ignores the fact that these organized feminist groups were actively involved in this protest and that both Amy Richlin and Phyllis Culham, coeditor of the book he mentions (Culham and Edmunds 1989), were prominent members of the WCC. Is this an example of revisionist history in the making?

36. All of the papers presented at this panel have been printed in the *Women's Classical Caucus Newsletter* 20.1 (1993): 20–53.

37. According to National Research Council statistics for 1993, which include only doctorates conferred by United States universities, 44% of classics doctorates were earned by women. Comparative figures for total doctorates and all humanities doctorates are 38% and 47.5%, respectively (Thurgood and Clarke 1995, 48–49).

38. Prior to 1996, the APA had never made any efforts to gather information on the sex ratio of its membership. Therefore, this figure is derived from an informal count

based on names listed in the 1995 edition of the *American Philological Association Directory of Members*.

39. The two sets of data in figure 4 do not correspond precisely. Figures for candidates come from the annual reports of the APA Placement Service and include only those job seekers who have registered with the service. Figures for appointments have been compiled from annual lists of classics appointments supplied to the APA by U.S. and Canadian institutions; the latter include unadvertised positions and individuals who were not registered candidates.

40. According to the National Research Council's 1991 survey of humanities doctorates, classics had the highest percentage of nontenure-track positions of all the humanities disciplines (14.8%), which was more than twice the national average among humanities doctorates (Brown and Mitchell 1994, 32–33).

41. The CSWMG placement service report for 1992 and 1993 (*APA Newsletter* 19.2 [1996]: 14–17) discusses the perception of some males that women are being favored over men in the interview and hiring process. The report concludes that statistical information does not support this perception, for "women are now entering the profession at about the same rate as men, but at somewhat lower levels" (17). One reason why this perception is so persistent may stem from the frequently noted phenomenon that dominant groups tend to perceive equality as a loss.

42. Although the CSWMG and WCC have been actively promoting strategies for increasing the attractiveness of classics for members of minority groups (including the institution of an APA classics minority scholarship and sponsorship of workshops and panels), the lack of progress in this area has led to painful self-examination and divisions. In 1993, Shelley Haley, a Black classicist and former WCC cochair and newsletter editor, resigned from the APA and the WCC: "There has been too much accommodation, too much rationalization, too much justification. I have never been a 'dutiful daughter' sitting at (P)APA's knee" (Haley 1993b, 3).

Chapter 3

1. Redfield's statement about "theory" does not mention feminism and names only male theorists, but I suspect that the omission is disingenuous, for feminism is the only theoretical position within classics that can be said to "function politically as a faction" (see chapter 2).

2. In fact, this type of search would have been virtually impossible before the advent of the *DCB* because of the number and variety of categories in which articles relevant to classical gender studies can be found. It is clear that *APh* uses the "Authors and Texts" rubric whenever possible; 40% of these works are so classified, involving 86 authors or texts (58% Greek and 42% Latin). Such a traditional method of classification frequently obscures the real focus of the articles, as for example when two articles dealing with Terentia and Tullia are listed under Cicero, husband of the first and father of the second (Carp 1981; Dixon 1984).

3. Marilyn Skinner, the new editor of the official journal of the American Philological Association *(TAPA)*, is one of the leading feminist classical scholars in America. In the editor's statement announcing her appointment, Skinner was not coy about her own "keen preoccupation with theory, including feminist theory, and with issues of gender and sexuality in antiquity" (Skinner 1995, 2). On the other hand, she sought to mitigate possible fears about the revolutionary nature of her appointment by emphasizing her belief in the mutual interdependence of theory and philology, perfectly illustrating one of her own earlier contentions: "If women scholars are to revo-

lutionize classical studies, they will doubtless insist upon doing it slowly and tact-fully, enlisting, if possible, the support of the entire classics establishment" (Skinner 1987a, 186).

4. Indeed, I have been told by graduate students that dissertation titles are not always indicative of the scholarly approach because the students feel constrained to employ traditional titles, which sometimes conceal the use of feminist or other con-temporary theoretical frameworks. However, the fact that such pressure still exists in graduate programs is itself significant. Graduate students' responses to my question-naire on feminism and classics, to be discussed later, suggest that many of them are quite familiar with and interested in feminist approaches, though they do not neces-sarily feel free to employ these in their dissertations.

5. This type of textual change is particularly insidious in editions that are fre-quently used by nonspecialists, such as the Loeb, for readers may not realize that the modern editor has created not only the translation but even some of the words in the text.

6. In fact, Sarah Pomeroy (1991a) and Bella Zweig (1991) both point out the recent phenomenon of books whose titular focus on women is actually misleading, concealing the author's real interest, presumably to attract purchasers interested in gender studies.

7. One male faculty member responding to my survey of classicists (see chapter 5) indicated that he had filled out the questionnaire based on his direct contact with feminism, which was "not extensive." However, he went on to say, "in light of things like Amy Richlin's *Helios* article on Foucault et al. [Richlin 1991], I wouldn't be sur-prised to find that the other theoretical approaches that have shaped my scholarship (and to a slightly lesser extent my teaching) are themselves significantly dependent on feminist scholarship."

8. The move away from an isolationist "history of women" to a more inclusive "history of gender" does not imply another erasure of women but rather a more sophisticated attention to the manifold complexities of the category "women" and of gender performance for both males and females within the specific cultural context under study. This is convincingly demonstrated in Mary Beard's rereading of her early work on vestal virgins: "This is a story not just about gender and its ambiguities (though it is no doubt partly that); it is a story about gender (and its uncertainties) mapped on to other cultural categories (and their uncertainties)—civic identity, nationhood, and imperialism" (Beard 1995, 174).

9. It is important to note that the overwhelming majority of books and articles cited in the new bibliography Humphreys provides were written by and about males, and by British and European scholars. Her ten pages of bibliography include only five pieces that focus on women by American scholars (one of whom was British born and educated). Since American scholars created and still lead the subfield of women in antiquity, it would seem that anyone who wishes to make pronouncements about the field should take this major body of work into consideration.

10. Skinner notes that this type of publication is not only "a characteristic and insti-tutionalized mode of dissemination" for work on women in antiquity but is also highly unusual in the discipline of classics, which has always emphasized individual-istic, not to say adversarial, scholarship. A 1985–86 American Council of Learned Societies survey of scholars in seven disciplines found that classicists ranked very low on collaborative scholarship. Only 38% of classicists reported having published a chapter in an edited book; this was 9% lower than history and 10% lower than En-glish and American literature, the other two closest disciplines (Morton and Price 1989, 32). Moreover, only 10% of classicists reported having ever coauthored a

paper or publication with a departmental colleague, and only 27% reported coauthorship with a classicist at another institution. Classics was the lowest on departmental collaboration and only 5% higher than literature, the lowest discipline on extrainstitutional collaboration (25). These statistics support Skinner's claim that the edited collection of articles is an innovative feature of classical scholarship on women.

11. Sarah Pomeroy, one of the authors of this book, initiated the collaborative mode of working during an NEH grant of which she was project director, producing a text jointly written by a group of faculty (Hunter College Women's Studies Collective 1983). I first experienced this process in Pomeroy's 1983 NEH Institute on Women in Classical Antiquity, when all the participants jointly produced the first draft of *Women in Classical Antiquity: Four Curricular Modules*, which was later edited by Pomeroy with the assistance of Helene Foley and Natalie Kampen, who also coauthored *Women in the Classical World*. Kampen's introduction to her new collection (1996) directly credits feminism with prompting collaboration among the contributors to the volume.

12. In his introduction to the special issue of *Helios* on "Documenting Gender: Women and Men in Non-Literary Classical Texts," David Konstan notes that "interest in the construction of gender identities in the ancient world is now well established within the discipline of classical philology"; he highlights this collection's attention to various types of noncanonical texts as part of an "integrated anthropological approach that is increasingly a hallmark of research on women in antiquity" (Konstan 1992, 6).

13. In contrast, Beth Cohen's *The Distaff Side: Representing the Female in Homer's Odyssey* (1995) centers on a literary work and includes a number of articles that do not discuss visual evidence. Unlike Kampen's collection, which explicitly acknowledges its feminist orientation, the preface of Cohen's collection states that the work is "feminine in orientation, but not solely feminist in approach" (viii). It is unfortunate that the advertisements for the book use this phrase but change the word "solely" to "narrowly," a significant change that suggests some ambivalence about feminism.

14. "Feminist analyses of ancient art undertaken in the past decade have appeared in volumes edited by classicists, anthropologists, and art historians rather than by classical archaeologists" (Brown 1993, 245). Cohen, Kampen, and Reeder are art historians.

15. Amy Richlin alludes to this potential when she proposes that there may be "something revolutionary about knowing the past" (Richlin 1993, 294), and the collection of essays that she edited concretely demonstrates the heuristic value of studying the destructive consequences of gender ideology in antiquity with regard to pornography and sexualized violence (Richlin 1992c).

16. Jennifer Roberts (1994) has admirably carried out this hard intellectual work with regard to writings about Athenian democracy, which she traces from antiquity to modern times, explaining various positions in the context of the political and ideological matrix from which they arose. One cannot read her book *Athens on Trial* without gaining a clearer recognition of the political underpinnings of all scholarship, including Roberts's own, as she readily acknowledges.

17. In an article cowritten with Barry Strauss, Ober discusses drama in more detail, concentrating particularly on Sophocles' *Antigone* and Aristophanes' *Ecclesiazusae (Women in the Assembly)*. Apart from a reference to Antigone as "a subject and a female" (Ober and Strauss 1990, 260), their discussion of the tragedy manages to avoid mention of gender at all, presumably because their focus is on the *political* dimension of drama. Only in their discussion of the comedy do the authors confront

the gendered nature of Athenian politics (this would be hard to ignore in a play about women wearing male clothes who vote themselves into power), but they emphasize the play's allegorical representation of other political concerns: "The most glaring inequalities within Athenian political society were the result of the unequal distribution of wealth" (266). Compare this with Taaffe (1991), discussed earlier, who sees the interconnection of gender ideology and political ideology as central to the play's meaning.

18. For contemporary feminist discussion of the gendered nature of politics, see Wendy Brown's *Manhood and Politics* (1988), Anne Phillips's *Engendering Democracy* (1991), and Kathleen Jones's *Compassionate Authority* (1993).

19. Cynthia Patterson has produced one of the few less than glowing reviews of Ober's work that I have found; emphasizing somewhat different problems than I have stressed here, she points out his lack of attention to the role of the Athenian *oikos* (household) and to "the integrating power of religion, ritual, and ceremony," both areas that involved women more directly than the political arena. Noting the tendency of many writers on democracy to deplore the exclusion of Athenian women, she states that "this is not a particularly useful attitude for understanding Athenian social history and may be for some simply a convenient back door to '(male) history as usual' " (Patterson 1992, 113, 111). In a review of the recent English edition of Loraux's *The Children of Athena* (originally published in French in 1981), Simon Goldhill (1994) laments this book's lack of influence on current Anglophone scholarship, where he feels its emphasis on the integration of gender, myth, and rhetoric in Athenian cultural ideology would be especially relevant.

20. Evans mentions "the feminist movement" (Evans 1991, ix) and Bauman, less directly, "the explosion in women's studies" (Bauman 1992, xi) as catalysts for their books.

21. For pertinent reviews that discuss these problems in more detail, see Culham (1993) and Bendix (1994). The absence of feminist theory, which is designed to deal with the bias and limitations of male-authored sources, may in fact account for some of these problems.

22. Mireille Corbier (1995) discusses how Augustus's lack of surviving male heirs led him to use a traditional Roman practice (marital alliances between elite families) to construct a new kind of family unit, the *domus Augusta*, that ultimately gave women a new responsibility for "the transmission of legitimacy."

23. One respondent to my survey of individual classicists, although speaking about her own reaction to feminism, could have been describing feminist influence on classical scholarship that is not directly connected with the study of ancient women: "slow progressive minor changes and shifts of attention starting to have cumulative effects."

Chapter 4

1. Although it includes an excellent article on how to teach the *Aeneid* from the perspective of cultural diversity (Haley 1995a), the *Teacher's Guide to Advanced Placement Courses in Latin* (Brucia 1995) perpetuates the traditionally masculine focus of Vergilian pedagogy; the suggested bibliography for Vergil AP courses contains only one work influenced by feminist scholarship (Wiltshire 1989) and includes only 6 women among the 64 authors listed. Of course, this does not mean that individual teachers do not emphasize gender in their own classes; to note just two promising developments, Eileen Mooney (1995) addresses the issue of "Gender

Equity in the Latin Classroom" in a recent article, and the theme of the University of Maryland's 1995 Latin Day was "Women in Ancient Rome," including a "dux femina facti" campaign video contest and a skit written by Lillian Doherty and Eva Stehle in which Venus teaches her son Aeneas about legendary and historical Roman women.

2. Only one of the many feminist collections devoted to gender studies in classical antiquity contains an article on the *Aeneid*— Foley (1981), which includes Christine Perkell's "On Creusa, Dido, and the Quality of Victory in Virgil's *Aeneid.*" This article, arguing that Aeneas's inattentive and irresponsible behavior toward Creusa and Dido reflects "an incomplete humanity in Aeneas and in the *pietas* which he exemplifies" (Perkell 1981, 370), is one of the earliest feminist readings of the epic; later readings that draw on feminist principles also tend to emphasize the female characters either as a potential locus of opposition to the dominant ideology (Nugent 1992) or as an alternative perspective to the political and public focus of the epic (Wiltshire 1989). The most recent Vergilian bibliography published in *Vergilius* (McKay 1995) is indicative of the general pattern of recent work on Vergil. Of 154 entries whose names indicate the sex of the author, only 32 are women, and half of these women appear in the section dealing with "Vergil and Later Ages." Significantly, this section also contains the only three titles in the entire bibliography that explicitly mention gender or women (all in female-authored entries). Indeed, most of the work on Vergil that shows strong feminist influence can be found in studies that range beyond the strictly classical and cover several centuries (for example, Desmond 1994; Pavlock 1990; Suzuki 1989; Wofford 1992).

3. Despite my admiration for the studies of Brooks Otis (1964) and Viktor Pöschl (1962), my conclusions were more in line with what later came to be called the "pessimistic" reading of the epic, at that time most clearly represented in the work of Michael Putnam (1965). For a summation of the two main strands of modern criticism of the *Aeneid* up to that time, see Johnson (1976, 1–16).

4. This sentence appeared in the context of a discussion of *Aeneid* 10.468–69: "sed famam extendere factis, / hoc uirtutis opus" [but to prolong one's fame by deeds, this is the task of true merit].

5. When Juvenal seeks to caricature female intellectuals in his sixth satire, he imagines a woman praising Vergil and exculpating Dido ("laudat Vergilium, periturae ignoscit Elissae" 6.435). In connection with this passage, Marilynn Desmond asserts, "Juvenal assumes that for a woman reader . . . reading Virgil means reading Dido" (Desmond 1994, 45).

6. The Latin is "nam quae docta nimis cupit et facunda uideri / crure tenus medio tunicas succingere debet, / caedere Siluano porcum, quadrante lauari."

7. Although Wofford is sensitive to issues of gender, that is not her main focus in this book. To my mind, her analysis of the *Aeneid* makes a very significant contribution to Vergilian scholarship, for she brilliantly demonstrates *how* Vergil's famous ambiguity and lack of ideological closure are achieved: "The separation of action and figure permits the representation of a version of experience that is denied, displaced, or suppressed by the poem's figurative scheme: the figures work to contain the more disruptive implications of this representation, but they can never be entirely successful. . . . The action serves to reveal the limited success of the ideological shifts and transformations that constitute the poem's figurative argument" (Wofford 1992, 9–10). My own early study of the *Aeneid* in some ways parallels Wofford's (though on a much less sophisticated level), for I distinguished a tripartite temporal focus in the epic: narrative (present = time focus of characters); historical (present = time focus of readers contemporary with Vergil); and cosmic (divine perspective in which events

are points within the unfolding of universal destiny). I argued that the indeterminate time of the first perspective was separable from the apocalyptic time of the other two and served to disrupt their ideological message. My current analysis is deeply indebted to Wofford's central insight about the tension between figure and action.

8. All quotations from the *Aeneid* refer to the edition of Mynors (1969); all translations are my own.

9. "The allusions to female sexuality thus participate in a politics of scapegoating by which female eroticism becomes both the figure that hides the poem's imperialism and the source blamed for most of the obstacles to Aeneas's 'success' as founder of Rome" (Wofford 1992, 107).

10. The *Dirae* are said to "attend" Jupiter ("apparent" 12.850), suggesting that they serve much the same function as the public attendants *(apparitores)* of Roman magistrates, such as the lictors. Making them female here highlights the text's ideological compulsion to displace violence onto feminine figures.

11. Grace Starry West (1980) argues that Dido is presented in masculine terms; I do not find her argument convincing, however, because she cannot adduce any words or images that specifically describe Dido as "manly." Her assertions are based on parallels like that of Dido and Ajax in the underworld, or on the way she herself reacts to Dido's words: "We spontaneously praise these words for their heroic and manly qualities" (322). According to the concepts I have been using here, West is thus contending that the political Dido is not transgendered but is rather a sex-role crossover. West uses the mythical figure of Caeneus, a woman-man-woman who quite literally crossed over sexes, to claim that Dido's story supports gender polarization: "Through Caeneus' proximity to Dido in the catalogue Vergil suggests that Dido's masculine role has been ultimately unnatural too, that is, has been undertaken against the grain of her nature as a woman" (323).

12. This lack of attention to the difference gender makes also undercuts Monti's comparison of the Dido-Aeneas *hospitium* with those of Latinus-Aeneas and Evander-Aeneas. Vergil may describe the associations in similar terms, as Monti points out, but Aeneas himself accepts full political consequences only for his alliances with men. For example, he seems totally unmoved by Dido's accusation that he has betrayed his *fides* in their association ("nusquam tuta fides" 4. 373), simply arguing that he has discharged his obligation to her by gratitude, while he bitterly accuses himself of betraying his *fides* to Evander after the death of Pallas ("haec mea magna fides?" 11.55).

13. Jones calls for such a reconceptualization of authority because its traditional construction, by excluding the symbolically feminine, makes it difficult for actual females to be seen as authoritative: "When political authority is defined as the rightful imposition of order on disorder, ... it excludes women and the symbolically female from its practice axiomatically. Women represent disorder" (Jones 1993, 21). This statement could easily be construed as a description of the gender ideology presented at the figurative level of the *Aeneid;* compare Van Nortwick's statement of this ideology: "[T]he progress of destiny, of the heroic mission, requires the imposition of male order on female disorder" (Van Nortwick 1992, 131).

14. Glenda McLeod (1991) points out that later writers, such as St. Jerome and Boccaccio, classify Camilla with the viragoes, whom they assimilate to a masculine paradigm; for Jerome, such virgins "transcend their gender through their chastity" (McLeod 1991, 40). Christine de Pizan, however, emphasizes the viragoes' feminine gender, treating them in a fashion that I have been calling transgendered: "Nowhere does she suggest that their courage is unfeminine, nor does she use the traditional epithet of manly" (McLeod 1991, 124).

15. Both Dido (in a passage immediately preceding her entrance) and Camilla are linked with Penthesilea, who is presented with more ambivalence than either of the transgendered female characters: "bellatrix, audetque uiris concurrere uirgo" [a warrior-woman, this maiden dared to join battle with men], 1.493. However, it must be remembered that this passage belongs to the figurative level of the epic, since it is part of the temple frieze.

16. An interesting article by Grace Starry West (1985) focuses on issues of gender in this scene but is weakened by West's conflation of sex and gender. After pointing out that Chloreus is identified as a priest of Cybele (thus, most likely a eunuch, though Vergil does not say this), she assumes that he is "unfit to do the work of men" (27), unsexed and therefore automatically gendered as feminine, although all the text describes is the luxurious and gorgeous nature of his weapons and armor. In a complementary way, she argues, Camilla's female sex makes her heroism "fatally flawed through nature," as the warrior's "heretofore respectable though often dangerous desire to wear the armor of the enemy he has killed becomes the vain love of a naive girl for pretty ornaments" (24). It appears that West would deny the possibility of the transgendered; both Chloreus and Camilla, she maintains, are "revealed as travesties of heroic warriors" (25).

17. Although the *Aeneid* has been termed misogynistic, I agree with Desmond (1994, 33) that the epic as a whole scapegoats "unconstrained sexuality" rather than females, but the figurative ideology seeks to associate this sexuality most closely with females.

18. In a fascinating article, Maria Wyke (1992) discusses how Cleopatra is presented in the various monuments (sculpture, architecture, coins, poetry) constructed to celebrate and validate the accession of Augustus; she concludes that Cleopatra was a "problematic signifier" deeply implicated in the discourses of Orientalism, sexuality, and gender who "entered the Augustan texts possessed of extraordinary ideological potency" (128).

19. According to Stewart Justman (1993), the economist and philosopher Adam Smith faced a similar problem when he wrote *The Theory of Moral Sentiments;* Justman argues that this dilemma accounts for the ubiquity of references to Roman Stoicism in this work: "I theorize that it was in part to avert the shaming implications of his own 'feminine paradigm' that Adam Smith exalted the stoic principle of self-command . . . a stoicism teaching submission to the order of things" (26).

20. Most commentators on the characterization of Aeneas do not explicitly acknowledge the important role that gender expectations play in creating the "problem." Few are as open as Mark Van Doren (1946), who sees the *Aeneid* as a "relative failure" in comparison with the Homeric epics (xii). He chides Vergil's style as "soft and sad" rather than "forthright, confident, and masculine" (96), criticizes the characterization of Aeneas as "prettified" (103), and describes all the male characters as "pale, sad specimens of their sex" (107). Perhaps Van Doren could be so direct precisely because he was not a classicist (though he was a well-known literary scholar in his time). However, an unconscious defense of Aeneas's masculinity seems to underlie many classicists' discussions of Aeneas's character, as, for example, when Gordon Williams (1983) keeps referring to Aeneas's "frontier spirit" (shades of Natty Bumppo) or W. R. Johnson (1976, 15) insists, "This is not to say that Aeneas is not heroic in precisely the way that his champions claim him to be: he is a deeply humane and profoundly good man; he is also fearless and courageous, as powerful and as energetic as he is compassionate and gentle" (note the double negative). It is only recently that this gender dimension has become more explicit among classical

scholars, particularly in the perceptive study by Thomas Van Nortwick (1992), who suggests that there is perhaps a "gender ambiguity" (157) in the depiction of Aeneas's heroism: he is "not aggressive enough, not masculine enough, not driven to achieve the goals the gods have chosen for him" (118–19). I have already noted how this reading prompted an explicit defense of Aeneas's masculinity from Karl Galinsky (1992b; see also 1992a). However, even in the rare cases where the issue of gender does become explicit, the discussion is couched in terms of a sex-role crossover rather than transgendering.

21. In a playful article, Barbara Kellum analyzes the architectural and sculptural program of the Forum of Augustus not only as a visual embodiment of the civic and social ideology of the regime but also as "a sexually fraught theater for the engendering of the masculine" (Kellum 1996, 171).

22. When Karl Galinsky (1992a, 80–87) argues for the "masculinity" of Aeneas on the grounds that Roman concepts of manliness were linked with a sense of social responsibility, which he terms "one of the cardinal Roman virtues," he does not pay attention to the contested nature of this link. Certainly, masculinizing the concept of social responsibility was central to the political and moral program of Augustus, but this was a link that had to be constructed and constantly reaffirmed (hence the need for the extensive imagistic program discussed in Zanker 1988). While a concept of social responsibility was not foreign to elite Roman males of the Republic, such social responsibility was never separable from the individual status and power it was supposed to confer. What is *not* manly (in a Roman sense) about the social responsibility imposed upon Aeneas is that it diminishes rather than enhances his personal power, status, and satisfaction.

23. Vergil's description of this tableau resembles the depiction of Achilles' slaying of Penthesilea on the famous drinking cup by the "Penthesilea Painter" (for an illustration, see Keuls 1985, figs. 28–29). The Amazon, unarmed, is kneeling in front of Achilles, gazing up into his face and stretching out her hands in supplication as the warrior plunges his sword into her breast. I am not suggesting that Vergil's description alludes to this cup; I am only suggesting that the sexual/gender symbolism is similar: the macho Turnus, who once contemptuously dismissed Aeneas as effeminate, has been reduced to a feminine posture, while Aeneas forcibly asserts his masculinity. The story of Penthesilea relates that Achilles immediately regretted his action as he fell in love with the Amazon he had just slain, but Vergil permits us no glimpse of Aeneas's afterthoughts; we see only the passion with which he buries his sword in the breast of Turnus (Aeneas is "feruidus" [intensely hot, blazing], 12.951).

24. Focalization is a narratological term that describes the process whereby a story is told through the perspective of one of the characters; the reader, to a greater or lesser extent, enters the mind of the character and sees the action through her/his eyes (for a fuller explanation, see Doherty 1995, 18–19).

25. Doherty critiques examples of both types of readings of the *Odyssey* and presents a compelling argument for "a closed oppositional reading as an antidote to the Siren songs with which the *Odyssey* woos its female audience" (Doherty 1995, 63). Her own reading of the epic draws upon the principles of narratological and reader-response criticism, which are explained with exceptional clarity.

Chapter 5

1. In an article on "Self-Promotion and the 'Crisis' in Classics," Heath places feminists among the extremist elites in classics "*both* left and right, whose primary concern is with self-promotion (grounded in ideological posturing and research 'agen-

das')" and who are draining resources from "the vast majority of classicists whose careers depend upon quality teaching, successful program development, institutional service, and research" (Heath 1995b, 5).

2. This would seem to undermine Marilyn Skinner's observation that women in antiquity was "a fully established area of specialization within classical scholarship" by the mideighties (Skinner 1986, 1).

3. The amazement expressed by scholars outside of classics when they do discover our work should remind us of how much communicating remains to be done. A case in point is provided by the medieval scholar Marilynn Desmond, whose study of Dido led her to feminist classicists: "I might easily insert here a narrative of my own sense of intellectual comradery [sic] as I researched this book and came upon the dazzling work of women scholars in classical studies such as Maria Rosa-Lida de Malkiel, Mary Louise Lord, Judith Hallett, or Christine Perkell who suggest ways of revising traditional approaches to classical studies" (Desmond 1994, 226).

4. The site is designed and maintained by Ross Scaife and Suzanne Bonefas; the URL is http://www.uky.edu/ArtsSciences/Classics/gender.html.

5. Ten years ago, Judith Stacey and Barrie Thorne argued that a discipline's basic epistemology helped to determine its reaction to feminism; fields "with strong traditions of interpretive understanding," such as literature and history, have responded most positively, while fields "more deeply anchored in positivist epistemologies," such as sociology and economics, have posed more obstacles to feminist transformation. (Stacey and Thorne 1985, 309). But both types of epistemology are "basic" to classics, as I argue in chapter 1, and the discipline keeps their contradictions at bay only by refusing to theorize—hence, the particularly complex and conflicted nature of classics' response to feminism.

6. In 1990, Amy Richlin summed up her perception of what feminists had and had not accomplished in classics over the previous 15 years: "We have begun the process of recovering women's lived reality, as best it can be done. . . . We have begun to look at texts in a new way—something that must be done, for we can hardly burn them. We have woven a network for political action. What have we not accomplished? Look in any Women's Studies section in a university bookstore and count the number of books by classicists; then count the ones that use feminist theory. And look through the contents of any "mainstream" Classics journal (an oxymoron), and see if any of the critics or historians who write there so much as acknowledge the existence of feminist criticism. And look at the graduate programs and count how many feminists teach there" (Richlin 1990, 183). Well, I have done much of the "counting" that Richlin recommended, and I have documented that substantial progress has been made in the last five years. Even in graduate programs, there is some progress, though minimal in comparison with the other areas Richlin mentions.

REFERENCES

Adcock, F. E. 1927. The Breakdown of the Thirty Years Peace, 445–431 B.C. In *The Cambridge Ancient History*. Vol. 5, *Athens 478–401 B.C.* Edited by J. B. Bury, S. A. Cook, and F. E. Adcock, 165–92. Cambridge: Cambridge University Press.

Agard, Walter R. 1967. Classical Scholarship. In *American Scholarship in the Twentieth Century*. Edited by Merle Curti, 146–233. New York: Russell & Russell.

AJP Today. 1987. *American Journal of Philology* 108.3: vii–ix.

Archer, Léonie J., Susan Fischler, and Maria Wyke. 1994. *Women in Ancient Societies: An Illusion of the Night*. New York: Routledge.

Arthur, Marylin B. 1973. Early Greece: The Origins of the Western Attitude toward Women. *Arethusa* 6 (1): 7–58. Reprinted in Peradotto and Sullivan 1984: 7–58.

———. 1976. Review Essay: Classics. *Signs: Journal of Women in Culture and Society* 2 (2): 382–403.

———. 1977. The Liberated Women of the Classical Era. In *Becoming Visible: Women in European History*. Edited by Renate Bridenthal, Claudia Koonz, and Susan Stuard, 60–89. Boston: Houghton Mifflin.

———. 1987. From Medusa to Cleopatra: Women in the Ancient World. In *Becoming Visible: Women in European History*, 2d ed. Edited by Claudia Koonz and Susan Stuard, 79–105. Boston: Houghton Mifflin.

Ascher, Leona. 1973. Women in Classical Studies: Victorian and Modern. *Classical Journal* 68 (4): 354–65.

Bachofen, J. J. 1861. *Das Mutterrecht: eine Untersuchung über die Gynaikokratie der alten Welt nach ihrer religiosen und rechtlichen Natur*. Stuttgart: Krais and Hoffmann.

Badian, Ernst. 1975. The Lives of Ancient Women. *New York Review of Books*, 30 October, 28–31.

Balsdon, J. P. V. D. 1962. *Roman Women: Their History and Habits*. London: Bodley Head.

———. 1977. Women. *Classical Review* 21 (2): 207–8.

Bauman, Richard A. 1992. *Women and Politics in Ancient Rome*. New York: Routledge.

Beard, Mary. 1992. What Is a Goddess? *Times Literary Supplement*, 19 June, 12–13.

———. 1995. Re-reading (Vestal) Virginity. In *Women in Antiquity: New Assessments*. Edited by Richard Hawley and Barbara Levick, 166–77. New York: Routledge.

Belenky, Mary F., Blythe M. Clinchy, Nancy R. Goldberger, and Jill M. Tarule. 1986. *Women's Ways of Knowing: The Development of Self, Voice, and Mind*. New York: Basic Books.

Bem, Sandra Lipsitz. 1993. *The Lenses of Gender: Transforming the Debate on Sexual Inequality*. New Haven: Yale University Press.

Benario, Herbert W. 1977. An Addendum to "Women in Classical Studies: Victorian and Modern." *Classical Journal* 72 (3): 258–60.

Bendix, John. 1994. Review of *Women and Politics in Ancient Rome,* by Richard Bauman. *Bryn Mawr Classical Review* 94.2.2.

Berman, Kathleen. 1974. A Basic Outline for Teaching *Women in Antiquity. Classical World* 67 (4): 213–20.

Bernal, Martin. 1987. *Black Athena: The Afroasiatic Roots of Classical Civilization.* Vol. 1, *The Fabrication of Ancient Greece 1785–1985*. New Brunswick: Rutgers University Press.

———. 1989. Classics in Crisis: An Outsider's View In. In *Classics: A Discipline and Profession in Crisis?* Edited by Phyllis Culham and Lowell Edmunds, 67–74. Lanham, Md.: University Press of America.

Bertram, Stephen. 1971. The Generation Gap and Aeneid 5. *Vergilius* 17: 9–12.

Blais, Madeleine. 1995. *In These Girls, Hope Is a Muscle*. New York: Atlantic Monthly Press.

Blok, Josine. 1987. Sexual Asymmetry: A Historiographical Essay. In *Sexual Asymmetry: Studies in Ancient Society*. Edited by Josine Blok and Peter Mason, 1–57. Amsterdam: J. G. Gieben.

Blundell, Sue. 1995. *Women in Ancient Greece*. Cambridge: Harvard University Press.

Boatwright, Mary T. 1991. The Imperial Women of the Early Second Century A.C. *American Journal of Philology* 112: 513–40.

Bradley, Keith. 1992. "The Regular, Daily Traffic in Slaves": Roman History and Contemporary History. *Classical Journal* 87 (2): 125–38.

———. 1994. *Slavery and Society at Rome*. Cambridge: Cambridge University Press.

Briggs, Ward W., Jr. 1991. The Past Lies before Us: CAMWS 1905–2000. *Classical Journal* 86 (3): 268–76.

———, ed. 1994. *Biographical Dictionary of North American Classicists*. Westport, Conn.: Greenwood Press.

———. Forthcoming. Abby Leach. *Classical World*.

Briggs, Ward W., and William M. Calder III, eds. 1990. *Classical Scholarship: A Biographical Encyclopedia*. New York: Garland.

Bright, David F. 1981. Ovid. vs. Apuleius. *Illinois Classical Studies* 6 (2): 356–66.

Brittain, Alfred. 1907. *Woman: In All Ages and in All Countries*. Vol. 2, *Roman Women*. Philadelphia: George Barrie & Sons.

Broughton, T. Robert S. 1990. Lily Ross Taylor. In *Classical Scholarship: A Biographical Encyclopedia*. Edited by Ward W. Briggs and William M. Calder III, 454–61. New York: Garland.

Brown, Prudence, and Susan Mitchell. 1994. *Humanities Doctorates in the United States: 1991 Profile*. Washington, D.C.: National Academy Press.

Brown, Shelby. 1993. Feminist Research in Archaeology: What Does It Mean? Why Is It Taking So Long? In *Feminist Theory and the Classics*. Edited by Nancy Sorkin Rabinowitz and Amy Richlin, 238–71. New York: Routledge.

Brown, Wendy L. 1988. *Manhood and Politics: A Feminist Reading in Political Theory*. New Feminist Perspectives. Totowa, N.J.: Rowman & Littlefield.

Brucia, Margaret A., ed. 1995. *Teacher's Guide to Advanced Placement Courses in Latin*. Princeton: College Entrance Examination Board and Educational Testing Service.

Bruns, Ivo. 1900. *Frauenemancipation in Athen: ein Beitrag zur attischen Kulturgeschichte des fünften und vierten Jahrhunderts*. Kiel: Schmidtii & Klaunigii.

Burnett, Anne Pippin. 1991. Signals from the Unconscious in Early Greek Poetry. *Classical Philology* 86 (4): 275–300.

Cairns, Francis. 1989. *Virgil's Augustan Epic*. Cambridge: Cambridge University Press.

Calder, William M. III. 1992. The Refugee Classical Scholars in the USA: An Evaluation of Their Contribution. *Illinois Classical Studies* 17 (1): 153–73.

———. 1994. Classical Scholarship in the United States: An Introductory Essay. In *Biographical Dictionary of North American Classicists*. Edited by Ward W. Briggs Jr., xix-xxxix. Westport, Conn.: Greenwood Press.

Cameron, Averil, and Amélie Kuhrt, eds. 1983. *Images of Women in Antiquity*. Detroit: Wayne State University Press.

Carp, Teresa. 1981. Two Matrons of the Late Republic. In *Reflections of Women in Antiquity*. Edited by Helene P. Foley, 343–54. New York: Gordon and Breach. Reprinted from *Women's Studies* 8 (1981): 189–200.

Carroll, Mitchell. 1907. *Woman: In All Ages and in All Countries*. Vol. 1, *Greek Women*. Philadelphia: George Barrie & Sons.

———. 1909. The New Classical Philology. *Classical Weekly* 2 (20): 154–56.

Clark, Elizabeth A., and Diane F. Hatch. 1981. Jesus as Hero in the Vergilian *Cento* of Faltonia Betitia Proba. *Vergilius* 27: 31–39.

Clayman, Dee L., ed. 1995. *The Database of Classical Bibliography*. Atlanta, Ga.: Scholars Press. Featuring *L'Année Philologique* 47–58 (1976–1987).

Cohen, Beth, ed. 1995. *The Distaff Side: Representing the Female in Homer's Odyssey*. New York: Oxford University Press.

Cole, Susan Guettel. 1983. Women and Men in Classics in the United States and Canada. In *APA Committee on the Status of Women and Minority Groups Report on 1979 Survey*. New York: American Philological Association.

———. 1992. *Gunaiki ou themis*: Gender Differences in the Greek *leges sacrae*. *Helios* 19 (1–2): 104–22.

Connor, W. R. 1989. The New Classical Humanities and the Old. In *Classics: A Discipline and Profession in Crisis?* Edited by Phyllis Culham and Lowell Edmunds, 25–38. Lanham, Md.: University Press of America. Reprinted from *Classical Journal* 81 (1986): 337–47.

Conway, Jill K. 1989. Politics, Pedagogy, and Gender. In *Learning about Women: Gender, Politics, & Power*. Edited by Jill K. Conway, Susan C. Bourque, and Joan W. Scott, 137–52. Ann Arbor: University of Michigan Press.

Corbier, Mireille. 1995. Male Power and Legitimacy through Women: The *domus Augusta* under the Julio-Claudians. In *Women in Antiquity: New Assessments*. Edited by Richard Hawley and Barbara Levick, 178–93. New York: Routledge.

Coser, Rose Laub. 1973. Sex Roles and Economics. *Science* 182 (411): 471–73.

Culham, Phyllis. 1986. Ten Years after Pomeroy: Studies in the Image and Reality of Women. *Helios* 13 (2): 9–30.

———. 1990. Decentering the Text: The Case of Ovid. *Helios* 17 (2): 161–70.

———. 1992. Imperial Ideology and Perceptions of Women's Roles. Paper delivered at Feminism and Classics: A Symposium, 5–7 November, University of Cincinnati, Cincinnati, Ohio.

———. 1993. Review of *War, Women and Children in Ancient Rome*, by John K. Evans. *American Journal of Philology* 114: 171–74.

———. 1996. Did Roman Women Have an Empire? In *Inventing Ancient Culture: Historicism, Periodization, and the Ancient World*. Edited by Mark Golden and Peter Toohey. New York: Routledge.

Culham, Phyllis, and Lowell Edmunds, eds. 1989. *Classics: A Discipline and Profession in Crisis?* Lanham, Md.: University Press of America.

Dean-Jones, Lesley. 1992. The Politics of Pleasure: Female Sexual Appetite in the Hippocratic Corpus. *Helios* 19 (1–2): 72–91.

DeJean, Joan. 1989. *Fictions of Sappho 1546–1937*. Chicago: University of Chicago Press.

Delia, Diana. 1991. Fulvia Reconsidered. In *Women's History and Ancient History*. Edited by Sarah B. Pomeroy, 197–217. Chapel Hill: University of North Carolina Press.

Desmond, Marilynn. 1994. *Reading Dido: Gender, Textuality, and the Medieval Aeneid*. Medieval Cultures, vol. 8. Minneapolis: University of Minnesota Press.

Dickison, Sheila K. 1976. Women in Antiquity: A Review-Article. *Helios* 4 (2): 59–69.

Dixon, Suzanne. 1984. Family Finances: Tullia and Terentia. *Antichthon* 18: 78–101.

———. 1988. *The Roman Mother*. Norman, Okla.: University of Oklahoma Press.

Doherty, Lillian Eileen. 1991. The Internal and Implied Audiences of *Odyssey* 11. *Arethusa* 24 (2): 145–76.

———. 1995. *Siren Songs: Gender, Audiences, and Narrators in the Odyssey*. Ann Arbor: University of Michigan Press.

Donaldson, James. 1907. *Woman: Her Position and Influence in Ancient Greece and Rome, and among the Early Christians*. London: Longmans, Green, and Company.

Donlan, Walter. 1981. A Brief History of the Classical Association of the Atlantic States and *The Classical World*: 1907–1980. *Classical World* 75 (1): 3–25.

Duerst-Lahti, Georgia, and Rita Mae Kelly. 1995a. Introduction to *Gender Power, Leadership, and Governance*. Edited by Georgia Duerst-Lahti and Rita Mae Kelly, 1–7. Ann Arbor: University of Michigan Press.

———. 1995b. On Governance, Leadership, and Gender. In *Gender Power, Leadership, and Governance* Edited by Georgia Duerst-Lahti and Rita Mae Kelly, 11–37. Ann Arbor: University of Michigan Press.

Duff, J. Wight. 1936. Social Life in Rome and Italy. In *The Cambridge Ancient History*. Vol. 11, *The Imperial Peace* A.D. *70–192*. Edited by S. A. Cook, F. E. Adcock, and M. P. Charlesworth, 743–74. Cambridge: Cambridge University Press.

Dupont, Florence. 1992. *Daily Life in Ancient Rome*. Translated by Christopher Woodall. Oxford: Blackwell.

Dyson, Stephen L. 1989. Complacency and Crisis in Late Twentieth-Century Classical Archaeology. In *Classics: A Discipline and Profession in Crisis?* Edited by Phyllis Culham and Lowell Edmunds, 211–20. Lanham, Md.: University Press of America.

Dzielska, Maria. 1995. *Hypatia of Alexandria*. Translated by F. Lyra. Cambridge: Harvard University Press.

Edmunds, Lowell. 1989. Introduction to *Classics: A Discipline and Profession in Crisis?* Edited by Phyllis Culham and Lowell Edmunds, ix-xxviii. Lanham, Md.: University Press of America.

Edwards, Catharine. 1993. *The Politics of Immorality in Ancient Rome*. Cambridge: Cambridge University Press.

Eliot, T. S. 1945. *What Is a Classic?* An Address Delivered before the Virgil Society on the 16th of October, 1944. London: Faber & Faber.

Engels, Friedrich. 1884. *Der Ursprung der Familie, des Privateigentums und des Staats. Im Anschluss an Lewis H. Morgans Forschungen.* Zurich: Schweizerische Genossenschaftsbuchdruckerei.

Evans, John K. 1991. *War, Women, and Children in Ancient Rome.* New York: Routledge.

Evans-Grubbs, Judith. 1993. "Marriage More Shameful than Adultery": Slave-Mistress Relationships, "Mixed Marriages," and Late Roman Law. *Phoenix* 47 (2): 125–54.

Fairclough, H. R. 1908. Review of *Greek Women,* by Mitchell Carroll. *Classical Weekly* 2 (3): 22–23.

Fantham, Elaine, Helene Peet Foley, Natalie Boymel Kampen, Sarah B. Pomeroy, and H. A. Shapiro. 1994. *Women in the Classical World: Image and Text.* New York: Oxford University Press.

Faraone, Christopher A. 1991. Binding and Burying the Forces of Evil: The Defensive Use of "Voodoo Dolls" in Ancient Greece. *Classical Antiquity* 10 (2): 165–220.

Fetterley, Judith. 1978. *The Resisting Reader: A Feminist Approach to American Fiction.* Bloomington: Indiana University Press.

Fleming, Thomas. 1986a. Des dames du temps jadis. *Classical Journal* 82 (1): 73–80.

———. 1986b. Old Adam, New Eve: Lies, Damn Lies, and Feminist Scholarship. *Chronicles: A Magazine of American Culture* 10 (6): 8–9, 15.

Flory, Marlene B. 1993. Livia and the History of Public Honorific Statues for Women in Rome. *Transactions of the American Philological Association* 123: 287–308.

Foley, Helene P., ed. 1981. *Reflections of Women in Antiquity.* New York: Gordon and Breach.

———, ed. 1994. *The Homeric Hymn to Demeter: Translation, Commentary, and Interpretive Essays.* Princeton: Princeton University Press.

Fowler, R. 1983. "On Not Knowing Greek:" The Classics and the Woman of Letters. *Classical Journal* 78 (4): 337–49.

Frank, Tenney. 1908. Review of *The Latin Language,* by Charles E. Bennett. *Classical Weekly* 1 (13): 100–101.

Franklin, Susan Braley. 1908. First Year Latin. *Classical Weekly* 1 (13): 98–100.

Gagarin, Michael. 1992. "Flow Backward Sacred Rivers": Tradition and Change in the Classics. *Classical Journal* 87 (4): 361–71.

———. Forthcoming. Gertrude Elizabeth Smith (1894–1985). *Classical World.*

Galinsky, Karl. 1992a. *Classical and Modern Interactions: Postmodern Architecture, Multiculturalism, Decline, and Other Issues.* Austin: University of Texas Press.

———. 1992b. Review of *Somewhere I Have Never Travelled,* by Thomas Van Nortwick. *Vergilius* 38: 156–58.

Gamel, Mary-Kay. 1990. Reading "Reality." *Helios* 17 (2): 171–74.

Gardner, Jane E. 1986. *Women in Roman Law and Society.* Bloomington: Indiana University Press.

Garrison, Elise P. 1991. Attitudes toward Suicide in Ancient Greece. *Transactions of the American Philological Association* 121: 1–34.

Gleason, Maud W. 1995. *Making Men: Sophists and Self-Presentation in Ancient Rome.* Princeton: Princeton University Press.

Gold, Barbara K. 1993a. The APA Panel on Sexual Harassment: Background. *Women's Classical Caucus Newsletter* 20 (1): 16–19.

————. 1993b. "But Ariadne Was Never There in the First Place": Finding the Female in Roman Poetry. In *Feminist Theory and the Classics*. Edited by Nancy Sorkin Rabinowitz and Amy Richlin, 75–101. New York: Routledge.

Goldberger, Marvin L., Brendan A. Maher, and Pamela Ebert Flattau, eds. 1995. *Research-Doctorate Programs in the United States: Continuity and Change*. Washington, D.C.: National Academy Press.

Goldhill, Simon. 1994. Review of *The Children of Athena: Athenian Ideas about Citizenship and the Division between the Sexes,* by Nicole Loraux. *Bryn Mawr Classical Review* 94.1.11.

Gomme, A. W. 1925. The Position of Women in Athens in the Fifth and Fourth Centuries. *Classical Philology* 20 (1): 1–25. Reprinted in *Essays in Greek History and Literature*, 89–115. Oxford: Blackwell, 1937.

Goodstein, Leonard D. 1988. From Learned Society to Professional Association. *ACLS Newsletter* 1 (4): 5–6.

Goodwater, Leanna. 1975. *Women in Antiquity: An Annotated Bibliography*. Metuchen, N.J.: Scarecrow Press.

Goold, G. P. 1992. Paralipomena Propertiana. *Harvard Studies in Classical Philology* 94: 287–320.

Gordan, Phyllis G., Harry C. Avery, and George Kennedy. 1971. Report of the Committee on Academic Employment and Placement. *Transactions and Proceedings of the American Philological Association* 102: liii–lviii.

Gould, John. 1980. Law, Custom and Myth: Aspects of the Social Position of Women in Classical Athens. *Journal of Hellenic Studies* 100: 38–59.

Grafton, Anthony, and Lisa Jardine. 1986. *From Humanism to the Humanities: Education and the Liberal Arts in Fifteenth- and Sixteenth-Century Europe*. Cambridge: Harvard University Press.

Graham, Patricia Albjerg. 1978. Expansion and Exclusion: A History of Women in American Higher Education. *Signs: Journal of Women in Culture and Society* 3 (4): 759–73.

Greene, Ella Catherine. 1907. The Elements of the Translation of Latin. *Classical Weekly* 1 (1): 2–5.

Gutzwiller, Kathryn J., and Ann Norris Michelini. 1991. Women and Other Strangers: Feminist Perspectives in Classical Literature. In *(En)gendering Knowledge: Feminists in Academe*. Edited by Joan E. Hartman and Ellen Messer-Davidow, 66–84. Knoxville: University of Tennessee Press.

Gutzwiller, Robert. 1989. Classics in the Courts. In *Classics: A Discipline and Profession in Crisis?* Edited by Phyllis Culham and Lowell Edmunds, 351–61. Lanham, Md.: University Press of America.

Hadas, Moses. 1936. Observations on Athenian Women. *Classical Weekly* 29 (13): 97–100.

Haley, Shelley P. 1993a. Black Feminist Thought and Classics: Re-membering, Re-claiming, Re-empowering. In *Feminist Theory and the Classics*. Edited by Nancy Sorkin Rabinowitz and Amy Richlin, 23–43. New York: Routledge.

————. 1993b. Editorial: Pro-Choice. *Women's Classical Caucus Newsletter* 21 (2): 2–3.

————. 1995a. Cultural Diversity and the Advanced Placement Latin Syllabus. In *Teacher's Guide to Advanced Placement Courses in Latin*. Edited by Margaret A. Brucia, 19–22. Princeton: College Entrance Examination Board and Educational Testing Service.

———. 1995b. Introduction to *Reminiscences of School Life, and Hints on Teaching,* by Fanny Jackson Coppin, i-xxxvi. African American Women Writers, 1910–1940. New York: G. K. Hall.

Hallett, Judith P. 1977. *Perusinae glandes* and the Changing Image of Augustus. *American Journal of Ancient History* 2: 151–71.

———. 1983. *Classics and Women's Studies.* Working Paper No. 119. Wellesley College Center for Research on Women.

———. 1984. *Fathers and Daughters in Roman Society: Women and the Elite Family.* Princeton: Princeton University Press.

———. 1985. Buzzing of a Confirmed Gadfly: *Ho de anexetastos bios ou biôtos anthropôi. Helios* 12 (2): 23–37.

———. 1989a. Women as *Same* and *Other* in the Classical Roman Elite. *Helios* 16 (1): 59–78.

———. 1989b. The Women's Classical Caucus. In *Classics: A Discipline and Profession in Crisis?* Edited by Phyllis Culham and Lowell Edmunds, 339–50. Lanham, Md.: University Press of America.

———. 1992a. The Case of the Missing President: Werner Jaeger and the American Philological Association. In *Werner Jaeger Reconsidered.* Edited by William M. Calder III, 37–68. Illinois Studies in the History of Classical Scholarship, vol. 2. Atlanta, Ga.: Scholars Press.

———. 1992b. Martial's Sulpicia and Propertius' Cynthia. *Classical World* 82 (2): 99–123.

———. 1993. Feminist Theory, Historical Periods, Literary Canons, and the Study of Greco-Roman Antiquity. In *Feminist Theory and the Classics.* Edited by Nancy Sorkin Rabinowitz and Amy Richlin, 44–72. New York: Routledge.

———. Forthcoming/a. Edith Hamilton (1867–1963). *Classical World.*

———. Forthcoming/b. *Feminae doctissimae atque praestantissimae:* Six North American Women Classicists, an Introduction. *Classical World.*

Hallett, Judith P., and Lee T. Pearcy. 1991. *Nunc meminisse iuvat:* Classics and Classicists between the World Wars. *Classical World* 85 (1): 1–27.

Hawley, Richard, and Barbara Levick, eds. 1995. *Women in Antiquity: New Assessments.* New York: Routledge.

Heath, John. 1995a. *Omnis effusus labor:* On Futile Efforts and Inevitable Results: A Reply from John Heath. *Classical World* 89 (1): 53–60.

———. 1995b. Self-Promotion and the "Crisis" in Classics. *Classical World* 89 (1): 3–24.

Henderson, Jeffrey. 1991. Women and the Athenian Dramatic Festivals. *Transactions of the American Philological Association* 121: 133–47.

Henry, Madeleine M. 1995. *Prisoner of History: Aspasia of Miletus and Her Biographical Tradition.* New York: Oxford University Press.

Herzog, Reinhart. 1983. On the Relation of Disciplinary Development and Historical Self-Presentation—The Case of Classical Philology. In *Functions and Uses of Disciplinary Histories.* Edited by Loren Graham, Wolf Lepenies, and Peter Weingart, 281–90. Dordrecht: D. Reidel Publishing Company.

Horowitz, Helen Lefkowitz. 1984. *Alma mater: Design and Experience in the Women's Colleges from Their Nineteenth-Century Beginnings to the 1930s.* New York: Alfred A. Knopf.

———. 1995. A Man's and a Woman's World. *Academe,* July-August, 10–14.

Horowitz, Maryanne Cline. 1976. Review of *Goddesses, Whores, Wives, and Slaves: Women in Classical Antiquity,* by Sarah Pomeroy. *American Historical Review* 81 (4): 825.

Horton, George. 1909. Review of *Greek Women*, by Mitchell Carroll. *Classical Journal* 4 (6): 283–85.

Humphreys, S. C. 1993. *The Family, Women and Death: Comparative Studies*. 2d ed. Ann Arbor: University of Michigan Press.

Hunter College Women's Studies Collective. 1983. *Women's Realities, Women's Choices: An Introduction to Women's Studies*. New York: Oxford University Press.

Jardine, Alice A. 1985. *Gynesis: Configurations of Woman and Modernity*. Ithaca: Cornell University Press.

Johnson, W. R. 1976. *Darkness Visible: A Study of Vergil's Aeneid*. Berkeley: University of California Press.

Jones, Kathleen B. 1993. *Compassionate Authority: Democracy and the Representation of Women*. New York: Routledge.

Joplin, Patricia Klindienst. 1990. Ritual Work on Human Flesh: Livy's Lucretia and the Rape of the Body Politic. *Helios* 17 (1): 51–70.

Joshel, Sandra R. 1992. The Body Female and the Body Politic: Livy's Lucretia and Verginia. In *Pornography and Representation in Greece and Rome*. Edited by Amy Richlin, 112–30. New York: Oxford University Press.

Juffras, Diane M. 1991. Sophocles' *Electra* 973–85 and Tyrannicide. *Transactions of the American Philological Association* 121: 99–108.

Just, Roger. 1975. Conceptions of Women in Classical Athens. *Anthropological Society of Oxford Journal* 6: 153–70.

Justman, Stewart. 1993. *The Autonomous Male of Adam Smith*. Oklahoma Project for Discourse and Theory, vol. 14. Norman, Okla.: University of Oklahoma Press.

Kallendorf, Craig. 1991. Recent Trends in Vergilian Scholarship. *Helios* 18 (1): 73–82.

Kampen, Natalie Boymel. 1981. *Image and Status: Roman Working Women in Ostia*. Berlin: Gebrüder Mann Verlag.

———. 1995. Looking at Gender: The Column of Trajan and Roman Historical Relief. In *Feminisms in the Academy*. Edited by Domna C. Stanton and Abigail J. Stewart, 46–73. Ann Arbor: University of Michigan Press.

———, ed. 1996. *Sexuality in Ancient Art: Near East, Egypt, Greece, and Italy*. Cambridge: Cambridge University Press.

Katz, Marilyn A[rthur]. 1990. Sexuality and the Body in Ancient Greece. *Trends in History* 4 (4): 97–125.

———. 1992. Ideology and "the Status of Women" in Ancient Greece. *History and Theory* 31 (4): 70–97.

Keller, Evelyn Fox. 1992. Gender and Science: An Update. In *Secrets of Life, Secrets of Death: Essays on Language, Gender and Science*, 15–36. New York: Routledge.

Kellum, Barbara. 1996. The Phallus as Signifier: The Forum of Augustus and Rituals of Masculinity. In *Sexuality in Ancient Art: Near East, Egypt, Greece, and Italy* Edited by Natalie Boymel Kampen, 170–83. Cambridge: Cambridge University Press.

Kennedy, George. 1984. Afterword: An Essay on Classics in America since the Yale Report. In *Classica Americana: The Greek and Roman Heritage in the United States*, by Meyer Reinhold, 325–51. Detroit: Wayne State University Press.

Kerber, Linda K. 1987. Daughters of Columbia: Educating Women for the Republic, 1787–1805. In *Our American Sisters: Women in American Life and Thought*. Edited by Jean E. Friedman, William G. Shade, and Mary Jane Capozzoli, 96–114. Lexington, Mass.: D. C. Heath. Reprinted from *The Hofstadter Aegis:*

186REFERENCES

A Memorial. Edited by Stanley Elkins and Eric McKitrick. New York: Alfred A. Knopf, 1974.
Keuls, Eva C. 1985. *The Reign of the Phallus: Sexual Politics in Ancient Athens*. New York: Harper & Row.
King, Helen. 1983. Bound to Bleed: Artemis and Greek Women. In *Images of Women in Antiquity*. Edited by Averil Cameron and Amélie Kuhrt, 109–27. Detroit: Wayne State University Press.
———. 1995. Self-Help, Self-Knowledge: In Search of the Patient in Hippocratic Gynaecology. In *Women in Antiquity: New Assessments*. Edited by Richard Hawley and Barbara Levick, 135–48. New York: Routledge.
Kitto, H. D. F. 1951. *The Greeks*. Baltimore: Penguin Books.
Koenen, Ludwig. 1994. John Patrick Sullivan. *Women's Classical Caucus Newsletter* 21 (1): 21–22.
Kokkinos, Nikos. 1992. *Antonia Augusta; Portrait of a Great Roman Lady*. New York: Routledge.
Koloski-Ostrow, Ann O., and Claire L. Lyons, eds. In press. *Naked Truths: Women, Sexuality, and Gender in Classical Art and Archaeology*. New York: Routledge.
Konstan, David. 1989. What Is New in the New Approaches to Classical Literature. In *Classics: A Discipline and Profession in Crisis?* Edited by Phyllis Culham and Lowell Edmunds, 45–49. Lanham, Md.: University Press of America.
———. 1990. Classics. In *Encyclopedia of the American Left*. Edited by Mari Jo Buhle, Paul Buhle, and Dan Georgakas, 141–42. New York: Garland.
———. 1992. Introduction. Special issue, "Documenting Gender: Women and Men in Non-Literary Classical Texts." *Helios* 19 (1–2): 5–6.
Kraus, Christina S. 1991. *Initium turbandi omnia a femina ortum est*: Fabia Minor and the Election of 367 B.C. *Phoenix* 45 (4): 314–25.
Lateiner, Donald. Forthcoming. Elizabeth Hazelton Haight and the Ancient Novel. *Classical World*.
Lefkowitz, Mary R. 1985. Response I. *Helios* 12 (2): 17–22.
———. 1989. Writing about Women in Greek Literature. In *Classics: A Discipline and Profession in Crisis?* Edited by Phyllis Culham and Lowell Edmunds, 251–56. Lanham, Md.: University Press of America.
Lefkowitz, Mary R., Annette H. Eaton, Roger A. Hornsby, Janet M. Martin, and Ann N. Michelini. 1973. Report of the Committee on the Status of Women. *Proceedings of the American Philological Association* 104 (1): 22–28.
Lefkowitz, Mary R., and Maureen B. Fant. 1982. *Women's Life in Greece and Rome: A Source Book in Translation*. Baltimore: Johns Hopkins University Press.
Lloyd-Jones, Hugh. 1975. Ancient Women. *Times Literary Supplement*, 26 September, 1074–75.
Loraux, Nicole. 1987. *Tragic Ways of Killing a Woman*. Translated by Anthony Forster. Cambridge: Harvard University Press.
———. 1993. *The Children of Athena: Athenian Ideas about Citizenship and the Division between the Sexes*. Translated by Caroline Levine. Princeton: Princeton University Press.
Macan, R. W. 1927. Herodotus and Thucydides. In *The Cambridge Ancient History*. Vol. 5, *Athens 478–401 B.C.* Edited by J. B. Bury, S. A. Cook, and F. E. Adcock, 398–419. Cambridge: Cambridge University Press.
Macurdy, Grace Harriet. 1932. *Hellenistic Queens: A Study of Woman-Power in Macedonia, Seleucid Syria, and Ptolemaic Egypt*. The Johns Hopkins University Studies in Archaeology, vol. 14. Baltimore: Johns Hopkins University Press.

————. 1937. *Vassal Queens and Some Contemporary Women in the Roman Empire*. The Johns Hopkins University Studies in Archaeology, vol. 22. Baltimore: Johns Hopkins University Press.

McGinn, Thomas A. J. 1991. Concubinage and the *Lex Julia* on Adultery. *Transactions of the American Philological Association* 121: 335–75.

McGregor, Malcolm F. 1971. Democracy: Its Admirers and Its Critics. *Echos du Monde Classique/Classical Views* 15 (2): 53–63.

McKay, Alexander G. 1995. Vergilian Bibliography 1994–1995. *Vergilius* 41: 93–111.

McLeod, Glenda. 1991. *Virtue and Venom: Catalogs of Women from Antiquity to the Renaissance*. Ann Arbor: University of Michigan Press.

McManus, Barbara F. 1976. *Inreparabile tempus*: A Study of Time in Virgil's *Aeneid*. Ph.D. diss., Harvard University.

————. 1990. Multicentering: The Case of the Athenian bride. *Helios* 17 (2): 225–35.

McNally, Sheila. 1978. The Maenad in Early Greek Art. *Arethusa* 11 (1–2): 101–35. Reprinted in Peradotto and Sullivan 1984: 107–141.

Metzger, Walter P. 1987. The Academic Profession in the United States. In *The Academic Profession: National, Disciplinary, and Institutional Settings*. Edited by Burton R. Clark, 123–97. Berkeley: University of California Press.

Meyer, Eduard. 1920. *Die Vereinigten Staaten von Amerika: Geschichte, Kultur, Verfassung und Politik*. Frankfurt am Main: H. Keller.

Michels, Agnes K. L. 1969. A Memorial Minute for Lily Ross Taylor. *Transactions and Proceedings of the American Philological Association* 100: xvii-xix.

Monti, Richard C. 1981. *The Dido Episode and the Aeneid: Roman Social and Political Values*. Leiden: Brill.

Mooney, Eileen M. 1995. Gender Equity in the Latin Classroom. *American Classical League Newsletter* 18 (1): 14–19.

Moore, Frank Gardner. 1919. A History of the American Philological Association. *Transactions and Proceedings of the American Philological Association* 50: 5–32.

Morris, Ian. 1994. Archaeologies of Greece. In *Classical Greece: Ancient Histories and Modern Archaeologies*. Edited by Ian Morris, 8–47. Cambridge: Cambridge University Press.

Morton, Herbert C., and Anne J. Price. 1989. *The ACLS Survey of Scholars: Final Report of Views on Publications, Computers, and Libraries*. Lanham, Md.: University Press of America.

Myerowitz, Molly. 1992. The Domestication of Desire: Ovid's *Parva Tabella* and the Theater of Love. In *Pornography and Representation in Greece and Rome*. Edited by Amy Richlin, 131–57. New York: Oxford University Press.

Mynors, R. A. B., ed. 1969. *P. Vergili Maronis opera*. Oxford: Clarendon Press.

National Center for Education Statistics. 1994. *Digest of Education Statistics 1994*. Washington, D.C.: U.S. Department of Education.

National Research Council. 1978. *A Century of Doctorates: Data Analysis of Growth and Change*. Washington, D.C.: National Academy of Sciences.

Nimis, Steve. 1984. Fussnoten: das Fundament der Wissenschaft. *Arethusa* 17 (2): 105–34.

Nugent, S. Georgia. 1992. Vergil's "Voice of the Women" in *Aeneid* V. *Arethusa* 25 (2): 255–92.

Nussbaum, Martha C. 1986. *The Fragility of Goodness: Luck and Ethics in Greek Tragedy and Philosophy*. Cambridge: Cambridge University Press.

Ober, Josiah. 1989. *Mass and Elite in Democratic Athens: Rhetoric, Ideology, and the Power of the People*. Princeton: Princeton University Press.

Ober, Josiah, and Barry Strauss. 1990. Drama, Political Rhetoric, and the Discourse of Athenian Democracy. In *Nothing To Do with Dionysos? Athenian Drama in Its Social Context*. Edited by John J. Winkler and Froma I. Zeitlin, 237–70. Princeton: Princeton University Press.

Ong, Walter, S. J. 1959. Latin Language Study as a Renaissance Puberty Rite. *Studies in Philology* 56: 103–24.

———. 1962. Latin and the Social Fabric. In *The Barbarian Within and Other Fugitive Essays and Studies*. New York: Macmillan.

Osborne, Robin. 1994. Looking On—Greek Style. Does the Sculpted Girl Speak to Women Too? In *Classical Greece: Ancient Histories and Modern Archaeologies*. Edited by Ian Morris, 81–96. Cambridge: Cambridge University Press.

Otis, Brooks. 1964. *Virgil: A Study in Civilized Poetry*. Oxford: Clarendon Press.

Padel, Ruth. 1990. Between Theory and Fiction: Reflections on Feminism and Classical Scholarship. *Gender & History* 2 (2): 198–210.

Page, T. E., ed. 1900. *The Aeneid of Virgil, Books I-VI*. London: Macmillan.

Panel Discussion of Doctoral Programs in the Classics. 1972. *Classical World* 65 (8–9): 245–61.

Pantel, Pauline Schmitt. 1992. Women and Ancient History Today. Translated by Arthur Goldhammer. In *A History of Women in the West*. Vol. 1, *From Ancient Goddesses to Christian Saints*. Edited by Pauline Schmitt Pantel, 464–71. Cambridge: Harvard University Press.

Paterno, Joseph. 1989. *Paterno: By the Book*. New York: Random House.

Patterson, Cynthia. 1986. *Hai attikai*: The Other Athenians. *Helios* 13 (2): 49–67.

———. 1992. Review of *Mass and Elite in Democratic Athens: Rhetoric, Ideology, and the Power of the People*, by Josiah Ober. *American Journal of Philology* 113 (1): 110–15.

Pavlock, Barbara. 1990. *Eros, Imitation, and the Epic Tradition*. Ithaca: Cornell University Press.

Peradotto, John. 1989. Texts and Unrefracted Facts: Philology, Hermeneutics, and Semiotics. In *Classics: A Discipline and Profession in Crisis?* Edited by Phyllis Culham and Lowell Edmunds, 179–98. Lanham, Md.: University Press of America. Reprinted from *Arethusa* 16 (1983): 15–33.

Peradotto, John, and J. P. Sullivan, eds. 1984. *Women in the Ancient World: The Arethusa Papers*. Albany: State University of New York Press.

Perkell, Christine G. 1981. On Creusa, Dido, and the Quality of Victory in Virgil's *Aeneid*. In *Reflections of Women in Antiquity*. Edited by Helene P. Foley, 355–77. New York: Gordon and Breach. Reprinted from *Women's Studies* 8 (1981): 201–223.

Phillips, Anne. 1991. *Engendering Democracy*. University Park, Pa.: Pennsylvania State University Press.

Pomeroy, Sarah B. 1973. Selected Bibliography on Women in Classical Antiquity. *Arethusa* 6 (1): 127–57. Reprinted in Peradotto and Sullivan 1984: 315–42.

———. 1974. Women's Classical Caucus. *Proceedings of the American Philological Association* 104 (1): 66–67.

———. 1975. *Goddesses, Whores, Wives, and Slaves: Women in Classical Antiquity*. New York: Schocken Books.

———. 1976. A Classical Scholar's Perspective on Matriarchy. In *Liberating Women's History: Theoretical and Critical Essays*. Edited by Berenice A. Carroll, 217–23. Urbana: University of Illinois Press.

————. 1984. Selected Bibliography on Women in Classical Antiquity, Part 2. In *Women in the Ancient World: the Arethusa Papers*. Edited by John Peradotto and J. P. Sullivan, 343–72. Albany: State University of New York Press.

————. 1991a. The Study of Women in Antiquity: Past, Present, and Future. *American Journal of Philology* 112: 263–68.

————, ed. 1991b. *Women's History and Ancient History*. Chapel Hill: University of North Carolina Press.

————. 1994. Macurdy, Grace Harriet. In *Biographical Dictionary of North American Classicists*. Edited by Ward W. Briggs Jr., 392–93. Westport, Conn.: Greenwood Press.

————. 1995. The Contribution of Women to the Greek Domestic Economy: Reading Xenophon's *Oeconomicus*. In *Feminisms in the Academy*. Edited by Domna C. Stanton and Abigail J. Stewart, 180–95. Ann Arbor: University of Michigan Press.

Pomeroy, Sarah B., Marylin B. Arthur, Leona Ascher, Judith P. Hallett, Agnes K. Michels, and Dorothea S. Wender. 1973. Report of the Women's Caucus. *Proceedings of the American Philological Association* 104 (1): 28.

Pöschl, Viktor. 1962. *The Art of Vergil: Image and Symbol in the Aeneid*. Translated by Gerda Seligson. Ann Arbor: University of Michigan Press.

Post, L. A. 1926. The Feminism of Menander. *Classical Weekly* 19 (24): 198–202.

————. 1940. Woman's Place in Menander's Athens. *Transactions and Proceedings of the American Philological Association* 71: 420–59.

Purcell, Nicholas. 1986. Livia and the Womanhood of Rome. *Proceedings of the Cambridge Philological Society* 32: 78–105.

Putnam, Michael C. J. 1965. *The Poetry of the Aeneid: Four Studies in Imaginative Unity and Design*. Cambridge: Harvard University Press.

Quint, David. 1993. *Epic and Empire: Politics and Generic Form from Virgil to Milton*. Princeton: Princeton University Press.

Rabinowitz, Nancy Sorkin. 1993a. *Anxiety Veiled: Euripides and the Traffic in Women*. Ithaca: Cornell University Press.

————. 1993b. Introduction to *Feminist Theory and the Classics*. Edited by Nancy Sorkin Rabinowitz and Amy Richlin, 1–20. New York: Routledge.

Rattenbury, R. M. 1943. Review of *Essays on the Greek Romances*, by Elizabeth Hazelton Haight. *Classical Review* 57: 114–15.

Rayor, Diane, trans. 1991. *Sappho's Lyre: Archaic Lyric and Women Poets of Ancient Greece*. Berkeley: University of California Press.

Redfield, James. 1991. Classics and Anthropology. *Arion* 3d ser. 1 (2): 5–23.

Reeder, Ellen D. 1995. *Pandora: Women in Classical Greece; With Essays by Sally C. Humphreys et al*. Baltimore, Md.: Trustees of the Walters Art Gallery, in association with Princeton University Press.

Reinhold, Meyer. 1984. *Classica Americana: The Greek and Roman Heritage in the United States*. Detroit: Wayne State University Press.

Richard, Carl J. 1994. *The Founders and the Classics: Greece, Rome, and the American Enlightenment*. Cambridge: Harvard University Press.

Richlin, Amy. 1983. *The Garden of Priapus: Sexuality and Agression in Roman Humor*. New Haven: Yale University Press.

————. 1988. Is Classics Dead? *Women's Classical Caucus Newsletter* 13 (1): 13–27.

————. 1990. Hijacking the Palladion. *Helios* 17 (2): 175–85.

————. 1991. Zeus and Metis: Foucault, Feminism, Classics. *Helios* 18 (2): 160–80.

————. 1992a. Introduction to *Pornography and Representation in Greece and Rome*. Edited by Amy Richlin, xi-xxiii. New York: Oxford University Press.

————, ed. 1992b. *Pornography and Representation in Greece and Rome*. New York: Oxford University Press.

————. 1992c. Roman Oratory, Pornography, and the Silencing of Anita Hill. *Southern California Law Review* 65 (3): 1321–32.

————. 1992d. Sulpicia the Satirist. *Classical World* 82 (2): 125–40.

————. 1993. The Ethnographer's Dilemma and the Dream of a Lost Golden Age. In *Feminist Theory and the Classics*. Edited by Nancy Sorkin Rabinowitz and Amy Richlin, 272–303. New York: Routledge.

————. 1994. Review of *Daily Life in Ancient Rome*, by Florence Dupont. *The Historian* 56 (2): 370–71.

Richter, Donald. 1971. The Position of Women in Classical Athens. *Classical Journal* 67 (1): 1–8.

Roberts, Jennifer Tolbert. 1994. *Athens on Trial: The Antidemocratic Tradition in Western Thought*. Princeton: Princeton University Press.

Ruscio, Kenneth P. 1987. Many Sectors, Many Professions. In *The Academic Profession: National, Disciplinary, and Institutional Settings*. Edited by Burton R. Clark, 331–68. Berkeley: University of California Press.

Rush, Benjamin. [1798] 1988. *Essays: Literary, Moral and Philosophical*. Edited by Michael Meranze. Schenectady, N.Y.: Union College Press.

Schwager, Sally. 1988. Educating Women in America. In *Reconstructing the Academy: Women's Education and Women's Studies*. Edited by Elizabeth Minnich, Jean O'Barr, and Rachel Rosenfeld, 154–93. Chicago: University of Chicago Press. Reprinted from *Signs* 12.2 (1987): 333–372.

Scott, Joan Wallach. 1988. *Gender and the Politics of History*. New York: Columbia University Press.

Sealey, Raphael. 1990. *Women and Law in Classical Greece*. Chapel Hill: University of North Carolina Press.

Segal, Charles. 1971. Humanism and Classical Literature: Modern Problems and Perspectives. *Classical Journal* 67 (1): 29–37.

————. 1978. The Menace of Dionysus: Sex Roles and Reversals in Euripides' *Bacchae*. *Arethusa* 11: 185–202. Reprinted in Peradotto and Sullivan 1984: 195–212.

————. 1994. The Gorgon and the Nightingale: The Voice of Female Lament and Pindar's Twelfth *Pythian Ode*. In *Embodied Voices: Representing Female Vocality in Western Culture*. Edited by Leslie C. Dunn and Nancy A. Jones, 17–34. New Perspectives in Music History and Criticism. Cambridge: Cambridge University Press.

Selden, Daniel L. 1990. Classics and Contemporary Criticism. *Arion* 3d ser. 1 (1): 155–78.

Seltman, Charles. 1955. The Status of Women in Athens. *Greece & Rome* 2 (3): 119–24.

————. 1956. *Women in Antiquity*. London: Thames and Hudson.

Shapiro, H. A. 1991. The Iconography of Mourning in Athenian Art. *American Journal of Archaeology* 95: 629–56.

Shaw, Brent D. 1991. The Paradoxes of People Power. *Helios* 18 (2): 194–214.

Shero, L. R. 1932. Xenophon's Portrait of a Young Wife. *Classical Weekly* 26 (3): 17–21.

Shero, Lucius Rogers. 1963. The American Philological Association: An Historical Sketch. *Transactions and Proceedings of the American Philological Association* 94: x-l.

Shorey, Paul. 1919. Fifty Years of Classical Studies in America. *Transactions and Proceedings of the American Philological Association* 50: 33–61.

Skinner, Marilyn B. 1980. Putting It Back Together. *Women's Classical Caucus Newsletter* 5 (2): 1–2.

———. 1985. Classical Studies vs. Women's Studies: *Duo moi ta noêmmata. Helios* 12 (2): 3–16.

———. 1986. Rescuing Creusa: New Methodological Approaches to Women in Antiquity. *Helios* 13 (2): 1–8.

———. 1987a. Classical Studies, Patriarchy and Feminism: The View from 1986. *Women's Studies International Forum* 10 (2): 181–86.

———. 1987b. Des bonnes dames et méchantes. *Classical Journal* 83 (1): 69–74.

———. 1989. Expecting the Barbarians: Feminism, Nostalgia, and the "Epistemic Shift" in Classical Studies. In *Classics: A Discipline and Profession in Crisis?* Edited by Phyllis Culham and Lowell Edmunds, 199–210. Lanham, Md.: University Press of America.

———. 1992. Our Voices, Ourselves. Paper delivered at Feminism and Classics: A Symposium, 5–7 November, University of Cincinnati, Cincinnati, Ohio.

———. 1993. Woman and Language in Archaic Greece, or, Why is Sappho a Woman? In *Feminist Theory and the Classics.* Nancy Sorkin Rabinowitz and Amy Richlin, 125–44. New York: Routledge.

———. 1995. Marilyn B. Skinner Appointed Editor of *TAPA. American Philological Association Newsletter* 18 (5): 1–2.

Skutsch, Otto. 1992. Recollections of Scholars I Have Known. *Harvard Studies in Classical Philology* 94: 387–408.

Snyder, Jane McIntosh. 1989. *The Woman and the Lyre: Women Writers in Classical Greece and Rome.* Carbondale, Ill.: Southern Illinois University Press.

Snyder, Jane M., Hugh M. Lee, Mary R. Lefkowitz, Janet Martin, and Gail Smith. 1977. Report of the Committee on the Status of Women and of Minority Groups. *Proceedings of the American Philological Association* 107 (1): 26–34.

Solomon, Barbara Miller. 1985. *In the Company of Educated Women: A History of Women and Higher Education in America.* New Haven: Yale University Press.

Sourvinou-Inwood, Christiane. 1995. Male and Female, Public and Private, Ancient and Modern. In *Pandora: Women in Classical Greece,* by Ellen D. Reeder, 111–20. Baltimore, Md.: Trustees of the Walters Art Gallery, in association with Princeton University Press.

Stacey, Judith, and Barrie Thorne. 1985. The Missing Feminist Revolution in Sociology. *Social Problems* 32 (4): 301–16.

Stehle, Eva. 1989a. Introduction. Special issue, "Studies on Roman Women," Part 2. *Helios* 16 (2): 115–18.

———. 1989b. Venus, Cybele, and the Sabine Women: The Roman Construction of Female Sexuality. *Helios* 16 (2): 143–64.

Stehle, Eva, and Amy Day. 1996. Women Looking at Women: Women's Ritual and Temple Sculpture. In *Sexuality in Ancient Art: Near East, Egypt, Greece, and Italy.* Edited by Natalie Boymel Kampen, 101–16. Cambridge: Cambridge University Press.

Stewart, Zeph. 1990. Changing Patterns of Scholarship as Seen from the Center for Hellenic Studies. *American Journal of Philology* 111: 257–63.

Sullivan, J. P. 1973. Editorial. *Arethusa* 6 (1): 5–6.

Suzuki, Mihoko. 1989. *Metamorphoses of Helen: Authority, Difference, and the Epic.* Ithaca: Cornell University Press.

Syme, Ronald. 1939. *The Roman Revolution*. Oxford: Oxford University Press.

———. 1986. *The Augustan Aristocracy*. Oxford: Clarendon Press.

Taaffe, Lauren K. 1991. The Illusion of Gender Disguise in Aristophanes' *Ecclesiazusae*. *Helios* 18 (2): 91–112.

Thomas, Richard F. 1992. Thomas Unbound. *Lingua Franca*, February/March, 3, 54.

Thornton, Bruce. 1991. Constructionism and Ancient Greek Sex. *Helios* 18 (2): 181–93.

Thurgood, Delores H., and Julie E. Clarke. 1995. *Summary Report 1993: Doctorate Recipients from United States Universities*. Washington, D.C.: National Academy Press.

Tompkins, Daniel. 1994. "What Has This To Do with the Praetor's Edict?" Classical Studies and Contemporary Society. *Arethusa* 27 (1): 11–39.

Toulmin, Stephen. 1972. *Human Understanding*. Vol. 1, *The Collective Use and Evolution of Concepts*. Princeton: Princeton University Press.

Trachy, Carole Law. 1976. Review of *Goddesses, Whores, Wives, and Slaves: Women in Classical Antiquity*, by Sarah Pomeroy. *Archaeological News* 5 (3): 87–89.

Tuana, Nancy, ed. 1994. *Feminist Interpretations of Plato*. University Park, Pa.: The Pennsylvania State University Press.

Van Doren, Mark. 1946. *The Noble Voice: A Study of Ten Great Poems*. New York: Henry Holt and Company.

Van Nortwick, Thomas. 1992. *Somewhere I Have Never Travelled: The Second Self and the Hero's Journey in Ancient Epic*. New York: Oxford University Press.

Versnel, H. S. 1987. Wife and Helpmate: Women of Ancient Athens in Anthropological Perspective. In *Sexual Asymmetry: Studies in Ancient Society*. Edited by Josine Blok and Peter Mason, 59–86. Amsterdam: J. G. Gieben.

Veysey, Laurence. 1979. The Plural Organized Worlds of the Humanities. In *The Organization of Knowledge in Modern America, 1860–1920*. Edited by Alexandra Olesen and John Voss, 51–106. Baltimore: Johns Hopkins University Press.

von Stadten, Heinrich. 1992. Women and Dirt. *Helios* 19 (1–2): 7–30.

Walcot, P. 1976. Review of *Goddesses, Whores, Wives, and Slaves: Women in Classical Antiquity*, by Sarah Pomeroy. *Greece & Rome* 23 (1): 98–99.

Walker, Susan. 1983. Women and Housing in Classical Greece: The Archaeological Evidence. In *Images of Women in Antiquity*. Edited by Averil Cameron and Amélie Kuhrt, 81–91. Detroit: Wayne State University Press.

West, Grace Starry. 1980. Caeneus and Dido. *Transactions of the American Philological Association* 110: 315–24.

———. 1985. Chloreus and Camilla. *Vergilius* 31: 22–29.

Wijsman, Henri J. 1992. Female Power in *Georgics* 3. 269/270. *Harvard Studies in Classical Philology* 94: 259–61.

Wilamowitz-Moellendorff, Ulrich von. 1893. *Aristoteles und Athen*. 2 vols. Berlin: Weidmann.

Williams, Dyfri. 1983. Women on Athenian Vases: Problems of Interpretation. In *Images of Women in Antiquity*. Edited by Averil Cameron and Amélie Kuhrt, 92–106. Detroit: Wayne State University Press.

Williams, Gordon. 1983. *Technique and Ideas in the Aeneid*. New Haven: Yale University Press.

Wiltshire, Susan Ford. 1989. *Public and Private in Vergil's Aeneid*. Amherst: University of Massachusetts Press.

Wofford, Susanne Lindgren. 1992. *The Choice of Achilles: The Ideology of Figure in the Epic*. Stanford: Stanford University Press.

Wyke, Maria. 1992. Augustan Cleopatras: Female Power and Poetic Ambiguity. In *Roman Poetry and Propaganda in the Age of Augustus*. Edited by Anton Powell, 98–140. London: Bristol Classical Press.

Zanker, Paul. 1988. *The Power of Images in the Age of Augustus*. Translated by Alan Shapiro. Ann Arbor: University of Michigan Press.

Zeitlin, Froma I. 1996. Playing the Other: Theater, Theatricality, and the Feminine in Greek Drama. In *Playing the Other: Gender and Society in Classical Greek Literature*, 341–74. Chicago: University of Chicago Press. Reprinted and revised from *Representations* 11 (1985): 63–94.

Zinsser, Judith P. 1993. *History and Feminism: A Glass Half Full*. The Impact of Feminism on the Arts and Sciences. New York: Twayne Publishers.

Ziolkowski, Theodore. 1993. *Virgil and the Moderns*. Princeton: Princeton University Press.

Zweig, Bella. 1991. Review of *Death and the Maiden: Girls' Initiation Rites in Greek Mythology*, by Ken Dowden. *Women's Classical Caucus Newsletter* 16 (1): 38–41.

———. 1993. The Primal Mind: Using Native American Models for the Study of Women in Ancient Greece. In *Feminist Theory and the Classics*. Edited by Nancy Sorkin Rabinowitz and Amy Richlin, 145–80. New York: Routledge.

INDEX

Aeneas: characterization of, 93–94,
108, 115, 175–76n. 20; identification with Hector, 111–12; in relation to feminized space, 92,
109–10; transgendering of,
110–14
Aeneid: feminist readings of, 92, 115,
173n. 2; gender ideology of figurative level in, 96–99, 102, 107,
109–10, 113, 114, 174nn. 9, 13;
pessimistic reading of, 173n. 3;
symbolic distortions in, 102–103;
teaching of, 92, 172–73n. 1; young
males and feminine imagery in,
113–14. *See also* Vergil
American Institute of Archaeology
(AIA), 73
American Philological Association
(APA), 20; attitude toward women
in, 29–31, 35–36; feminist organizations in, 35, 37–38, 48 (*see also*
Committee on the Status of Women
and Minority Groups; Women's
Classical Caucus); women presidents of, 27–29, 30, 141
androcentric norms, 59, 74, 117;
deconstruction of, 77–78, 118

Année Philologique, L' (Aph), 52; classification rubrics of, 52, 67, 73,
160, 169n. 2
anonymous refereeing: of journal submissions, 39, 54; of paper submissions, 38–39
APA. *See* American Philological
Association
appointments in classics. *See* placement statistics in classics
archaeology, classical, xiii, 4, 72–73
Arethusa, 1973 special issue on
women, 15–16, 18–19, 37
Aristophanes, 63, 171–72n. 17
Aristotle, 78
art exhibitions on ancient women, 72,
138
art history, classical: as scholarly
focus, 52, 72, 171n. 14; gender-
related studies in, 63, 72, 81, 171n.
13, 176n. 21
Arthur, Marylin. *See* Katz, Marilyn
articles in classical journals: categories defined, 57, 145; category 1
discussed, 57–58; category 2 discussed, 60–62; category 3 discussed, 62–64; category 4 dis-

THE AUTHOR

Barbara F. McManus is a professor of classics at the College of New Rochelle. An interest in feminist theory, feminist cultural studies, and feminist pedagogy provides a unifying foundation for her work in apparently diverse areas, ranging from classical antiquity to Renaissance England to the humanistic potential of computers. She is coauthor of *Half Humankind: Contexts and Texts of the Controversy about Women in England, 1540–1640* (1985) and has published articles in *Classical World, Helios, Women's Studies Quarterly,* and several edited collections. A longtime promoter of gender equity and professional inclusiveness, she is an active member of the Women's Classical Caucus and the American Philological Association.

THE EDITOR

Claire Sprague is Professor Emerita of the Department of English, Brooklyn College of the City University of New York. She has also taught at New York University, John Jay College, the University of Zaragoza, Reed College, and the University of Wisconsin. Her publications include *In Pursuit of Doris Lessing: Nine Nations Reading* (1990), *Rereading Doris Lessing: Narrative Patterns of Doubling and Repetition* (1987), *Van Wyck Brooks: The Early Years* (1968, 1993), *Virginia Woolf* (1970). She was the first president of the Doris Lessing Society and a past editor of the *Doris Lessing Newsletter* (1979–1986). She is the coproducer of *Sister Talk,* a radio program aired over WOMR, Provincetown, and WTJU, Charlottesville. Her current work in progress is a study of five artist and writer couples in twentieth-century America.